Neil LaBute received his master of Fine Arts degree in dramatic writing from New York University and was the recipient of a literary fellowship to study at the Royal Court Theatre, London. He also attended the Sundance Institute's Playwrights Lab and is the Playwright-in-Residence with MCC Theater in New York City.

LaBute's plays include: *bash: latter-day plays*, *The Shape of Things*, *The Mercy Seat*, *The Distance From Here*, *Autobahn*, *Fat Pig* (Olivier Award nominated for Best Comedy), *Some Girl(s)*, *This Is How It Goes*, *Wrecks*, *Filthy Talk for Troubled Times*, *In a Dark Dark House*, *Reasons to Be Pretty* (Tony Award nominated for Best Play), *The Break of Noon*, *In a Forest, Dark and Deep*, *Lovely Head*, *Reasons to be Happy* and *The Money Shot*. He is also the author of *Seconds of Pleasure*, a collection of short fiction which was published by Grove Atlantic.

His films include *In the Company of Men* (New York Critics' Circle Award for Best First Feature and the Filmmaker Trophy at the Sundance Film Festival), *Your Friends and Neighbours*, *Nurse Betty*, *Possession*, *The Shape of Things*, a film adaptation of his play of the same title, *The Wicker Man*, *Lakeview Terrace*, *Death at a Funeral*, *Some Velvet Morning* and *Dirty Weekend*. He has also created the TV series *Full Circle* and *Ten X Ten* for DirecTV.

NEIL LABUTE

Plays One

Filthy Talk for Troubled Times

The Mercy Seat

This Is How It Goes

Some Girl(s)

Helter Skelter

A Second of Pleasure

with an introduction
by the author

FABER & FABER

First published in 2014
by Faber and Faber Limited
The Bindery, 51 Hatton Garden, London ECIN 8HN

Typeset by Country Setting, Kingsdown, Kent CT14 8ES
Printed in England by CPI Group (UK) Ltd, Croydon CRO 4YY

A CIP record for this book is available from the British Library

ISBN 978-0-571-30785-2

4 6 8 10 9 7 5

Contents

Introduction

As a writer, I barely feel started with my life's work and yet surely this must be at least the halfway point (and that's being generous).

I've been lucky enough to be around in the business of theatre for almost thirty years now (over half of my actual lifetime) and with that has come an almost equal number of accolades and rebukes. My work has been publicly loved and hated, and I suppose that's ultimately the best place I could imagine being – in the middle is too safe and too mundane a spot for the likes of me.

That said, there's nothing I love more than working with actors on a new play, regardless of how a particular show may have been received by critics and/or the public. I remember each of the situations that created the works in this volume in vivid and loving detail. Whether they were well reviewed or dispatched with little or no interest, the six plays contained in these pages mark a kind of evolution in my writing, like little signposts carved into trees along a wooded trail.

Filthy Talk for Troubled Times started as a series of sketches while I was still in school. Graduate school at the University of Kansas, to be exact, and the play was put together with friends as a kind of 'nasty cabaret' with few theatrical trappings but an energetic audience and me trying my best to sound like Mamet while doing a tentative two-step forward as a writer with my own voice. I kept adding to the piece – a new scene or monologue every time some other director or theatre company asked to produce the play – and it remains a living thing. Even now, as it finds a printed home in this edition, I've continued to tweak the material and to let it evolve as it desires. The structure of the thing certainly allows for the pieces to ebb and flow in a way that a more formally written play might not. The idea was to create the sense and mood of an evening being played out in a bar or a strip club, with less emphasis on real time than in some of my later plays. The men and women are types, relying strongly on casting to give individual characteristics to each person, since I saw the universe as a whole made up of people who were as similar as they were different. A living, breathing, throbbing puddle of need and neuroses.

One of my most savage and immediate reviews of the play came from an audience member when I staged the show as a graduate student at New York University. A monologue about midway through the play talks about AIDS (one of several that do, in fact) and during a performance one of our spectators shouted out, 'Kill the playwright!' The actors kept going, I settled down a bit lower in my seat and we got through the rest of the show. It was frightening but also a little thrilling, to know that simple words on the page could prompt someone to that kind of action (one that usually doesn't happen in the live theatre these days). It gave me a rush and also reminded me that I have a duty as a playwright always to say the truth and to push boundaries and ask questions. That's the job and it's a job I love. You'll have to drag me out of here screaming if you want me to quit now.

The Mercy Seat came many years later – just after the tragedy of 9/11 – and grew out of me asking that important storytelling question: 'What if?' I'm not the most topical or political of writers, I prefer gender politics over the other kind, but I did see a moment where a profoundly personal question could be asked on stage while utilising the backdrop of a public outrage as its platform. The question was: 'Can a person still be selfish in a time of national selflessness?' Sadly, the answer was a resounding 'yes' for both my characters and the nation as a whole, as time would show. Even when writing this more newsworthy place, I still found myself interested in a man and a woman, how their love (or lack of it) was affected by a crisis. The play was given two beautiful productions, first in 2002 in New York, followed by a towering one in London at the Almeida Theatre in 2003.

This Is How It Goes and *Some Girl(s)* premiered barely days apart in London during the summer of 2005. One began life at the Donmar Warehouse (still one of the finest spaces I've worked in) while the other sprang up in the West End at the Gielgud Theatre in a production fronted by the actor David Schwimmer. This was a textbook example of how different two experiences can be for a writer having their work done in the same city. I only spent a little time with either production as I was not directing them, but the scope of one naturally dwarfed the other (a commercial production v. a smaller subscription house) and where I felt like I was constantly rewriting on one, the other seemed to have come out of me finished and ready for production. It was a schizophrenic experience but I feel so lucky to have had them together at one time (during another summer of turmoil – this time in England with the London bombings that put fear in the hearts of even the sturdiest of theatre patrons).

Both plays feature a writer (or would-be writer) creating confusion in the lives of people that they've grown up around, so I must've been working something out in my own life or just stuck on a particular theme. I've learned not to ask too many questions of my muse: when she comes and offers up a story, I am thankful and take what she has to offer. This is not an easy profession. It's not digging ditches, I grant you that, but it's hard work and I love it and so when I get an idea I roll up my sleeves and get down to business. That's how it goes. Inspiration followed by perspiration.

A side note is in order: the original title of *Some Girl(s)* was *Some Girls (I Fucked Over)* but producers ultimately did not agree with my sense of this having great commercial appeal. Therefore, *Some Girl(s)* was born with me holding fast to at least my set of parentheses.

Helter Skelter and *A Second of Pleasure* are two more recent works that came out of commissions for short-play festivals. I love the short form and still write as many of these pieces as time allows. You have a freedom of form and idea that is much harder to sustain in a full-length play. I can take an idea that is just a flicker and turn it into something playable for ten or fifteen minutes on the stage out of which I could never create a two-act play. I am at home in this form, playful and mischievious, and it's still a joy to be asked to write a short play and know that it has a home somewhere. *Helter Skelter* was written for a German theatre who put on a collection of my short plays, and was then done at the Ensemble Studio Theatre in New York during their marathon of short plays under the alternate title *Things We Said Today* (substituting one stolen Beatles title for another). *A Second of Pleasure* was taken from one of my stories in the collection of nearly the same name and first staged at 59E59 in New York as part of the 'Summer Shorts' festival that I've been happy to be a part of five times over now. Both are portraits of men and women in moments of crisis – a topic I just can't stop picking at. Hey, if it was good enough for Eric Rohmer and John Updike and Edward Albee, it's good enough for me.

I can't finish this introduction without thanking the good people at Faber & Faber for their sustained interest and commitment to my writing. It's nice to have a home. I am also very excited by the cover art to this volume; I've always admired the pop world of Roy Lichtenstein and this piece in particular spoke directly to both myself and my editor as a perfect representation of my thematic universe. Thank you, Roy, for being so damn clever.

So there you have it: Neil LaBute in six easy steps. The plays represent a fair amount of time in my actual life and a great learning curve in my artistic education. I think that I've found my voice along the way and I've enjoyed nearly every minute of the journey. I have found myself to be a thorough and quick-witted theatre artist and a person of many and profound personal faults. I will continue to hone the one and to work on the other. I'd like to achieve a more perfect balance but we all have things we need to work on. That's what makes us human.

Well, most of us, anyway.

Neil LaBute
May 2014

FILTHY TALK FOR TROUBLED TIMES

Scenes of Intolerance

Filthy Talk for Troubled Times was first produced in February 1990 at the Westside Dance Project, New York City, in a production directed by Neil LaBute.

Previous versions of this text, under the same title, were presented at various regional locations, beginning with the University of Kansas in 1988.

Characters

Man One
Man Two
Man Three
Man Four
Man Five
Waitress One
Waitress Two

Silence. Darkness.

Lights up slowly to reveal five men huddled in small pockets around a bar and various tables. Two topless cocktail waitresses move about them, silently filling orders and cleaning up.

After a brief tableau, Man Two moves to Waitress One. Speaks quietly in her ear.

Waitress One (*to Man Two*) . . . No, I don't think so.

Man Two moves back to his place near Man One.

Man Two Fuck 'em.

Man One Right . . . Fuck 'em.

The other Waitress looks down at the filthy table before her. There is no tip.

Waitress Two Fuck 'em.

Man Four makes an obscene gesture at an unseen person.

Man Four Fuck 'em.

Man Three responds.

Man Three Fuck 'em, yeah . . . you bet.

Man Five looks around the room with disgust.

Man Five Fuck 'em. Definitely . . . fuck 'em all.

Long silence.

7

Man One . . . Alright! So you found her attractive . . . big fucking deal, right?

Man Two Sure. But I'm not gonna let my guard down, correct?

Man One No chance in hell. Fuck, you let slip you admire the bitch, you're picking out nursery wallpaper next week . . .

Man Two Hey, nothing wrong with being conservative.

Waitress Two (*overlapping*) . . . Tell me this isn't true. If we could get one really good penis – I mean, take turns keeping it in our freezers, bring it out at parties, that kind of thing – fuck, we could do away with men entirely!

Man Five (*overlapping*) . . . Shit, it's not like I'm dying to meet somebody. I mean, with all this new data they're throwing at us, science says I'm sleeping with like, everybody she's screwed in the last five, maybe ten, years. So if she's at all promiscuous . . . Fuck, that makes me a fag. (*Beat.*) I mean, at least in theory . . .

Man Three (*overlapping*) . . . But if she invites me in, okay.

Man Four That's it, huh?

Man Three Fuck yes . . . I mean, I don't expect anything for buying dinner, springing for a movie, shit like that . . .

Man Four Yeah, that's low class . . .

Man Three But some chick, she lets me in the front door? Then hey, I figure it it's open season . . .

Man Four Seems reasonable.

Man Three Otherwise, she's a tease, right? Now, I can see making clear on the porch she's a prude bitch, doesn't go in for all the humping and what have you – in fact, I kinda admire that – then it's a handshake and 'I will see you soon'. Fine. (*Beat.*) I never call the gash again so long as I live, but fine . . .

Man Four That I can handle . . .

Man Three Right. But if it's in over on the couch . . . 'Is there a late movie on? I've got a nice Chablis . . . ' Bunch of shit like that . . . (*Beat.*) Fuck it, the bitch is mine.

Man Four Seems reasonable.

Man Three Yep. The way I see it . . . she opens one door, she opens 'em all.

Waitress One (*overlapping*) . . . I mean, what is going on out there? Huh? Honestly. It's safer in here – with my tits out and all of these guys around – then it is out on the street these days. And I'm being completely serious . . .

> *Long silence.*
> *Waitress One crosses the room, taking a drink order from the men. They watch her in turn.*

Man One Would you look at that –

Man Four – bitch over there?

Man Three I wonder if she's –

Man Five – wearing anything under that skirt?

> *She exits.*
> *Man Two watches her leave with contempt.*

Man Two . . . Ahh, who cares? Fuck 'em.

> *The men return to their cabals for more private conversation.*
> *Brief tableau.*

Bar lights fade down as Man Three is highlighted: (each pocket of conversation will be illuminated one after the next as the evening moves along).
Man Three sits at the bar.

Man Three . . . Fine then, I'm not gonna lie to you . . . it scares me shitless. Hey, I don't look forward to sprouting lesions down at the free clinic because some loose-bummed eunuch screwed the friend of a friend somewhere down the line . . . that's not fair. I never did anything to him . . . not unless I was pretty drunk!

He laughs.

I'm kidding . . . but AIDS is some spooky shit, don't you think?

Pause.

Still . . . I'll do whatever I can to help. Answer phones, collect money at shopping malls, knock on doors, whatever. Put me down for it. And why? Because it's an 'issue', and issues are important, so, whatever they need . . .

Pause.

I just wish people'd do me one favour: don't try and tell me that Rock Hudson was queer, okay? I mean, I'll sit and look at their charts and filmstrips for weeks . . . that's fine. Just don't say that about Rock. You ever see him in *Pillow Talk* . . . with Doris Day? You know he was fucking her offscreen . . . Come on! Had to be . . . How about *Giant*? There's a great movie . . . and you wanna sell me the notion that Hudson'd rather be popping little Jimmie Dean than Liz Taylor? I say go fuck yourself . . .

Pause.

Hey . . . you must've at least watched an episode of
McMillan and Wife, right? Well, you see it . . . it's still on
cable . . . and I'm saying there's no way that McMillan
ever got down on his knees for some other guy – if you
knew anything about that character you'd know that
Hudson just did not have that in him!

Pause.

I'll be glad to do what I can to help . . . but seriously, lay
off Rock. That's where I draw the fucking line.

Man Two stands with Man One.

Man Two . . . Where the fuck is she?

Man One Who?

Pause.

Man Two I don't know . . . haven't met her yet.

Man Four stands talking to Man Five.

Man Four . . . Look, I'm not saying it's for everybody . . .
right? Overall, pushing shoes for a living is a gigantic pile
of shit . . . no question. I am, however, suggesting an
alternative reality here . . . offer up a few of its advantages.

Pause.

Yes, sure, there's the low pay, hustling for commissions . . .
fine, agreed, that's bullshit. And yeah, some old cunt
staggers in with her fucking gams shoved down in boots
she's been traipsing around the mall in all day . . . frankly,
the stench makes my balls crawl up in my throat . . .
no man deserves that. And there are those days when
you're sitting on that stool tying a pair of Buster Browns
on some screaming preschool bitch or helping one of
those poor crippled fucks find a reasonable-looking gimp
shoe – you know, with the big heel and the soft insole –

that kind of thing. Times like that, you figure . . . fuck, life as I know it is over.

Pause.

But then . . . suddenly . . . it happens. A fucking miracle transpires.

He savours this thought a moment.

I'll be helping one of the usuals, like I said, and I will happen to glance over, very casual, into the mirror next to me . . . occasionally I'll score a little pantie action or a touch of thigh . . . and . . . shit, there it is. My reason for living this otherwise very fucked existence.

Pause.

Some broad, maybe thirty, thirty-five – still firm is the point I am making here – she's sitting back in one of our captain's chairs with a leg up on the shoe bench. I mean, she has the right, doesn't she? It's a big fucking mall, kids are really chapping her ass with their whining . . . so she's sitting there, waiting for one of our lazy high-school pricks to get her some sandals or something . . . and, I mean, she's really relaxing so, if I lean down just enough and the light is with me – yes, certain factors are key – but if things are working in my favour . . . shit, I can see all the way to Antarctica! I could just reach over and plant my territorial flap . . . I mean, fuck, I am right there!! Ohhh . . . no briefs, nothing. Nothing but snatch. (*He smiles.*) Snatch à la mode . . .

Pause.

So I'm sitting there, minding my own business, playing my natural part in the food chain, as it were . . . and I swear to God, I'm starting to see, like, daylight coming up from down there! And why is this? Because . . . this bitch has got her mouth open and she's smiling . . . right at me. She smiles, and she's creating a natural shaft of sorts . . . sunlight is just streaming through!

Pause.

Fuck . . . drop my shoehorn, snap a lace . . . whatever. Lose the sale, tough shit! She's got me now, I'm in for the ride on this one. She moves a bit, arches her back a touch, for effect . . . and I'm not kidding you, she's starting to prism down there . . . I mean, it's a fucking rainbow. This cannot be happening!! I look up . . . the smile. I look down . . . the sun sets in the west . . . I look up again . . . she's still got that grin on her face! So . . . I smile the fuck back until she's halfway out to the car.

Then . . . I stroll back into the stock room and get down on my knees – I don't care who's watching – and I give thanks for being gainfully employed. I mean, a guy sees a vista like that one . . . he's gotta have faith that a greater being than himself is running this show. You know?

Waitress Two stops at a table, wiping it with a rag.

Waitress Two . . . Yep. He was a real fucker, that one . . . I mean, a first-class, cock-sucking, piece of shit . . . fucker! You bet he was . . .

Pause.

I mean, he was a . . . well, he wasn't totally fucked, I guess . . . but he was a prick. Treated me like shit! Oh yeah . . . a real prick sandwich, he was, no doubt about it. I mean, he could . . . well at best he was a true son-of-a-bitch. That much I know . . . I mean, some bitch, somewhere, is plenty proud to call him 'son'. Trust me . . .

Pause.

Bastard! Yeah . . . that's more like it. That rolls off the tongue more freely when I picture him. He was a complete bastard! I mean . . .

Pause.

Well, he . . . he was not very nice. Okay? I don't care
what you say. He wasn't very, ahh . . . I mean . . .

Pause.

What the fuck do I mean? Well . . . I mean . . . (*Beat.*)
Shit, but you see what I'm getting at, don't you?

Man One talking to Man Four.

Man One . . . So these gals just think I'm gonna hump
their legs like some fucking mongrel, anytime they
want . . . right there in the office. Whatever moves them,
you know? Like I just need it all times of the day, can't
make it till we're back at my place . . . don't have the
fucking decency that God gave a two-legged creature or
something, right? (*Beat.*) Got a touch a' colour-blindness
. . . doesn't make me a sons a' bitching Shar Pei, does it?

Pause.

I could see it coming, once I got that dog food account –
which is so shitty, I mean, nobody wants to push those
fucking 'Puppy Chunks,' it's our worst seller – it's simply
the fact that I'm now in this huge position of control.
Ever since I moved up I've had the whole junior staff
scratching at my office door like they were in heat . . .

Pause.

I'll tell you something: you can try and measure success
all you want – buy the 'Beamer', fly first-class, whatever –
but you're wasting your time. If you're a guy and you
achieve any kind of plateau in your career . . . power just
rolls out from between your legs like f-ing cologne, and
the iciest twat in the place – bitch who wouldn't tell you
the building's on fire eight months ago – she's down there
at your feet with the rest of 'em . . . begging for scraps.

Pause.

Here . . . lemme give you a piece of advice on how to survive in the business world. The best way I've found of staying on top of these ladder-licking animals . . . simple. You let them come around all they want – one at a time, you can't take on the whole pack at once, right? Then, let her roll over on her side there, like the poor stupid bitch she is, all warm and inviting . . . and right when she's making her move, all squatted down there like an asshole on her hindquarters . . . you lift your leg and shit in her face! (*Beat.*) Believe me, she'll get the point.

Pause.

Hey, it's not pretty . . . but when you're working with executives, it's effective as hell.

Man Five and Man Two stand at the bar.

Man Five . . . This is fucked!

Man Two What's that?

Man Five Look at all the guys here tonight! There's at least as many men as there are chicks! . . .

Man Two I know it . . .

Man Five These bitches . . . they really got it figured, don't they? It's like . . . all I see at work is pussy . . . I'm just about the only guy left in my division, practically . . . I mean it. It's like a travelling poontang exhibit! Course, what good is it? Can't touch a fucking one of 'em.

Man Two Yeah, those business things never work out . . .

Man Five No shit . . . but they're everywhere! And some of those rags are making, maybe upwards of twenty, twenty-five thousand now . . . a year! And I mean every year . . .

Man Two Yeah? Well, I suppose if they . . .

Man Five And I'm talking about more than one! Shit, these women execs are all over the place! Like fucking cockroaches . . . (*Beat.*) But okay, fine, equal rights, women's lib, fine . . . for women today, sitting in an office is the new masturbation. So be it. I don't wanna get off on a tangent here – but hey, seriously, what is the deal? I come here and I gotta stare at guy's asses all night? Where do all the career gals come dinner time? They gotta eat, don't they? Gotta have a drink sometime . . . fuck somebody . . . I mean, they're human, after all. Pretty much. But look at this! There are easily an equal number of guys floating around the place tonight . . . it's at least fifty–fifty . . . that like . . . umm . . .

Man Two Ahh, one to one . . .

Man Five Right! What the fuck kind of ratio is that? I'm a single guy . . . so, how's this work, I get one piece the entire night? Who wrote those fucking rules, I'd like to know . . .

   Pause.

And that's if all goes perfectly. No snags of any kind – but what if a set of twins stumble in here off the street? Huh? What about those two guys? What then? I suppose it cuts me out a little more, right? What am I standing at then, maybe three-tenths of a fuck? . . . Tit and maybe a handful of pubic hair . . . Fuck that! I'm throwing my money away being here tonight! I'm paying eight-fifty a pop on drinks to not even get a one-snatch minimum? I'm outta here.

   He starts off.

Man Two Hey . . .

Man Five Yeah, what?

Man Two Well . . . uh, what if the twins are girls? I mean, you might end up with both of them, right? Maybe. And that'd be . . . two. At least that would be something. I'm just saying 'maybe', It could happen . . .

Pause.

Man Five You know, I like the way you think . . . very optimistic. Okay, I'll buy us another round, see what happens . . . and listen, if any women come by, let me do the talking . . . okay? I know how to handle these things . . .

Waitress One stands alone. Stacking glasses.

Waitress One . . . Okay . . . I'm gonnna stand right here, you stand still, you're a better target, right? I'll stay right here, and the next guy that comes by . . . I'm gonna talk to him. I mean, really talk. Communicate.

Pause.

I just wanna reach out . . . make some contact, you know? A signal, that is all I need. A verbal sign that rises up – and this is important – not just between a man and woman, but simply . . . us as human beings. Two like creatures reaching out and saying 'Hey, I'm here. For God's sake, I'm here! I'm alive!'

Pause.

And if that works into dinner and a movie, well then . . . it's fate.

Pause.
　　Man Two moves past. She looks at him, then turns to look away. Awkwardly, he walks slowly off.

Waitress One Okay . . . the next guy who comes by, *he's* the one. I mean it . . .

Man Two sitting alone.

Man Two . . . Fuck.

He contemplates this.

What's the matter with that word, anyway? 'Fuck.' You say it to somebody, they're usually offended as hell. Well, fuck . . . at least I had the courtesy to say something.

Man Four stands in a corner of the room.

Man Four . . . I just refuse to believe that women could ever find me repulsive . . . it's a mind-set, I guess, but I know I'm correct in thinking this . . .

Pause.

And if, perchance, one does – well then, fuck her. There's more where she came from . . . trust me.

Man Five sits alone.

Man Five . . . Fuck it, that's it . . . one more person smiles at me, I'm gonna kick some ass . . .

Pause.

This is not a fucking game . . . You wanna smile, do it on your own time! You wanna fuck, pull up a chair . . .

Man Four chats with Man Two.

Man Four . . . Huh? 'Silence equals death'? Bullshit! 'Silence' is not speaking our loud. (*Beat.*) 'Death' is letting some guy put his thing up your ass, right?

Pause.

I mean, a person comes down with a cancer, some kind of Lou Gehrig's disease . . . hey, let's get Jerry out there, hustling for money . . . I am with you. But some dude is walking around after sex and he's got shit all over his dick, ya figure he's pretty much on his own. (*Beat.*) And I don't think that's so cold . . .

Waitress Two stands talking with Waitress One.

Waitress Two . . . Shit. He really just bent me over, and I don't mean in the good sense . . .

Pause.

I guess I opened myself up for it, but you figure . . . just . . . it stands to reason, doesn't it, that eventually things have gotta click? I mean, they can't *all* be motherfuckers ! Can they?

Pause.

God . . . who in the fuck goes to the trouble, huh? Why not say, 'Fuck off! Leave me alone!' Maybe I'd respect him more. I'm with the guy seven months, no questions, not any pushing – I learned my lesson with that shit years ago – and so, Sunday, he buys a ring, takes me to dinner and gives me the thing – and this was not shitty quality, it was a gem cluster, that had to cost something – so . . . what? What happened? I mean, I fucking paused for a second, a split second! I'm in my thirties, for chrissakes, a marriage proposal takes a minute to register, you know? Then . . . so he grabs it back, says, 'Actually, I've reconsidered. We should stop seeing one another . . . it'd be best. I've met someone . . . ' *What?* Is this a fucking joke?! Could he really be that . . . evil? I mean, you don't just do that . . . that kind of hurt takes planning, he had to wanna hurt me . . . right?

Pause.

Bastard! There's an unwritten law, isn't there? You don't even talk about weddings, shit like that, unless it's all the way. You just don't . . .

Pause.

So . . . you can imagine, I'm reeling by this time, fucking crying right there in the restaurant . . . Shit . . . I'm a mess. And he tells me to 'take it easy'. Easy! Here's a guy I'm all ready to take a blood test with and he says I'm making a scene . . . Well, I have this funny way of being hurt when I find out my steady is banging a teenager from his 'Intro to Lit' class . . . I'm silly that way. Anyway, there I am, weeping in my soup – this one's gonna hurt, I could feel it – and then he leans close, pats me on the head . . . says he'll cover the move-out, wants to pay for my new utilities, everything – and 'can we still see each other . . . dinner?'

She takes a quick drink.

My hand just shot out . . . even thinking back, I don't think I could've controlled it – maybe – but I didn't let go of his balls until he passed out in his salad. (*Beat.*) I just kept turning 'em, full revolutions like the whole scrotum would come free if I just worked on it awhile – for a minute there, I thought I could feel the fuckers giving way, I really did! – but, I couldn't get 'em to come off . . .

Pause.

You know, for all the stink guys make about them, those little bastards are pretty solid. (*Beat.*) Too bad, I could've used something to remember him by . . .

Man Three stands with Man Five. They watch Man Four pass by.

Man Three . . . Fuck, I'm glad I'm a guy! You know?

Man Five Yeah, why's that?

Pause.

Man Three Because then I don't have to date 'em.

Man One talking to Man Four.

Man One . . . And I was going into the racquet club –
this was a couple months ago – and out comes this
couple . . . regular people, sweats and whatnot on . . . but
the breeze is pretty solid and so one of them, the woman,
turns her face away from the wind, toward me . . . and
I'm staring into the face of death, I swear to God! I mean,
give this bitch a scythe and just save her some time, I'm
not kidding you! This is deathbed material here . . .

Pause.

Oh, no question she had it. (*Beat.*) Absolutely none . . .
Her eyes are, like, blinking 'HIV' in Morse code to me!
Seriously . . . but I smiled at her. I did. And you know
what? (*He smiles.*) Her face lit up, Jesus . . . you'd've
thought I was Jonas Salk or something, the smile that just
suddenly appears. And I felt good about that. I did . . .
It was just . . . my tiny bid for humanity. You know?

Pause.

But: the whole time – and this only took a few seconds,
but all while we were passing – I wasn't thinking
'humanitarian gesture, reach out to my fellow creatures'
crap. No. I'm noticing that her hair is wet and now I'm
trying to figure our if she used the hot tub, the ice plunge
or what. Same old me. (*Beat.*) Anyway, I shot baskets for
maybe twenty minutes and then went home.

Pause.

Obviously I showered at my place . . .

Man Five sits and talks.

Man Five . . . So this buddy of mine, and I'm – before I
say this I should mention that we were all pretty stoned
at the time – but me and a few guys I know . . . we

caught these two gays in the park one night, and they were fucking. Yeah. Not even very late, middle of this neighbourhood, over near the kiddy-slide. Seriously.

Pause.

So this friend – he's really a nut – he sneaks over to 'em, motions the rest of us to come with him, and suddenly, we, like, jump 'em and we pin these buttfuckers down. And he . . . well, he starts screwing the one on top, right? Seriously, guy drops his pants and – so we're all rolling around on the grass, holding these two down – the one on the bottom reveals himself to be this fucking Chinese dude – don't know what the fuck's going through the other queer's mind, stooping that low – but we're holding 'em down, and my buddy's forcing the guy on top, who is now in the middle – it was confusing when it was happening, too – but he's making this son-of-a-bitch hump the chink underneath while he rides this top guy. I mean the middle guy. Well, you know what I mean! Can you believe that?!

Pause.

Both these fags are weeping now, I mean, fucking gasping for air by the time it was over but he just kept doing it anyway, our friend does . . . screaming at 'em, 'That'll teach 'em!! That'll teach 'em!!' (*Beat.*) This guy *really* gets wired when he smokes . . .

Pause.

Anyway, I don't know what the *fuck* he thought he was teaching 'em . . . but it's still, you know, a pretty interesting story.

Waitress One stands talking with Waitress Two.

Waitress One . . . I kid you not . . . he stood there and called me a cunt. Figure that one out . . .

Pause.

'Cunt' . . . why is it that there is no moral equivalent to the degrading . . . scatological . . . slang that men use on us? Hmm? You know as well as I do that anything we fire off at them pales compared to the ammunition they have . . . right at their fingertips . . . 'Twat', 'gash', 'slash' . . .? Ohh, and . . . what about 'slit'? Huh? And, trust me, this is far from a comprehensive list . . .

Pause.

Listen to those words! God, they are hateful . . . violence-oriented . . . Hell, they've even got better consonant groupings than our slurs to them do! It is a real shame when we can't even keep up in a fucking name-calling contest! And the thing is, if you look at the words they use, and I mean, really study 'em, they apply to men much more readily than they do to us. (*Smiles.*) Listen, I speak from experience when I say . . . just because some man doesn't *have* one does not necessarily mean that he can't be one.

Pause.

Right? I mean . . . shit, look at that guy over there: now he's a cunt if ever I saw one. He just doesn't know it yet . . .

Man Four sits talking.

Man Four . . . Trust me. you can tell when some bitch wants you. I am not kidding, you really can . . . Something . . . in her eyes, maybe a touch of whisper in her 'Could you pass the salt?' Could be anything, but it'll be there . . . if she wants you. (*Beat.*) There's always some telltale flicker when they really mean it. You just gotta watch for it . . . keep your eyes open.

Pause.

Course . . . it's a hell of a lot easier if she just walks up and says, 'Now why don't I just slip you out of those jeans and spin around on your dick like a fucking Christmas ornament?'

Pause.

But, hey, you can't count on that, so, it's best to plan ahead . . .

Man Three sits with Man Two.

Man Three . . . But what if the bitch gives me a disease? Huh?

Pause.

Well, fuck . . . I guess it's better than leaving her phone number. I mean, penicillin's one thing, but ringing me up all hours and chatting . . . that's where this shit gets messy.

Waitress One stands alone.

Waitress One 'Commitment' . . . Com-mit-ment. Hearing that word come out of my mouth used to mean so much to me . . .

Pause.

Now it just means that when some guy wants to sleep with me *and* one of my friends . . . I promise to make it sound like it was my idea.

Man One stands at the bar.

Man One . . . You know, I have never cheated on any woman . . . I mean, that I've had a serious – and I'm emphasising serious here, but – a serious relationship with. *Ever.*

Pause.

Well . . . at least not that first night . . .

Man Three sits talking with Man Four.

Man Three ... And I don't mean this in a degrading way.

Man Four Right ...

Man Three I'm just offering it as an exhibit ... a truth ... a manifesto, if you will, of unbiased insight. See?

Man Four Okay. But what the fuck's your point?

Man Three I'm just saying ...

Man Four Yeah?

Man Three ... that as a basic fact ...

Man Four Okay ...

Man Three ... the male member's better than the female. That's all I'm saying. And, I'm not implying 'better' in the sense of 'better than' – not specifically, not in the physical sense, or mentally, or even religiously, although I personally do believe there is a slight spiritual advantage, or edge, if you will, to the male member. (*Beat.*) Honestly ... the female is inferior.

Man Four So, you're saying ... what? The male member is better?

Man Three Right. But in no way do I want to start a thing here, a scene of any kind. Too fucking easy ...

Man Four Okay, but ...

Man Three I just wanna entertain this idea, no more than a germ of a thought, really ... a nugget, but I think it holds true ... the superiority of the, umm ...

Man Four ... average male?

Man Three Right. (*Beat.*) The male member.

Man Four 'Member'?

Man Three Exactly.

Man Four Member of what? What the fuck's the guy a member of?

Man Three Excuse me?

Man Four What're we talking about here . . . is this a ball club or something?

Man Three Oh. No, no . . . I'm not referring to 'it' as a 'he' . . . I'm making 'it' an 'it' . . . spade a spade, really. *The* male member – actual appendage.

Silence.

Man Four What're you . . . you're not talking about some guy's thing?

Man Three Right . . .

Man Four His dick?

Man Three Well . . . yes. His member, penis. Whichever you prefer.

Man Four Ahh, I don't prefer anything – what are we talking about dicks for? Who the fuck is this guy?

Man Three No one, actually . . . just a hypothetical figure.

Man Four Well, I don't wanna . . .

Man Three I'm just suggesting this, and only in the broadest terms – as a thing, simply as an entity unto itself . . . the male member is better than the female. (*Beat.*) You see what I'm shooting for here? Just a kind of very open-ended thesis . . . something we can springboard from. Scientifically.

Man Four A thesis . . . about some guy's dick?

26

Man Three Right. Although it needn't be an actual dick . . . or member . . . of someone we know. As I stated earlier. That's the beauty of this whole concept . . . it's universal!

Man Four We're talking about . . . what? All the guys' . . . joints in the world? *Every*body?

Man Three Sure. All-encompassing. But again, only in the most polite, self-deprecating terms . . . this is not meant to drive a fucking wedge between the sexes!

Pause. Man Four considers this.

Man Four So you're saying that a guy's dick . . .

Man Three But again, very politely . . .

Man Four Okay, but . . . you're politely saying that a guy's penis –

Man Three – or member – they're synonymous, really . . .

Man Four Some guy's . . . fuck . . . 'member' . . . is better than some lady's?

Man Three Correct. All thing's being equal, the male member comes out the big winner.

Pause.

Man Four Okay. I can see that.

Man Three Sure. It's simple . . .

Man Four What you're *really* saying –

Man Three – just suggesting –

Man Four . . . is that the dick would kick some ass! If we compared the two.

Man Three Well . . . yes. It would certainly distinguish itself . . .

Man Four That I can believe!

Silence. Man Four about to say something else. Stops. Thinks.

Man Three Trouble? What?

Man Four In theory . . . I'm seeing a practical problem. My problem is . . . and this, I believe, is universal . . .

Man Three Yes?

Man Four Women . . . don't have 'em.

Pause.

Man Three Mmm . . .

Man Four See what I mean? How can you compare the two when . . .

Man Three Still, I believe comparisons could be drawn.

Man Four How?

Man Three I'm speaking of *broad* parallels, of course . . . but certain factors are still undeniable.

Man Four Like what?

Man Three Well . . .

Man Four Guys got 'em and women don't. Now sure . . . they got that other thing, their snatch, vagina . . . you know . . .

Man Three Their *member* . . .

Man Four But it's not . . . is it? Not really. It's different . . .

Man Three How so?

Man Four Well, fuck, I dunno . . . I'm shooting from the hip here, but wouldn't 'member' connotate an appendage? Kind of a dangling . . . free-hanging sorta thing . . . like a . . . dick?

Man Three Or member.

Man Four Whatever! Doesn't it?

Man Three Well, yes, but I'm speaking in the most generic way. Simply weighing the two . . .

Man Four Right, right, but how can you?

Man Three What? Taking two like things and holding them up for scrutiny . . .

Man Four Yeah, but . . . still . . .

Man Three It's only a hypothesis . . .

Man Four Look, I see what you're driving at and I admire the effort. I do. All *I'm* saying is that you go ahead and compare this shit all you want to. Eventually, the truth is gonna win out . . .

Man Three But . . .

Man Four *And* the result of all this is . . .

Man Three Fair enough. I'm only interested in end results . . .

Man Four The fact remains: women do not have dicks. No fucking way . . .

Silence.

Man Three Okay . . . you got me there.

Waitress Two stands at the bar.

Waitress Two . . . but why is it that if you give a guy an abortion, he'll give you the world . . . but it you give him a kid, he gives you the front door?

Pause.

Huh? Now explain that one to me . . .

Man Four and Man Five stand together.

Man Four . . . But . . . it's . . . (*Beat.*) Aww, screw it . . . Okay, I give up.

Man Five What . . . so easily? I thought you were seriously challenging my theory here . . .

Man Four No, you've convinced me. I just . . . *how* the fuck do I get into these conversations?

Man Five Come on . . . You can't think of one thing?

Man Four Uh-uh . . . I guess you're right. *Every*thing around us is phallic . . .

Man Five Fucking right . . . or based on the phallic image.

Pause.

Man Four You're certain, though? No doubts?

Man Five Absolutely none . . .

Man Four What about food? I know we touched on some things, but all food?

Man Five You shitting me? *Any*thing. Pasta, bananas. Whole cucumber family.

Man Four And candy? Children's candy?

Man Five Take a long, hard look at a Tootsie Roll some time and then we'll talk, okay? (*Beat.*) So?

Man Four Umm, shit . . . just choose something?

Man Five Sure . . .

Man Four Ahh . . . okay, bacon?

Man Five It comes in pretty long strips . . .

Man Four Oh yeah. Fine, what about yams?

Man Five I take it that you've never seen a fresh yam, then? Can make a woman fucking quiver just to pick one up in the vegetable section . . .

Man Four Okay, fine . . . Other store things . . . Uhhh, batteries?

Man Five Phallic.

Man Four Shopping cart?

Man Five Phallic.

Man Four A mop? Oh wait, what am I thinking? Of course it is . . . with the handle thingie and . . . the . . .

Man Five See how easy this becomes?

Man Four No, hold on . . . Fuck . . . What about a lobster? Like those lobsters they keep in the tank at the deli section . . . What about . . .

Man Five Fuck, even the *tank* they keep them in is phallic! Look at it, it is longer than it is wide – and that's the only standard we can honestly follow, right?

Man Four But there's gotta be . . . what about a building? Something like that, huh? With all the varieties of architecture that we've . . .

Man Five I don't wanna push this . . . but try to imagine a building that doesn't fall into the phallic category . . . Which way do we build?! Up! *Up!* And if not up, then out. We either go horizontal – which, to be fair, is how our dicks spend a good portion of their waking hours – or we clamour for the stars . . . see? Just like the penis, all things strive to turn their pathetic little heads skyward . . . It's a bit sad, but oh so true . . . it's up or out, right? Things that go down are wrong, frightening . . . let's face it, just plain *bad*. When the Dow Jones is fucked, where's it go? Down. You gotta eat out a woman's snatch, what'll they say to you? 'Go down on me' . . . And I guess we know that is no fucking treat . . . Hell? It's down . . . Fucking Satan, that's what you ultimately find if you keep going down, that or coal mines. You wanna work in a sons-a-bitching mine? Of course not, nobody does. *All* these things . . . holes, basements? Shit . . . what good is a basement? Those fuckers flood first sign of rain. You following this? Just use this as a rule of thumb . . . up is good, down is bad. Everything is phallic, any deviations to that idea suck shit . . .

Pause.

Look at us!! We are phallic by design . . . and more than that, by nature. I mean, the world just naturally yearns to be, or become, phallic. What living thing doesn't reach toward the heavens all during its brief stay on earth? Huh? It's a brotherhood . . . it is, even with women. You've heard of 'penis envy'? It's the very basis of my argument here! Hey, those with the cocks run this place, let's quit fucking around and admit it!

Pause.

Man Four Yeah, maybe you're on to something there . . . 'cause it's . . .

Pause.

Wait! What you said about women . . . What about their private . . . well, you know . . . their privates – fuck it, members – or whatever you wanna call 'em? Huh?

Man Five Yeah. So?

Man Four Well, think about it . . . you could hardly call that thing 'phallic' It's the complete antithesis . . . isn't it? It can't be . . . I mean, shit, there's hardly any fucking shape to the thing as it is!

Pause.

Look . . . I just had this argument a little while ago with somebody and I think I'm right in saying this. Okay? Now . . . a woman's genitals can't really be considered phallic. Can they?

Pause.

Man Five Hmm . . . maybe not. (*Beat.*) Well look, with all the phallic shit floating around, we gotta have some place to put it . . . so maybe *that's* why a gal's crotch is shaped the way it is. You gotta admit, it's not exactly the most enviable design . . . I mean, you ever look up under a woman before? Huh? It's like a fucking bowling ball down there . . .

Man Four Yeah . . . but you do agree, then, a woman – or her shit underneath, anyway – is not phallic . . .

Pause.

Man Five Fine. I agree . . . No, you're right. Women, unlike the norm, are not phallic . . .

Silence.

But we fucking make 'em pay for it, don't we?

Man Three and Man Two sit at a table lost in discussion.

Man Three . . . And I gotta stop right here and say, this whole concept? It springs from a genuine love for the female race . . .

Man Two Okay . . .

Man Three But . . . women! You can't fucking trust 'em . . .

Pause.

Man Two Why not?

Man Three Well . . . personally, I could never trust anything that bleeds for a week and doesn't die . . .

Silence.

Man Two Oh. Yeah.

Man Two stops near Waitress One, falters, then moves on.

Waitress One God, I wish he would stop approaching me! I mean . . . if he's not careful, I'm gonna go to bed with him tonight . . , and that's the last thing I want!

Pause.

Actually, the *last* thing I want is to be alone, but . . . the other last thing is to be with someone.

Man One is talking to Man Three and Man Four.

Man One . . . Hey, you can say whatever the hell you want, but I'm here to level with you . . . you guys are floating up to your eyebrows in shit . . . Rock and roll has always been full of wimpy ass fucks . . . All these guys . . . Springsteen, Jagger . . . Lennon . . . fuck, even Morrison. I'm telling you, no balls on any of them. Like it really takes a big set of brass ones to give it to some pubescent groupie hiding in your shower back in the hotel. Fuck, I do that now, and I'm nobody!

Pause.

You gotta look at the old guys, the Vegas set . . . Now these were men born with their dicks securely fastened between their legs. Am I right? Dean, Jerry, fuck, even little Sammy Davis . . . hey, he may have a gamey eye, but you point him in the right direction . . . and bam! Do not

be fooled by these guys. They may be pushing some
dopey floor show for a living – you gotta eat, right? – but
in their primes, these were *men's* men I'm talking about
here.

   Pause.

Course, the king of them all was Frank Sinatra . . . right?
Now there was a man. I like that guy! He's a role
model – and you just know every woman wanted him . . .
you can see it. You gotta like Sinatra! And . . . it's not just
the voice. Believe me, plenty of guys could sing rings
around him. Crosby, Nat King Cole? Golden voices –
but, and this is the key – just as limp as fucking garden
hose! I don't know what it is, but maybe only every
fourth or fifth male singer in the world can get it up. I've
actually read about this, freak of nature. Is that odd as
hell or not? Most singers, and this has been tested, a
hard-on is just not in their repertoire . . .

   Pause.

Isn't that amazing? Documented fact . . . a lot of these
vocalists just don't have the dick for the job.

   Pause.

Nope . . . I will always come round to Sinatra. And like
I said, it's not the singing, not the Mafia connections –
that's cool, but no big deal. The fact of the matter? The
reason I admire the guy? Because he fucks.

   Pause.

Hey, everything about Sinatra says 'fuck' . . . his life, his
wives, the look. You gotta like a guy, at his age, who
pulls the fucking teething spoon outta Mia Farrow's
mouth just to take her down hard a few times . . . huh?
And especially, the Sinatra sound. You might find a better
voice, I said you could . . . but Frank's music just . . .

'fucks.' You know? There's really no better way to describe it . . .

Pause.

You find yourself with some time on your hands, spin a little St Francis on the stereo . . . Now, you gotta listen close, but in the background, quiet-like, almost subliminal . . . back near the horn section where all those no-cock singers have a bit of 'do-be-do-wop' going down – you listen close. Frankie's back there whispering a primal chant to manhood everywhere! He had to be careful, I mean, fuck, even 'the voice' had to put up with the censors, right? But he's back there . . . and you know what he's saying? Ol' Frankie's saying, 'Hey, don't be an asshole. Get those pants off her and let's fuck!'

Pause.

Ya see what I mean? Sinatra *fuck*s! And that is the truth, my friends.

Waitress One alone.

Waitress One . . . See? It's funny, isn't it? I mean, I just don't follow the guy. It's like, nobody seems to want to have fun any more. I guess that's what it is now: we're all just too serious. I mean, I'm as fucked-up and miserable as the next person, but I don' t let it get me down. You know?

Pause.

It just stupefies me . . . can you understand this mess? I'm just toying with him, having some fun – I was on the rebound at that time from somebody – and I just, teasingly, undo his fly, give his thing a playful slap or two – and he starts bawling and puts his fucking head on my shoulder! Yeah. Figure that. I'm sitting there, naked, and he's loving it, I make this move toward shedding his clothes, and he, like bursts into tears. What the fuck? So, I did the only sensible thing: I just got up, grabbed my shit and went outside – I didn't even dress until I got to the bus stop 'cause I'll be damned if I'm gonna put up with that kinda bullshit my first night back dating!

Pause.

Look, I'm plenty happy to get off with some guy right away – hell, it gives us something to talk about – but I am not gonna be his fucking psychologist. Why should I? What'd he ever do for me? Right?

Man Five sits.

Man Five . . . Never did me any fucking good, I'll tell you . . . Seriously. I've been seeing this female shrink for maybe, four years . . . you know where it got me? Huh?

Pause.

Any ideas? A bill for six thousand dollars . . . and I was still waking up with the same shit-sucking headaches I had since I was a kid . . . So guess what I did? Huh? I found my own cure . . . started banging that good-for-nothing Freudian bitch! What the hell, I figured she might scream out something in bed that she was keeping from me during our sessions – there was a time I was desperate to try anything – plus, I figured I was getting a little return on my investment . . .

Pause.

But shit, here I'm still suffering while she pulls in the dough and gets it regular on the side now – she's married, some guy I never met – try and sort that shit out! The broad sits in this big chair, very cool, reserved, legs tightly pulled together . . . listening to me whine about my mom and dad for a couple hours a week and telling me to, like, 'get in touch with your feelings . . . don't be so physically

37

motivated'. Shit like that . . . and then when my time is
up, off comes the dress and she's over on the couch
chewing on my pecker like a fucking cocker spaniel. So,
I ask you, where is the treatment here? How am I gonna
get over my sexual anxieties at this rate? I am not fucked
up, by the way, I just have some questions . . . so don't
get me wrong. I mean, look, it's not that I mind the
method she's using, it just doesn't seem very scientific,
that's all . . .

Pause.

Still, to be fair, she did knock twenty bucks an hour off of
our sessions. Fuck, I know a cheaper rate's not exactly a
cure . . . but I figure I'm making progress, right?

Man Two sits with a few of the other men.

Man Two . . . You think I'm proud of what I did? Huh?
No. *But* at least I am able to stare my mistakes right in
the fucking face, okay? Now, you got me started, you
wanna hear the end of this or not?

Pause.

Alright then. Shut the fuck up and hear me out. So, here
I am, forty-five minutes after I delivered this package . . .
and this secretary is still pulling me down on the desk for
another round of sexual gymnastics! She's roaring
through full splits, these aerial twists, unbelievable shit!
This bitch is definitely talented . . . a very phenomenal
young lady.

Pause.

But, see, she's wasting her affections on me . . . because,
fuck, I'm scared! . . . The whole time, I'm trying to get
my clothes on, wrapping things up – I'm an errand boy,
for chrissakes, I got no business humping this working
woman in the middle of her boss's office! And then

suddenly, my wallet, it pulls a no-show. Oh come on, I can't believe this shit! First, I get a chance to fuck this . . . Athena – this was a beautiful woman, no more than twenty-two – and now suddenly the gods turn around and take a dump squarely on my head. I mean, where the fuck could my ID be? I've been face-first inside this babe for not even an hour: how far can it get? I know the bitch didn't grab it, she's got nothing on – I make her bend over and check her anyway, which, by the way, she does with relish – but that fucker's disappeared! Goddammit! So, I start taking the place apart . . . I mean, practically. But no luck. Fuck! Now I'm starting to go a bit insane. I mean, there is a fucking *law* office trying to run itself the other side of the door, this lawyer could show from his meeting at any moment . . . and me and this nude typist of his are scrambling about looking for my wallet as if we're the only two people on earth . . . Jesus! Life has a weird way of keeping you guessing, doesn't it?

Pause.

Actually, it's funny though, isn't it? I mean, how one minute this broad is the finest meat I've seen on the planet, next thing you know – at least in my mind – she's a notch below a couple pictures of my brother's wedding. Fuck, once my belongings come up missing, I don't even recall ever looking at the lady again. Seriously. But, you know where I'm coming from here . . . you can't lose your wallet. You know? A wallet is sacred! It's your temple, right? It's not like the stuff inside is of monumental value, but to me the shit in those two leather pockets is my world . . . I had to have it back! So, I don't know what to think. I figure it's now anywhere between the warehouse and that gal's thighs, so I better fucking start backtracking! I say a 'Thanks!' to the girl, give her my number – it's actually to the shipping room, I don't wanna start something serious here – and I'm outta that place . . .

Pause.

I search for two fucking weeks . . . nothing. Not a goddamn *trace*. So finally, I gotta face this . . . the thing might still be back in that office. Somewhere. I head over . . . right past the secretary's cubicle – I don't even look in, how's that for fucking cold? – and straight up to the guy's desk on which I had been banging this gal . . .

Pause.

And fuck . . . I shit you not, there it is. Sitting right next to this dude's calendar, stuck through on his note spindle. Just waiting for me. Okay, he's on to me . . . What'm I gonna do? Think fast. Not that I'm scared – you fuck an employee on a man's ink blotter, I figure you can usually look him in the eye – so I decide to come clean. I explain the situation to him. And then . . . he explains it to *me*.

Pause.

My luck! I run up against a queer! Secretary like that and this guy's looking for dick to suckle on . . . go figure. He says he likes my style and would I mind a repeat performance, with a slight variation? – Yeah, I'd call a prick up my butt a variation, if ever I heard one – so, fuck . . . this is not good. I beg him, I plead. I offer to talk with the girl out front so that he can at least indulge in some of that, but no dice. Deal is, my hide for the cowhide or I can get lost . . . that's his offer. Oh man, I gotta think this through . . .

Pause.

I look at him . . . Can I just beat the shit outta him? No chance, I'm just a boy. I glance over at the wallet, but I'm sure I could never just grab it and dash or you know that would've been my course of action, I swear to God! I weighed the consequences heavily. If you learn nothing else about me, you will find I'm no pushover . . . but I see no way out. It's a complete no-win! Shit. So, I finally think to myself, 'What the fuck, it's worth it!' You gotta realise, I'm no fag, but he's got my wallet, for chrissakes! This is my personal property I'm talking about! I must've had thirty bucks in Arby's coupons alone in there . . . so.

Pause.

The rest happened in a blur. I undid my belt, dropped my pants – this young exec has his grey dress-flannels around his ankles before I could bend over – and I just held on for the ride. And . . . that was that.

He looks at the others.

Fuck you guys . . . no details! (*Beat.*) Trust my better judgement . . . it was none too pretty. I just locked my eyes on that calfskin beauty waiting for me on the desk and made it through . . . I made it! I even used the old coin purse as a bite stick at one point – to keep from crying. Fuck, I'm not ashamed to say it, I almost cried! I've got dignity just like anybody else. Anyway, the point is, my ass healed . . . no harm done . . . and more importantly, I still carry that wallet to this day. I figure, sometimes in this world a guy's got to make a few sacrifices . . . right?

Pause.

Hey, come on . . . don't look at me like that. I told you this was a bit off the beaten path. Fuck, the guy had my *wallet*!

Long silence.

Man Four Wow. So . . . did you guys fuck?

Man Two What?

Man Four You and him . . . did you do it? Like, all the way?

Man Two Am I talking to myself here? 'Did we do it'?! Take a big, fat fucking guess . . .

Man Three It was sort of unclear . . .

Man Two I mean, what am I opening up to you guys for, my health? I thought I was sharing a pretty incredible example of what a guy will do to protect something he loves . . .

Man Three Hey, just asking . . .

The other men look at Man Two. Man One gets up, moves off.

Man Two Anyway, it's in the past. Besides, who can realistically sit here and say he wouldn't have done the same thing? Huh? (*Looking at his pals.*) I mean, who here's never had a gay experience . . . right? In college, or . . .

Pause.

Oh come on . . . really?

Man One stands at the bar.

Man One . . . It just seems like we're approaching this problem ass-backwards. I mean, you gotta treat women like anybody else, right? They're the same as you or me . . . basically . . . except maybe they get to sit down to piss. But that's not really an advantage . . . not the way I look at it.

Pause.

And anyhow, in no way should some broad be able to use squatting instead of standing as a bargaining chip in a relationship . . . She is still a human being. If anything,

42

slightly less mobile than we . . . I'm just saying that we can't go around making some gal a sex object on account of what she is sporting down there. There'll be hell to pay. I'm sure of it . . .

Pause.

Nice ass . . . some kind of tits . . . nothing fancy, a respectable package . . . okay! Fine. But what am I gonna do, fall down and fucking die because she smiles at me in the produce aisle? Well, perhaps I will, but I'm sure as shit not gonna let her in on it . . .

Pause.

It's a matter of splitting hairs, I suppose, but in my book, women: sex objects . . . no thank you. But, objects of sex . . . now we're getting somewhere. You see?

Pause.

I feel word placement is key to a manageable relationship.

Waitress Two stands speaking to Waitress One.

Waitress Two . . . Oh sure. I had an orgasm . . . Once. I mean, I guess it was a orgasm . . . a muscle in my left thigh twitched. Course, I thanked the guy . . . profusely. Otherwise, he never would've shut up and I had to work in the morning. I really hate that shit . . . like when they feign . . . interest, you know?

Pause.

All this crap about men are trying to be more caring and sensitive . . . bullshit! They can kiss my ass . . . it's the same old business. You can lick 'em until you start to black out, it'd still take a court order to get them down on you . . . Instead, you're treated to thirty, maybe forty seconds of tit-massage – thrilling – a couple minutes of clumsy humping in some god-awful position – his choice, always – and then you gotta lay there and watch him buck and snort like some rodeo animal for an hour until he falls off to sleep. (*Smiles.*) Ain't love beautiful?

Pause.

Then, the topper . . . an elbow to the ribs . . . 'Hey, you make it?' Really sensitive, like we've got a fucking recipe for an orgasm! Jesus . . . take my vagina and sew it the fuck closed! Please, do me the favour. This is not my idea of a hot fuck. I mean, I am up to here with these smarmy little one-nighters with some poor, limp CPA. A couple tickets to the Ice Capades, cheap wine back at his place, and then face down on the bathroom tile for the evening while he dabbles in 'something he's never done before . . . ' Shit! Give me some romance, for God's sake! Would someone please come along and drop a decent guy right in my lap . . . Can I get some service, please?! I don't think it's unreasonable . . . some flowers, touch of candlelight . . . What the hell's the matter with a fairy-tale ending? Look, you give me my Prince Charming, and don't worry . . . I'll fuck his brains out. So far, though . . . same old shit.

Pause.

Yeah . . . winter of . . . no, I guess it was spring, actually. Spring of '89 . . . I had my orgasm.

Man Four stands near the bar.

Man Four . . . That's right, every time. My women orgasm *every* fucking time. Guaranteed.

Pause.

No, I'm not saying right off . . . What am I, a magician? There is the occasional tryst when I gotta stick with a gal for a while . . . Hell, maybe even a day or two. I remember one time . . . Chicago . . . in springtime, I think . . . I was

44

doing this gal for probably thirty hours . . . straight. It is not a fucking lie. No rest . . . always going at it. Hey, it's possible . . . We ordered food up to the room! Sure, the waiter who brought the stuff in saw us pumping away . . . I was just in for a weekender, what the fuck did I care?

Pause.

And to be completely candid, I'm someone who finds it fulfilling to let another guy in on some of the techniques I employ on any given bitch . . . I'm a Samaritan, I admit it.

Pause.

Seriously . . . thirty hours. But I got her . . . and believe me, that bitch thanked me. *Profusely* . . .

Pause.

It's a matter of control . . . and I take it personally, don't think I don't. Some of them . . . they wanna fight you, make you work for it, then pretend they never got there. Bullshit! I fucking ask them outright . . . 'Hey, you make it or not?' Now, they may try and hide it, but if they're honest with themselves, in front of their God: they always orgasm. *Guaranteed.*

Man Five stands talking to another man.

Man Five . . . Hey, that's nothing. Listen . . . Any of you guys ever make it with a gay chick? No, seriously. Like a lesbian or something of a similar nature? Huh? Contrary to popular belief, I hear those bitches are really hot in the sack, you fuck 'em on an off-night . . . I mean it! Hell, they like to dabble in dick just like a normal gal, don't let that biker get-up fool you . . . See, to them, it's like toying with witchcraft or necromancy . . . shit like that. Now, I'm not saying that I understand it completely myself . . . but I guess to a woman whose diet consists mainly of tit and bush . . . you gotta figure that pulling the real thing

up outta somebody's boxers is a little like opening
Pandora's Box! And, trust me, I'm using 'box' in an
extremely figurative way here . . .

The men laugh aloud.

Right? I mean, think of the first time you grabbed it
yourself. It's a little bit of a rush, isn't it? Course it is!
Now, come on, admit it – you guys are adults – who's
wanted to try one just to see if you couldn't turn her
around? Huh? Open those queer fucking eyes up a bit,
give her a taste of the sweet life – touch of the old 'la
dolce vita' – you know what I'm saying? 'Fess up! You
know that all those bitches are just using that homo
number as a front – it's all 'catch me if you can' game-
playing bullshit. Correct? And I figure – if you take the
time to play some hardball with these chicks – couple of
them are gonna come on over to our side . . . it's the
fucking law of averages!

Pause.

So, come on now . . . I'm looking for honesty here: who's
ever wanted to tangle with a lesbian? Be truthful!

*He waits with his hand held high. No hands from
anybody else. Slowly Man Five drops his arm down.*

Well . . . fuck, me either! I was just curious, that's all . . .

Waitress One sits.

Waitress One What do I hope for in a guy? Everything . . .

Pause.

What do I expect? Not much . . .

Pause.

What'll I *take*? Anything . . .

Man Three sits talking with Man Four and Man One.

46

Man Three . . . no, I'm serious here. You ever see your parents doing it? That's an event you will never forget . . . believe you me. I mean, I never had any trouble walking in on my mother after she just got outta the shower. To be honest, when I was in, like, junior high . . . most weekdays, I'd skip home from football early so I could catch her towelling off – that's no problem. In fact, I'm of the opinion that it was actually healthy . . .

Pause.

But . . . I always had trouble with the idea of seeing my old man with his ass up in the air . . . I never could stomach that. Just didn't seem natural, you know? Here's my father, who was a dentist – and a good one, I hear – this is a man of responsibility . . . I never had a particular need to see this guy face down in my mom's privates and cooing like a fucking baby. (*Beat.*) No thank you.

Pause.

One time, I was maybe twelve – cub scouts – I came in the house with my pinewood derby . . . the old man had worked like a beaver on that thing! Carving it, checking the weight, applying those little decals – first time I'd ever seen the guy touch a piece of fucking wood! So, I get home, I'd just won a medal or some stupid ass thing, I'm dying to show him . . . I run into their bedroom and . . . here he is with his dick down my mom's throat!

Pause.

Whoa! You can imagine my surprise at this seemingly unnatural coupling! I mean, this is a new one to me. I'm a kid, like I said, so it caught me off guard . . . but I was old enough to know that my mom's wisdom teeth weren't giving her any trouble and dad probably had no good reason for having his wee-wee down her larynx . . .

47

Pause.

But I'm a model son, right? I'm not wanting to create a scene, so I stood and watched this spectacle for maybe . . . five minutes or so . . . I was transfixed! I mean, once my eyes adjusted to the dark.

Brief pause.

Damn. I just couldn't stand looking at his big ass . . . this dentist, my father . . . cramming his pe— his member – into my mom's face. It was kind of sad, actually . . .

Pause.

Then, just for a moment, a tiny shudder of ecstasy rolls through him and he pulls away . . . and . . . I'm staring into the face of Mrs Freeman, our next-door neighbour. Ohh, fuck! She sees me, screams, I'm standing there pissing myself and stuttering . . . and you know what? That old shit just leans back on the comforter and says, between gasps, 'How'd we do, son? Where's our trophy?"

Pause.

. . . I dove at him and crammed that fucking car in his ass right up to the cockpit. Like I said, I was a good kid, but everybody's got a breaking point, right? I snapped off one of the axles but, by and large, I got most of that thing firmly in place . . .

Pause.

Well . . . he never said a word about it . . . Mrs Freeman pulled her skirt down and went back across the fence, my dad went into the bathroom to see what could be done to save the derby, and I just took off. Running. You know what? He never asked me to keep quiet about it. He never asked for my confidence or scolded me . . . never even complained of rectal discomfort, for that matter . . .

although he did stand for dinner that night, come to think of it. Over at the kitchen counter.

Pause.

But: every week after that, on Mondays, and I mean without fail, I'd find a crisp new ten-dollar bill in my lunch box. Now try and fucking figure that one out! Yeah. The old man was complex, no doubt about that . . .

Pause.

So, fuck – it's been fifteen years, he and mom are still together, the same house – I'm guessing this cash is gonna taper off, right? Everything's forgotten, as far as I'm concerned . . . but last week, I get a Western Union for a hundred and twenty bucks with a note. Says, 'Sorry about the summer. We were vacationing in Canada. Love, Dad.'

Pause.

It's a funny fucking world, isn't it?

Man One alone.

Man One . . . Listen, you call it what you want, but it's a fucking plague, it really is. I mean, I can't even step in the jacuzzi at my building any more, it's that bad. Some guy, or some girl – where does it end, right? – up to their neck in those bubbles . . . how do I know if they've got some open sore or not? Is that true or not? Right? You can't ask about something like that without sounding personal. Believe me, I have tried.

Pause.

See, I'm taking no chances with this shit – you know my neighbourhood, no thank you. I turned away two girl scouts selling cookies the other day, for chrissakes! Somebody pinned a merit badge on them with an open cut . . . I'm on machines next week coughing up blood.

Nope, if I don't know 'em, they could be a carrier. Shit, two people I do know have it! Haven't talked to them in weeks. All this research they're doing, *nobody's* checked to see that it can't be transmitted electronically. What do I know about the phone lines, right? I say, put them all in a fucking pot and boil them . . . just as a precaution.

Pause.

Still, I'm not totally callous . . . It's not like I don't drop some change in those cans they have at the supermarket. I want a cure as bad as the next person! It's just not fair, that's all. I mean, who pays the price? I'm asking you . . . who pays the . . . Well, I guess they do *die* eventually, but that's not really the point. It's you and me. Think about it. We date, we try to fuck fairly respectable women – no, I mean it, I know your type – all on the level, the usual set of positions – am I right? I can tell these things . . . You don't do anything weird, like, ahh, fruit? Do you? 'Cause I don't think the research is in on stuff like that yet . . . Be careful. Still, you're normal! Very few drugs, you only dabble, same as me, no transfusions – I mean, God, I have not used a pint of blood in years . . . Basically, everything by the book.

Pause.

But . . . who has to go around slipping paper under their thighs on the toilet seat? I won't even sit any more – I just squat and hunch over – you know what I mean. Can't kiss your friends, shit, I'm bringing *canned* beverages out to dinner now! That is the fucking end! So, who pays the price? Right? I ask you. Jesus, those queer bastards!

Pause.

And all because someone wanted to get one up the ass or can't throw away a needle or grew up in fucking Haiti . . . (*Beat.*) You know what? Some people ruin it for everybody!

Man Five talks with Man Three.

Man Five . . . What the fuck are you talking about? Hmm? Where do you get off calling me 'insensitive'?

Man Three From listening to you! Don't you hear yourself? You're an insensitive bastard . . .

Man Five What?!

Man Three Fuck, wake up . . . face it. You're a prick, big deal . . .

Man Five Fine, and who the fuck are you?

Man Three I'm a piece of shit – but at least I recognise it.

Pause.

Man Five You're a crazy fuck. Insensitive? I'll tell you fucking insensitive. The other day, I'm in line at the supermarket – there's this guy in front of me with his hand full of change – and he's buying some fucking discount *vegetables*! Couple of eggplants, a mangy-looking carrot or two . . . but you know what? He's got a smile and 'Have a nice day' for the bitch at the register who is looking down her nose at him . . . that poor bastard is eating like a refugee and he's still got a sunny attitude! I tell you what, I nearly cried – I'm not fucking with ya, I nearly crawled on the floor and wept for this poor fuck, for all those poor, sad fucks like him . . . I was late for work so I couldn't stop and talk but it tore me up all the same. So next time, maybe you'd better just stop and *think* a minute before you start pointing your fucking finger, you son-of-a-bitch!

Pause.
Man Five moves off. Man Three looks after him.

Man Three Shit . . . I wasn't implying that insensitivity was a *bad* thing! (*Beat.*) You dumb fuck . . .

Man Four stands, talking.

Man Four . . . You know, one of these days I gotta stop fucking. I mean it . . .

Pause.

I gotta get on with my life.

Man One sits at a table with Man Two.

Man One Fuck . . . fuck it . . . I mean . . . Ahhh, fuck . . .

Man Two Yeah.

Man One Shit! Ohh . . . fuck. Fuck *that* . . . I'm just . . . ohh, fuck!

Man Two Hey, I'm here for you.

Man One But . . . she . . . awww, fuck this . . . This is . . . it's all fucked. I'm . . . Fuck, fuck! I mean, *fuck*!

Man Two Go on . . . Get it out . . . Go ahead.

Man One . . . fuck . . .

Man Two Sure . . . that's it.

Pause.

Man One You know? I mean . . . ahh . . . I really just . . . shit. I really needed her.

Pause.

Man Two What? The fuck you talking about?

Waitress One walking by, stops for a moment.

Waitress One . . . Thing is, I broke up with a guy not all that long ago so I'm, you know . . . yeah. I'm not really ready for too much of anything but it's just kinda, I dunno, weird maybe, even at my age, to be without someone. To not at least have that man who calls me up

and wants to take me out, even if I can't make it. Maybe
that's all I need. Is that. Someone to want me, or . . .
(*Beat.*) What I used to do, and this is so childish, I realise
that . . . But if I had a relationship end – and I mean if,
like, he ran out on me or that type of thing, cheated with
someone – I would go out a few nights later to the bars
and look around, it didn't matter where, could even be a
restaurant or maybe a car dealer or wherever, and I'd
find – there is no way I should be telling you this! – I'd
go after the biggest loser in the place and then I'd fuck
him. Yeah. Not as a revenge or, or, you know, anything
like that – and I'm not saying the ugliest one or a mean
guy, an asshole or anyone of that nature – but just the
guy who you'd spot – and you can find this kind of
person at nearly any place you go, the laundromat or in,
maybe, Blockbuster, places like that are good – and I'd go
right over to him and offer myself up . . . (*Beat.*) I don't
mean like it was obvious or anything, not like 'Here I am,
take me now' or shit like that, but just be really really
nice to him and laugh at his jokes maybe, let him ask me
out to dinner or even to a film – you can't imagine some
of the shit I've seen with these guys, like with the subtitles
at the bottom and all that! Ohhh Jesus, I thought I was
gonna die a few times – but that's what I'd do. I would
do that. Go out on the date and then back over to his
place, if he had one, and then let him fuck me. Fuck me
as many times as he could or, or wanted to . . . do
anything he might ever dream up – trust me, a man like
the kind I'm saying here is not all that super-inventive,
they just feel so lucky to be even near you that they cum,
like, in two seconds most of the time and spend the rest of
the evening on the edge of the bed apologising to you.
Seriously. (*Beat.*) Never twice, though, okay? Don't be . . .
that mistake is one I've made so don't do it. It's not even,
I dunno, not that it's so bad or like you're starting up
some sort of relationship or anything, but if you see that

kind of guy again – any kind at all, really, but definitely
the needier ones – then you're just getting yourself in
deeper. You know? I mean, I saw this one again, type I
mentioned, took me to the local aquarium or some deal
and then out for ice creams – whatever – we fucked that
night. Like I said, how I described. Fine. Something in
me, though, and I've tried to go back and track it down,
see what it was that was so different about him but, see,
I left him my number. Yep. And of course, I mean, yes,
he calls me again – picked another moment where I was
feeling low about something, might have been about
work or, shit, I dunno, but I said alright, yeah, that I'd
see him for a second time. I think his name was Chip.
Yes, it was, because when I heard it I was, like, 'Fuck,
what? Chip?' Anyways, we go to Six Flags (you know,
with all those rides and games and things) which is pretty
fun, I have to admit, and the whole time he's a complete
gentleman . . . No sense of a 'date' where I have to hold
his hand or be all smiley, no, we're just laughing and . . .
eating pizza and a ton of good stuff, *but*, back at his
apartment that night, he's totally different. I'm serious.
Just more, and this is slightly, that's all, just slightly, but
still – wants me to undress in front of him and a little
rougher going inside me, just a few things that a girl
would notice, he's like that this time. *And* he tricks me!
He does, he totally turns a blow-job around on me where
I've been really specific in that I don't swallow – I mean,
only for a guy who's, not even just special but like 'the
one', you know? 'Him.' Marriage-guy. So I've told him
that, this Chip, he definitely knows the rules and he says
'Okay, no problem,' and so I trust him to follow the
guidelines and whatever, to just do his thing and then,
you know . . . right? But Chip gets all, I mean, he is
totally shallow breathing me here, as if we've just started
and he could go on for however long and then he's, like,
blam! He quivers and shoots a quart of his . . . I don't even

like thinking about it, so imagine when it goes everywhere, my mouth, my face, Stones T-shirt I'm wearing – ppplllttt! Okay, that's lovely! *And* as I look up at him, getting ready to head off to the bathroom to clean up, he has this look on his face. Not a smile, it's not quite that, but in his eyes, this sort of a gleam or something. The way a regular guy might look at me if he'd done that. Some good-looking guy who gets away with that kinda shit in bed or even life because of his face or what he does for a living or maybe his family . . . Chip is sitting there, off in the shadows and watching me, with this faint little grin and his pupils flaring up . . . excited by what he's just done to me. We don't say a word about it to each other and I leave not that much later, *but* he hardly even seems interested in me after that – with these big yawns and, ahhh, this continuous stream of 'I have to work in the morning' just to let me know I wasn't invited to stay over. My Stones shirt is ruined and I'm sure I definitely downed some of his nasty jizz and *that's* what I get from my second date with Chip? I'm not welcome to sleep over for a few hours? Nice. So I'm just saying, and your life is your own so do what you wanna, but hey: beware. Okay?

She nods and looks around for a moment.

However, if you wanna fuck someone so so grateful the first time around . . . and I'm saying, like, in tears and shit – *that* type of grateful – then you so have to screw a guy like the ones I was mentioning earlier. You really really do. But yeah, be careful – just the one time. Oh, and they will totally eat your pussy, and as many times as you ask them to, so that's something – not that they know what they're doing down there but most times it's still good enough to be at least okay. I mean, end of the day, it's just licking, right? Anybody can do it. (*Beat.*) But yeah. That's what I've done sometimes . . . when I'm feeling down or I find out the dude I'm with is actually married, I'll go do that. I mean, I don't end up dating 'em or anything, I'm not crazy! Right? It's just a little thing that I'll do, like a habit, or, or, or – I dunno, what else would you call it? A hobby, maybe. Yeah, like that. This thing you do every so often, makes ya feel good about yourself, nobody's the wiser. It's a hobby. (*Beat.*) I know it's not the best thing, it's probably pretty dangerous and crap like that, too, I know that, so I do try and curb that side of me these days, I really really do. But sometimes I can't help it . . . I'm a bad girl. And honestly, there is nothing like a super lame guy with his cock inside of you and sobbing as he goes to make you feel pretty alright about yourself. It's true.

She stops for a moment, thinks about it. shrugs.

Hey, I'm not pretending it's the smart choice or, or, like, the most adult thing to do in the world. I'm just saying that it works for me. Okay? (*Beat.*) Alright then. Jesus . . .

Man Two stands alone.

Man Two . . . Me? Why am I smiling? Because I know. You know? I mean, 'I *know*.' I'm aware of what's going on, okay? (*Beat.*) I'm the quiet one, guy who doesn't say much, speak unless I'm spoken to. Nod my head and 'Yeah, yeah, yeah' all night, not bat an eye, so be it. Easygoing. Like . . . some boy your sister dated in high school. Harmless . . .

Pause.

And it doesn't matter what's going on – genocide, an African village, a tractor-trailer jumps the median and jackknifes on a school van, some gal has a bleeding spell, it seeps all over my new 'posturepedic' – doesn't get me down. I just keep smiling. (*Beat.*) Why? Because inside, I'm talking it all in . . . and God, I'm laughing! I'm doubled over, tears running down, I can't catch my breath I find it all so fucking funny. 'Cause everywhere I look, far as the human cornea can make out . . . all I see are niggers, and women, and old folks and fucking foreign types. And all of 'em, scrambling around, clawing each other just to get my crumbs! It's like a vision, like some fucking revelation . . . them scattered around, like worker ants, cowering at my feet, as I tower over 'em, chewing down anything in my path.

Pause.

So some black person elbows me, knocks me off my bike in the park. Wave of the hand. Some cunt cuts in front, checkout, 'ten items', she's juggling seventeen . . . Let it go. (*Beat.*) See, I've got 'em in the long run. Because I'm a guy. And I'm white. And I've got a job. *And* I'm alive. That's right – I am not going anywhere and that, *that* just makes me howl with pleasure! 'Cause it's so perfect . . . and so dangerous.

Pause.

Fucking . . . some fucking homeless dick, snot running down, hundred degrees, the subway . . . he's staring *me* down? Go for it, pal! Mixed-up fuck'll never realise that I eat dudes like him for breakfast, and later on? I shit out diamonds . . . (*Beat.*) See, you can't do anything wrong when you're one of us.

Pause.

So, they can push and shove, gimme the finger or make eyes at me across the room. Doesn't matter a single bit. 'Cause they're lepers. They are, every last one of 'em . . . fucking freaks and monsters and I can't get enough. I can't! I wanna hold 'em, I want to scoop them up in my arms and say, 'Thank you! Thank you all for being so much less than me!' Seriously, they make me so very happy. (*Beat.*) And *that* is why I'm smiling, okay?

57

Waitress Two talks.

Waitress Two . . . So, I got the results back on Tuesday.
I passed it with flying colours . . . is that sweet? Shit, I
was sure that guy I was with at Club Med had it – body
like a god, beautiful – got him back to the room, we're in
the shower . . . his fucking crotch is the color of *rhubarb*!
I mean, nasty shit – and I still fucked him! Jesus, I need
some serious therapy, ya know? But I passed the fucker . . .
not a trace.

Pause.

They found a lump – fucking clinic! It's not even their job.
It was a 'freebee,' I guess. Little bastard is lodged right up
under my boob. I probably should've caught it . . . but I
could never get into all the self-check bullshit. Fuck that,
I have guys fondling me night and day, you'd think
someone would've had the courtesy to pass it along.

Pause.

Oh well . . . big fucking deal. Cut my tits off, see if I care!
(*Beat.*) Least I'm not gonna die of some fucking STD. I'll
still have my pride . . .

Man Three alone.

Man Three . . . And then sometimes I see myself as shit.
No, I do. 'Cause I will be out there, times it hits me, at
the pharmacy, the street, video store, maybe – snatching
the last copy of a new release, out from under some
handicapped lady. I could give two shits about it, just
wanna see her eyes well up – and I'll be doing this and
I nearly stop. Right? Stop and think to myself, 'Christ,
what the fuck am I doing? Huh?!' And I wanna go to her,
turn her around in line there and say, 'Hey, listen, whatever
it is that's wrong with you, I mean, whatever the fuck it is
about your person that irritates me so fucking much . . .

I don't care. I do not care. It's okay.' And I just give her the thing. Yeah, and we'd, I don't know, you know, stand there, I guess, or maybe go get a cup a' coffee – just let the world and all its worries pass us the fuck by.

Pause.

But then I think, 'What good would that do?' So I don't. (*Beat.*) But I suffer because of it. Seriously . . . Things I say, guys I fuck over at work, the drop of a hat, or women. *All* those women. I reflect now and then about that stuff. Question it or study myself in the mirror. I'm always looking, asking, 'Who am I? Am I indeed the shithead that I imagine myself to be?'

Pause.

But the answer is always the same. 'No.' No, I'm not. I am just fucking human. That's all. This very *human* being. Not good, not bad . . . just me. Just little ol' me.

Lights slowly fade to original tableau.
The men stand or sit apart now, more alienated than before. The waitresses are cleaning up.

Man One . . . Alright, so you found her attractive . . .

Man Three . . . Hey, nothing wrong with being conservative . . .

Waitress Two . . . We could do away with men entirely . . .

Man Five . . . It's not like I'm dying to meet somebody . . .

Man Three . . . But if she invites me in . . .

Man Four . . . Yeah, that's low class . . .

Man Two moves to Waitress One. He whispers in her ear.

Waitress One . . . No, I don't think so.

59

Man Two starts to move off.

Man Two Fuuuc . . .

He stops himself and turns to Waitress One. He smiles thinly.

Man Two . . . Thanks anyway.

He returns to a corner as the men stare off in silence. The waitresses return to clearing up.

Silence. Darkness.

THE MERCY SEAT

The Mercy Seat was first produced at the Manhattan Class Company (MCC), New York City, on 26 November 2002. The cast was as follows:

Ben Liev Schreiber
Abby Sigourney Weaver

Director Neil LaBute
Set Designer Neil Patel
Costume Designer Catherine Zuber
Lighting Designer James Vermeulen
Original Music and Sound Designer David Van Tieghem

The British premiere opened at the Almeida Theatre, London, on 30 October 2003. The cast was as follows:

Ben John Hannah
Abby Sinead Cusack

Director Michael Attenborough
Set Designer Robert Jones
Lighting Designer Mark Henderson
Sound Designer John Leonard

Characters

Abby
about forty-five

Ben
maybe thirty-three

A slash (/) indicates the point
when the following speaker begins to overlap

Silence. Darkness.

A spacious loft apartment, well appointed. Doors leading off in several directions, suggesting a hallway to bedrooms and a bathroom or two. A stainless steel kitchen, visible. Three large arched windows display a view of other buildings across the street.

A kind of amber haze in the air.

This is a large sitting room with lovely couches and chairs. Bookshelves heaped high. Framed pictures. A television plays quietly in one corner.

And a layer of white dust on everything. Absolutely everything.

Ben, maybe thirty-three, sits pressed into the corner of one loveseat, staring straight ahead. A cell phone rests in one hand. It rings and rings.

After a long moment, the front door opens and a woman of about forty-five enters, also covered in dust and carrying several plastic bags. This is Abby. She sees Ben as she removes a Hermes scarf from around her mouth but she says nothing, continuing on to the kitchen. She takes off her coat and hat, then begins putting groceries away. When she can't stand it any longer, she walks over and takes the phone out of his hand and pushes a button. The ringing stops. White clouds of dust follow her every move.

Abby . . . save it.

Ben Hmm?

Abby The phone. I turned it off to save it.

Ben That's okay.

Abby I know it's okay, I know that. That's why I did it, because it's okay.

Ben Right. / Sure.

Abby If you're not going to call then you should keep it off. / Save the battery.

Ben Uh-huh.

Abby Plus the sound . . . drives me crazy. You know?

Ben Sorry . . . I didn't hear it.

Abby Oh. (*Laughs.*) Okay . . .

Abby stands over Ben until he finally looks up. Doesn't say anything else. She shakes her head and moves back to the kitchen.

Abby So . . . you didn't call, did you?

Ben Huh?

Abby 'Call.' I asked if you called, but you didn't do it, right?

Ben Umm . . .

Abby Of course you didn't. I know you didn't.

Ben No, I didn't . . .

Abby I knew it.

Ben I mean, I didn't yet. Not *yet*. (*Beat.*) Didn't answer it, either . . .

Abby But you're going to?

Ben I'm . . . I was, ahh . . . I was going to maybe . . .

Abby Yeah, that's pretty much where I left you. At the 'babbling-to-myself' stage.

68

Ben I keep trying to. I do. To call, I mean, but . . .

Abby Really?

Ben Yeah, but . . . but I'm . . .

Abby Huh.

Abby walks over again, billowing little clouds of white behind her. She takes back the phone for a moment, turns it on. Waits. Checks something.

Abby The last number you called was the Chinese place. Yesterday morning, for your shirts. *I* called, actually . . . remember?

Ben . . . Yes. / I do.

Abby Good. / Just so we're on the same page here . . . (*Phone rings in Abby's hand.*) It's for *you* . . .

Abby sighs and holds it out. Ben takes it back and shuts it off.

Ben What I meant was . . . in my head, I was gonna . . . several times. But I . . .

Abby You couldn't. Right? / Just *couldn't* do it . . .

Ben No. I guess not. / Not yet.

Abby So, you want to, then? You haven't, but you want to . . .

Ben I dunno. I guess so . . . Shouldn't I?

Abby Oh, I can't help you with this one. Uh-uh . . . *this* one's all up to you.

Ben I know, I know . . . I just . . .

Abby You should, of course. Call, I mean. You know that, right?

Ben Yes. (*Beat.*) Yeah, I do . . . Yes.

Abby But that doesn't mean you will . . .

Ben . . . No. It doesn't.

Abby I mean, it's the decent thing to do.

Ben That's true . . .

Abby It's the *only* thing to do, really . . .

Ben I know that.

Abby But that in no way means you'll do it. Right?

Ben Pretty much, yeah.

Abby Yeah. (*Beat.*) Funny thing is, you were going to, anyway. I mean, for a *different* reason, obviously, but that's what you said.

Ben I did. / I did say that . . .

Abby That's what you told me. / You said, 'I'm going to call. I am. Right now.' You were sitting on the couch, the same *spot*, really, and I was kneeling between your legs when you told me that. Five minutes before it happened. Like, a *minute* before all this . . . happened. (*Beat.*) Of course, we've heard about that one a few times now, haven't we? The 'BIG' call.

Ben . . . Yes.

Abby Yeah, just a couple. / 'I'm going to do it, I promise. This time I mean it . . .' (*Beat.*) I even threw in a little incentive, didn't I? Down there on my hands and knees . . .

Ben I'm aware of that. / Yes. I did say it, I know . . . and I should. Call.

Abby . . . But that doesn't really mean shit. Does it?

Ben . . . I guess not.

Abby That's what I like about you, Ben. Your absolutely rigid commitment to being a flake.

Ben Thanks.

Abby You're welcome . . .

Ben A lot.

Abby You're welcome a lot. (*Beat.*) You want a snack? It's cheese.

Ben No, thanks, but . . . no.

Abby I'm gonna have some. I'm going to have some cheese . . .

Ben That's alright.

Abby I know it is! I know it's alright and that's why I'm going to have some. I'm going to fix myself a plate of this nice Havarti that I bought for you and a few crackers and then I'm . . . I'm going to . . .

Ben Go ahead . . .

Abby Oh, I will, I will . . . I'm . . . I think I'll just . . .

Abby doesn't finish the sentence but just nods to herself. She begins to cut into the fleshy white cheese and then stops as the tears come. She puts her head down but her shoulders betray her. After a moment, she calms herself and looks over at Ben, who hasn't moved but is looking at her.

That was a test, by the way . . . to see if you have a decent fucking bone in your body. / Which you failed.

Ben I just . . . / I'm sorry, Abby, but . . .

Abby What? You what . . . ? Tell me.

Ben I just can't right now.

71

Abby 'Can't'?

Ben No . . . not at the moment.

Abby 'Can't' what? Be human?!

Ben . . . No. I can't, no. / Not at this time.

Abby Jesus, you're amazing . . . / Seriously.

Ben I'm just telling you how it is . . .

Abby Oh great. Thanks, Ben, thanks a *bunch*.

She takes a piece of cheese and shoves it in her mouth. Chews. Ben sits up a bit, brushes off his legs. He turns on the phone and looks at it. It rings.

Ben Should I . . . ?

Abby Answer it or keep it off. It's up to you.

Ben Maybe I should . . . I mean . . .

Abby Yeah, maybe you really, really should.

Ben . . . Just say I'm doing alright or . . . / You know . . .

Abby Go on. / Do it. Answer.

Ben Yeah . . . I probably should.

Just then the phone stops ringing. Dead quiet. Maybe the sound of sirens way off.

Abby Too late. You're too late, Ben. As always . . .

Ben I see that.

Abby Once again, your ability to be completely off the mark is uncanny.

Ben . . . Thanks, honey.

Abby Fuck. You.

Ben Thanks again.

Abby Welcome.

They look at one another and almost smile. Almost. Ben fiddles with his cell phone a bit while Abby nibbles at a cracker.

Abby It's been nearly a day . . .

Ben I know.

Abby Almost an entire day since it happened.

Ben I know that.

Abby I mean, the world has gone absolutely *nuts* out there, it really, really has . . . No idea what's happening, no one does, the army patrolling around – there are people in *camouflage* on the Brooklyn Bridge – and you're, I don't know, just . . . I don't know where you are . . .

Ben Abby, I'm right here.

Abby . . . Why is that not comforting when you say it?

Ben I . . . I'm just saying that I know what's happening. I do. I'm aware of the situation here. / And out there . . .

Abby You are? / Really?

Ben Yeah, really. Yes . . .

Abby Huh . . . (*Beat.*) And all that knowledge of yours . . . it doesn't make you wanna do something? I mean, not even just a little bit?

Ben Of course . . . yeah, of course it does. But . . .

Abby Ahh, 'but'. There's always a 'but' when you talk to Ben Harcourt.

Ben Abby, that's not . . .

Abby 'I'd love to, but . . .' 'This Friday would be great, but . . .'

73

Ben Stop . . .

Abby 'Sure, you can suck my dick, but . . .'

Ben Abby, STOP IT!

Abby Why don't you just change your name? It's only two letters and you're there. 'B-U-T' instead of. 'B-E-N'. / It's not a bad little nickname . . .

Ben Abby, I said . . . / Why are you doing this?

Abby Because it makes me curious, that's all . . . (*Beat.*) When I was out there, walking around, staring at people . . . I suddenly wondered how you feel about it. I mean, *really* feel about what's happened . . .

Ben . . . I feel like everybody else does. / I do!

Abby I don't think that's true. / No, uh-uh . . . (*Beat.*) 'Cause after the shock of it, okay, after the obvious sort of shock that anyone goes through . . . your first thought was that this is an opportunity . . .

Ben Yeah, but, I mean . . . for us. / Just as a *possibility* for *us* . . .

Abby Who does that?! / Who in their right mind is going to see . . . *this* . . . as having 'unlimited potential'?

Ben I didn't mean it like *that* . . . / No, I just meant that . . .

Abby A meal ticket, that's exactly what you said! / 'Our meal ticket' to a banquet that, lately, you haven't seemed all that eager to attend . . . / Meaning, 'me' . . .

Ben Abby, that's not . . . / No, that is not the . . .

Abby And so that's why I'm wondering, I just wanna know . . . how does Mr. Ben Harcourt feel inside about all this? Hmm?

Ben I feel . . . you know . . . / I'm very . . . I mean . . .

Abby No, Ben, I don't know. That's why I'm asking you. / How do *you* feel? Hmm?

Ben . . . Not good.

Abby 'Not good.' Well, that's succinct, anyway.

Ben I do! I feel . . . it's awful, I mean, my God. I can't even . . .

Abby Sure, you can. Go on.

Ben What do you want me to say, Abby? Jesus . . . (*Beat.*) It's horrific. A complete and, and, and utter . . .

Abby Fill-in-the-blank . . .

Ben . . . tragedy. It's beyond belief. Biblical.

Abby Jesus, you sound like *Dan Rather*. 'Beyond belief. Biblical.'

Ben Hey, I'm a little . . . / Oh, yeah, it's so goddamn easy to . . .

Abby You left out 'calamity' and 'moral abyss'. / Tell me how it makes you *feel*!

Ben Shitty, okay?! I feel shitty about it!!

Abby And why's that?

Ben You know why . . . / Come off it . . .

Abby No, I don't, no . . . not really. / No, we talked about 'Thank God you weren't in there' and other survivor guilt-type shit, but we haven't really discussed how you –

Ben Jesus, Abby, this is . . . what do you want? I can't believe it! I'm in shock! I feel like I'm gonna throw up, okay, like I might just heave my guts out here on your . . . faux-Persian rug or something. How's that? I – feel – shitty! Is that enough?

Abby . . . It's a start. (*Beat.*) The rug's real, by the way.

Ben I don't know what to say.

Abby Well, that's nothing new . . . (*Beat.*) So . . . how shitty?

Ben Abby!

Abby No, I just mean, 'shitty' enough to walk out and do something about it? To go pitch in down at a hospital, or hand out food . . . on a 'shitty scale' of one to ten, how shitty is your shitty feeling?

Ben You're just trying to provoke something here . . .

Abby No, I'm not at all. I'm really interested. I am. (*Beat.*) I was thinking about this last night, woke up next to you on the couch there and I started thinking. I mean, I know how *I* feel, I know that, and I just wanted to be clear about where you and I stand on this thing. As a couple, I mean . . .

Ben What 'thing'?

Abby Just this whole . . . 'morality' thing. You know.

Ben I mean . . . shit, it's obvious that it's a catastrophe, right? That's . . . Why even mention that? It's beyond. I can't really find words that're even . . .

Abby Of course you can.

Ben No, I can't! They all sound . . . lame. / No. It's impossible.

Abby comes out into the living area now, provoking Ben. He stirs.

Abby Try. / Okay, no words, then. Action. That's what I'm saying. Do you feel 'not good' enough – your words, not mine – to go out and take some action, back this feeling up with a little . . . I dunno . . . some kind of . . .

Ben You want me to, what, go down on the street . . . ?

Abby Only if you feel like it . . .

Ben Of course I do. Of course, Abby, *but* . . . / I can't.

Abby Thank you! / I knew it was coming . . .

Ben You know I *can't*. You already know that!

Abby . . . Yeah, yeah, I know. I just wanted to hear that you wished you could . . .

Ben . . . I do. Obviously I do.

Abby I don't believe you.

Ben Well . . . whatever. That's not my problem . . .

Abby Yeah. (*Beat.*) On my way back down here, from the store, I followed someone. I mean, I saw this woman, wandering along, putting up xeroxes of this guy. A young man. Probably not her husband, looked too young for her, but then, hey . . . (*Points to herself and Ben.*) I don't think so, though. But she's just shuffling along in the dark with *sunglasses* on and this stack of pages, some masking tape, doing it at random. Street lamps, the sides of buildings, even on a car or two. Seriously. Didn't put the thing under the wiper but taped it right to the window. A picture of this smiling young man. In a tuxedo. 'Have You Seen Him?' and a phone number . . . (*Beat.*) I must've trailed her for, like, ten blocks or so before I realised I'd missed my street . . .

Ben Wow. / Huh . . .

Abby Yeah, 'wow'. / This whole city's covered in copies . . .

Ben Uh-huh. They said that on the news . . .

Abby Somebody at Kinko's corporate is probably laughing his ass off right now.

Ben Yep. (*A thin smile.*) . . . So, did you help her?

Abby What?

Ben I'm saying, did you help her out at all? Taping the signs up or anything?

Abby No, I didn't. / I had the . . . groceries and everything . . . but, umm . . . I was just trying to . . .

Ben Oh, okay . . . / Ahh, 'but' . . . I see.

Abby I get where you're going . . . / I get it, Ben.

Ben Fine. / Good. (*Beat.*) Look, it's sad, Abby, we already know that. It is. But my standing around and giving out *Twix bars* or shit like that is not gonna mean a damn thing . . . it isn't.

Abby I *know*. It'd just be nice if you were that kind of guy . . .

Ben Well, I'm sorry.

Abby . . . that's all.

Ben You know why I can't, anyway. / We've discussed it . . .

Abby Yeah, I know. / I *know* . . .

Ben Why I'm not answering the phone, or . . . I mean, come on.

Abby . . . The 'meal ticket', I know.

Ben So alright, then. (*Beat.*) Doesn't mean I'm not torn up about this, that it doesn't, you know, cover my soul . . .

Abby 'Cover my soul'? / Jesus, Ben, please . . .

Ben It 'moves' me . . . / Of course it does! But we've gotta look at the implications here. What it means to *us*, our future. I mean, I don't wanna sound crass here or unfeeling . . .

Abby No, that could *never* happen . . .

Ben Listen to me, I don't! But do you honestly think we're not gonna rebound from this? And I don't mean just you and me, I don't, I'm saying the country as whole. Of course we will. We'll do whatever it takes, go after whoever we need to, call out the *tanks* and shit, but we're gonna have theWorld Series, and Christmas and all the other crap that you can count on in life. We do it, every year, no matter what's going on, we still go to the movies and buy gifts and take a two-week vacation, because that's-the-way-it-is. (*Beat.*) I'm not making light of anything, either, when I say that, or making excuses for what we've decided – you know – this is not about that. I'm saying the American way is to overcome, to conquer, to come out on top. And we do it by spending and eating and screwing our women harder than anyone else. That's all I'm saying . . .

Abby That's really moving . . . / It's like seeing a Norman Rockwell for the first time . . .

Ben It is, though! That's what we do. It's what we're good at . . . / Come on, gimme a break . . .

Abby It's just . . . I mean, it's sooo, what, *outlandish*, you saying that! I don't even know where to . . .

Ben I'm not saying it's 'great', I'm saying it's a fact! This is a national disaster, yes . . . *until* the next time the Yankees win the pennant, then we'll all move on from there. Sorry, but it's true . . . (*Beat.*) And I do understand the 'big picture' here. The larger context, I mean. I do . . .

Abby Yeah? You've been keeping track on CNN, or . . .

Ben No . . .

Abby . . . somebody send by an inter-office memo?

Ben No, not exactly. I just . . . sort of . . . *know*. You know?

Abby You 'know'. Oh. (*Beat.*) You mean, like Kreskin or something? Like that?

Ben . . . You're being facetious now, right? / You didn't win the argument so now you're gonna . . .

Abby Very good. / See . . . you're not that much in shock, are you?

Ben Guess not. (*Beat.*) Actually, I don't know who 'Kreskin' is, I just figured you were being mean-spirited and went with it . . .

Abby Touché. (*Beat.*) You don't remember who 'The Amazing Kreskin' was? Seriously?

Ben No.

Abby Come on!

Ben I don't . . . I'm sure it's one of those 'you wouldn't understand' things. I probably wasn't old enough . . .

Abby Well, at least you're still sweet . . .

Ben I don't mean that you're . . . I'm just saying . . . whatever.

Abby Yep, that's us. 'Whatever.' Pretty much sums it up. (*Beat.*) Kreskin was a mystic. Well, not a mystic, really, not that, but just this guy on TV who would – looked a little like Austin Powers, in a way – he was a psychic, I guess, that's what you'd call him. Psychic. He'd walk around the studio, he had this show on television, Sundays, and he'd wander through the place telling people stuff about their lives. Reading their minds. Calling out the name of their dead dog, their mother's birth date, crap like that. Figuring out where they lost their keys or their way in life, that kind of thing. Even card tricks. Sort of.

80

That's who Kreskin was . . . around the time of *Wild Kingdom* and *Disney* and all those shows. Every Sunday night. When I was a teenager. (*Beat.*) Just forget it . . .

Ben No, but, I mean . . . what was the point of that?

Abby I don't know. I really don't . . .

Ben Oh. Okay . . .

Abby Yeah. Let's stop right there . . . at those frightening generational gaps that rage between us.

Ben . . . You're not that much older, Abby, really. I mean, a bit.

Abby Ben . . .

Ben Well, a dozen years, but . . .

Abby Just leave it.

Ben nods and stops there. The cell phone begins to ring again. They look at one another as he switches it off.

Abby Audie Murphy would be so proud . . .

Ben Who's that?

Abby No one. (*Chuckles.*) Don't worry about it.

Ben Another member of the ol' Sunday-night line-up or something?

Abby You're such a shit . . .

Ben Yeah, and don't forget I'm in shock. Imagine what I can do when I'm really firing on all cylinders . . .

Abby Oh, I'm well aware, believe me. Believe you me . . .

Ben No, come on, go ahead . . . who is this Murphy person?

Abby Geez, you're just, like, a complete cultural moron . . .

Ben Yep. Pretty much, yeah, and you know why?

Abby Yes . . . because it doesn't get you anything. There's no *reward* for knowing any of it. Trivia. / It's frivolous to you.

Ben Exactly! / That's *exactly* my point.

Abby You ever hear that 'knowledge is its own reward'?

Ben No. No, I haven't . . . and you know why?

Abby Why don't you tell me . . .

Ben Because . . . knowledge is shit, okay?. 'Knowledge for Knowledge's Sake' is pure *bull*shit. (*Beat.*) All learning ever does is remind you of what you haven't got. Teaches you about new stuff you'll never be or have. Because unless you can apply that knowledge and *do* something with it . . . it's useless. It's crap. Worthless shit. An MBA is one thing, but *Jeopardy!* is for assholes . . .

Abby Well, well . . . Goliath awakes.

Ben I'm just saying . . .

Abby I heard you.

Ben I'm just saying it, that's all.

Abby And it's been noted. (*Beat.*) Duly noted.

Ben . . . Don't.

Abby What?

Ben You know what. Just don't, okay?

Abby I don't know what you're talking about.

Ben Yes, you do. Of course you do. I've told you not to . . .

Abby And don't say 'just don't' to me, Ben.

Ben I'm saying 'don't say that', that's what I'm saying. You know what I'm saying, we've had this argument a hundred times since we've been . . . / Yes, we have, we're always . . .

Abby No, we haven't. / We never *get* to the argument because any time you've ever told me 'just don't' I tell you to *never* say that to me!

Ben Yeah, well, just don't . . . I mean it.

Abby Ooooh. You're so sexy when you're being a prick . . .

Ben Abby, just . . . don't.

Abby Stop it! / Don't say that!!

Ben You stop! / I said 'don't' first!!

Abby STOP THAT!!

Ben You!!

Abby What did I say?! *What?*

Ben You know what you said, what you always say!

Abby What?!

Ben 'It's been noted! Duly noted!' You know you said that, you say it all the time . . .

Abby Oh. (*Beat.*) I said that again?

Ben Yes, you did . . .

Abby I didn't even realise it, I'm sorry.

Ben Fine, then.

Abby Fine.

Ben I just don't want that. / I won't take it. Seriously.

Abby What? / What, Ben . . . What won't you 'take'?

Ben You know. / *That*. Being treated like one of your . . . underlings.

Abby No. / . . . You are, though. Ben.

Ben I am not! And I won't be treated like it.

Abby Well, I'm not trying to start something, I'm not . . . I promise, but . . .

Ben I do not work under you.

Abby No?

Ben No, I don't. I hold a position that supports yours . . .

Abby Yes, you do.

Ben . . . is subordinate to yours, maybe . . .

Abby True.

Ben I get paid less.

Abby Quite a bit less.

Ben *Somewhat* less. Right. That's all true . . .

Abby But . . . ?

Ben *But* I'm not 'under' you. You do not tower over me in some literal or figurative way.

Abby This may be drifting toward semantics . . .

Ben No, it's not. I have a point and it's not . . . (*Beat*.) I am your colleague. Your co-worker. Your partner.

Abby Okay, Ben, I get it . . .

Ben No, I just want to point out that . . .

Abby Geez, I wish you were this specific when you tell me to do that one thing with my tongue that you like . . .

Ben That's not funny.

Abby Yeah, it is.

Ben No, it isn't. At all.

Abby It's pretty funny.

Ben No, it's not. It's not at all funny . . . not when I'm trying to say something. Something about us.

Abby You've said it, Ben. I – get – it. I do. And I'm sorry if what I say sometimes hurts you.

Ben Well, it does. Sometimes. When you do.

Abby Was that a sentence?

Ben I'm serious!

Abby Fine.

Ben You belittle me. You make me feel small.

Abby And yet, somehow, I don't tower over you . . .

Ben Abby, stop it!

Abby Okay, okay. I was kidding. Please.

Ben Whatever.

Abby I was. Fair enough? Can we stop?

Ben . . . Yes. (*Beat.*) And I'm sorry I said the other thing. The 'just don't' thing . . .

Abby Alright . . .

Ben I wasn't saying it at you, anyway, I was . . .

Abby I know, but . . .

Ben I just meant don't say the 'duly noted' thing like I'm some . . . *Egyptian slave* or whatever. / Anyway . . .

Abby I accept your apology. / Yes, anyway . . .

Ben Okay . . . (*Beat.*) And if I am, 'under' you, I mean, if people would say that about me, behind my back, some Old World phrase like that . . . it's because you have never, in your infinite wisdom, seen fit to *promote* me . . .

A pause in which Ben suddenly stands and dusts himself off a bit. Moves the pillows around. Sits back down and ponders his cell phone. Abby watches.

Who the hell is Audrey Murphy, anyway?

Abby It's 'Audie'. He's a guy.

Ben Oh. 'Audie' is a guy's name?

Abby Yes. Anyway, it's no big thing.

Ben No, come on, you said it, you might as well . . .

Abby It was just a –

Ben He must be somebody important. Somebody who does some-thing better than me or you wouldn't have brought him up . . .

Abby Ben, honestly, it's not a big deal.

Ben I wanna know! I do.

Abby Oh, for God's . . . (*Beat.*) Did you ever see *To Hell and Back*?

Ben Uh-uh. What is that, on the TV?

Abby No. It's a movie. Well, he wrote the book first, and then . . .

Ben So he's an author. Big deal.

Abby He acted in it, as well. The movie.

Ben He did?

Abby Yes.

Ben Oh. Now he's an actor, too.

Abby Uh-huh.

Ben Did he play himself?

Abby Umm . . . yes, he did. I guess so, but . . .

Ben Well, that's not really acting then, is it?

Abby He was . . . Yes, of course it is! It's still acting.

Ben No, it's not . . . not technically.

Abby Ben, yes it is . . . he was re-creating what happened to him, during the war. World War II. But I'm sure they did many takes of each scene, over and over, like they do. Re-en*acting* it. So I'd call that acting, wouldn't you?

Ben I guess. Playing himself, though. That's kinda weak.

Abby He was very good. And he did that other movie . . . called, ahh, you know, the . . . / *Red Badge of Courage*.

Ben No . . . / The Civil War one?

Abby Yes! See, you're not an absolute moron . . .

Ben No, even I was forced to take a lit class or two. (*Beat*.) That was Stephen Crane. He died young. / Twenty-nine or something.

Abby Huh. / Well, he played the lead part in that as well.

Ben Another war part. It's the same thing . . .

Abby What do you mean?

Ben I'm saying the guy was no Brando, that's what I'm saying. And, yes, I know who 'Brando' is. (*Beat*.) He did a couple war pictures . . . What is the *point* here?

Abby No point. Sorry I brought it up.

Ben No, uh-uh, I turned off my phone. I didn't answer it and turned it off and you said your 'Andy Murphy' crack, so tell me why he's so . . .

Abby 'Audie'. His name was 'Audie Murphy'. Jesus . . .

Ben Why'd you say that to me?

Abby I was being ironic.

Ben Oh God . . . no . . . not that, please . . .

Abby I was.

Ben Not Abby Prescott's famous fallback position . . . Irony!

Abby I was and I'm sorry.

Ben And so . . . just where was the 'irony'? Huh?

Abby Ben, I don't want to get into . . . (*Beat.*) Look at the news . . .

Ben Fuck the news! I don't give a shit about the news!! I want to know what the hell is so *ironic* about some Audie Murphy in reference to me!!

Abby looks squarely at Ben and then picks up some cheese. Pops it in. Finishes it.

Abby . . . He was a hero.

Ben A what?

Abby Ha! (*Laughs.*) You don't even recognise the word . . .

Ben What do you mean, 'hero'? What kind of hero?

Abby A war hero. A hero in the world war. That's what he was, and that's why I said it.

Ben Oh. (*Beat.*) A hero, huh?

Abby Apparently so. Medal of Honor and all that.

Ben And so . . . the irony is . . .

Abby When juxtaposed with you . . .

Ben Got it. I get it. 'Duly noted.'

Abby glances sharply over at Ben, which makes him smile.

Ha-ha-ha. How ironic. How utter-fuckingly ironic.

Abby Just forget it.

Ben Wow, that was a good one! / Jesus, you oughta be on. 'Leno . . .'

Abby Ben . . . / Knock it off.

Ben No, I'm serious, you should've ended up in that one lesbian chick's video thing, you're so goddamn clever . . .

Abby Who?

Ben That long-haired chick, hates guys. The lesbian one. / You know, you've got the CD!

Abby I don't know who you're . . . / No . . .

Ben With the name . . . / The big-time name . . . from Canada.

Abby Who? / . . . Alanis Morissette?

Ben That's her! You should've been in that car with her and her three other *selves*, driving around, you're so wonderfully 'ironic'. (*Beat.*) You bitch, call me 'ironic'.

Abby She's not a lesbian. / I'm just telling you . . .

Ben So what? / What do I care?

Abby I know you don't care. Because it's trivia.

Ben No, trivial, that's what it is. *Trivial*. And she looks like one, anyway, so that's enough . . .

Abby God, you frighten me sometimes.

Ben I don't exactly sleep like a baby next to you, either, honey.

Abby No, I mean it. You really do. (*Beat.*) And how the hell did you remember she's *Canadian* if you don't like trivia?

Ben Because VH-1, as usual, played the shit out of it when it first came out . . .

Abby Yeah, but, why would you . . . ?

Ben I watch VH-1 . . .

Abby What? When do you ever sit down and watch . . . ?

Ben I do, and it was always on . . . with the 'pop-up' things . . .

Abby Yes, but that's still pretty . . .

Ben My daughter liked it! There, how's that? How's that for a little reality check, huh? Because *my* daughter liked the song.

Abby . . . Okay.

Ben Because my twelve year-old, who is probably sobbing her eyes out right now, wondering where her *daddy* is, likes the same fucking song that you just used to tease me with! That's how I know! (*Beat.*) Better?

Abby Alright, Ben, I'm sorry. / I am . . .

Ben Great, you're sorry. / That's really terrific. (*Beat.*) Yep.

Abby Don't.

Ben What?

Abby Stop it.

Ben Stop what?

Abby Just *stop* it . . . Don't make this about you.

Ben What do you mean?

Abby I'm saying don't make this thing that's happened, this whole . . . unbelievable thing that is going on out there right now . . . just about you. Because it's not. It isn't.

Ben Oh, it's not, huh?

Abby No. It – is – not.

Ben . . . Yeah, I know. I know that.

> *Ben is about to say something else but thinks better of it, bites his tongue. He crosses over to one of the windows and looks out.*

. . . Jesus.

Abby Indeed.

Ben I mean . . .

Abby I was just out there, remember?

Ben Yes.

Abby Getting you your cheese. I went out there to . . .

Ben I know you did.

Abby You know how *hard* it is to find Havarti at five in the morning? / The shelves are empty. People are snapping up shit like it was . . .

Ben No, but . . . / I'm sure they are . . .

Abby Well, they are. Since yesterday. (*Beat.*) Do you want some?

Ben No, it's okay. Thank you, though. (*Moves to another window.*) Look at the . . . un-fucking-believable.

Abby Uh-huh.

Ben You know? I mean, I know that's inadequate, but . . . shit. Look at it out there! It's . . . I mean, those buildings are just, like . . . gone.

Abby . . . Yes. (*Beat.*) The cheese is very good. You should eat something.

Ben No thanks.

Abby Alright. I'll put it in the fridge. Put it away.

Ben Okay.

Abby For later.

Ben Uh-huh. (*Beat.*) How many?

Abby What?

Ben People missing. Do they . . . ?

Abby I thought you were following the . . .

Ben I am, but . . . / CNN keeps upping the . . . tally thing.

Abby Thousands, I guess. / Something like that.

Ben Dead, or missing?

Abby Same thing. I mean . . . looks like, anyway.

Ben I suppose.

Abby They're saying close to five. Around there.

Ben God.

Abby All those people . . . just . . . (*Snaps her fingers.*)

Ben Yeah.

Abby Including you.

Ben Mmm-hmm.

Abby You've been lost, Ben. Just like that . . . up in smoke.

Ben nods thoughtfully at this, moves to yet another window. Tries to look down the street. Abby steps out towards him.

I wouldn't do that too much. People do know you around here. Well, they don't 'know' you, but . . . you know.

Ben Right. That's true . . .

Abby I mean, I'm not sure any one could ever really *know* Ben Harcourt, but you see what I'm saying.

Ben . . . Uh-huh. I get it.

Abby They know the face. That wonderful face of yours . . . / At the mailbox. Coming up the stairs. You are 'known.'

Ben Great. / Well, I'll be careful, then.

Ben steps away, wandering the room a bit. Stops in front of the TV.

Abby Good. I mean, you wouldn't wanna blow your cover just yet, right, sweetie?

Ben You know, Abby, that's . . .

Abby I just calls 'em like I sees 'em.

After a moment, Abby's phone rings. It stops after three rings. Silence as they look at each other.

Ben Looks like it might be higher. / Maybe six . . .

Abby Huh. / That's horrible . . .

Ben Shit . . . six thousand people. Fuck.

Abby . . . unless they're all hiding out at their girlfriends' houses.

Ben Jesus, that's cynical.

Abby Kidding! God, I'm only . . .

Ben Yeah, well, it's pretty . . .

Abby It's a *joke*. I thought that was one of the rules of disaster . . . to keep it light.

Ben Not *that* light.

Abby Sorry.

Ben Forget it . . . (*Beat.*) It's like February out there. You know? If I just woke up, from maybe a long sleep or something, and went to the window . . . I'd think it was the middle of winter.

Abby Well, it doesn't feel like winter. Not out there. / Not at all.

Ben I didn't say that . . . / I'm saying what it looks like, okay? It's not a definitive weather forecast, for chrissakes. I'm just saying how it *looks* . . . / Like the last place on Earth.

Abby Oh. / If it was snow we could go down and enjoy it.

Ben . . . Mmm-hmm . . .

Abby Make angels and go skiing and all that shit we used to do . . .

Ben Yep.

Abby Except you can't go outside, right? Don't wanna be *spotted* . . .

Ben Why do you have to keep saying that . . . ?

Abby Just pointing out the 'irony'. Sorry.

Ben Whatever . . .

Abby But if it was, snow, I mean, and none of this . . . stuff . . . had ever happened, then we could. We could go play.

Ben Yeah.

Abby . . . Like when we took that trip.

Ben Sure.

Abby Remember?

Ben Course. Vermont . . .

Abby Yeah . . . you sliced your hand open on the binding. (*Smiles.*) The edge of your ski binding . . .

Ben Right! Had to get a stitch or two, didn't I?

Abby Exactly. Three, I think . . .

Ben Stupid thing . . . the corner was all exposed. (*Beat.*) Still, it was a great time . . .

Abby Yep. Back when we liked each other . . .

Ben looks over at Abby, uncertain. Abby glances at him but returns to putting away the cheese and the rest of the groceries.

Ben What's that supposed to mean?

Abby Nothing.

Ben No, seriously . . .

Abby Nothing, Ben. Not anything.

Ben I still like you . . . What do you mean?

Abby I'm saying those first days were lovely. Really special. That's all I'm saying . . .

Ben I do, too! I mean, feel that way . . . (*Beat.*) Listen, God, Abby, you gotta know, I mean, I know that you *know* . . . This is not me. Like me, that is. This whole thing. Idea. I'm not normally like that. I just . . . but when I looked at it, for even a second, all I could see is, yeah, it's sad, it's just unbelievably *horrid* and all that shit, but . . . this is it. This is the moment. *Our* moment. Everything comes down to what we decide right here. Today. I use my Discover card or get picked up on a *mini-mart* video camera, it's over. Finished. The whole thing's lost. And so that's why I'm . . . you know . . . fuck. I dunno . . .

Abby Then good. (*Beat.*) I just wish, whatever happens, it could always be like that. Like Vermont.

Ben It can. Abby, that's what all this . . . (*Beat.*) Christ, that's what this is about! It can be like that now. Always. That's why we're . . . doing it . . .

Abby I guess so . . .

Ben Right? I mean, Jesus . . . you think I was born this way, like some cut-throat *pirate* of the high seas? Huh? Hell, I'm just trying to muddle through, that's all, just muddle my fucking way through to middle age, see if I can make it that far. You like trivia so goddamn much, well here's a little tidbit for ya . . . I'm *faking* it. Okay? Totally getting by on fumes. I put my game face on and go out there and I'm scared shitless. (*Beat.*) I've screwed up every step of my life, Abby, I'm not afraid to admit it. Happy to, actually, I am happy to sing it out there for anybody who wants to hear. I always take the easy route, do it faster, simpler, you know, whatever it takes to get it done, be liked, get by. That's me. Cheated in school, screwed over my friends, took whatever I could get from whomever I could take it from. My marriage, there's a goddamn fiasco, of which you're intimately aware. The kids . . . I barely register as a dad, I'm sure, but compared to the other shit in my life, I'm Doctor-fucking-*Spock*. No matter what I do or have done, they adore the hell out of me and I'm totally knocked out by that. What kids are like. Yeah . . . (*Beat.*) And you, let's not forget you. *Us*. Okay, yes, I haven't done all that I've promised, said I'd do, I fuck up along the way. Alright. But I'm trying, this time out – with you, I mean – I have been trying. Don't know what it looks like, feels to you, but I have made a real go of us and that is not a lie. It isn't. And so then, yesterday – through all the smoke and fear and just, I dunno, *apocalyptic* shit – I see a way for us to go for it, to totally erase the past . . . (*Beat.*) And I don't think it makes me Lucifer or a criminal or some bad man because I noticed it. I really don't. We've been given something here, a chance to . . . I don't know what, to wash away a lot of the, just, rotten crap we've done. More than anything else, that's what this is. A chance. I know it is . . .

Abby Yeah, but it's tainted . . . / It's a fluke.

Ben What? / No, it's not that, no, it's . . .

Abby We got lucky. Or, more specifically . . . *you* did. But you didn't earn it.

Ben What're you talking about?

Abby I'm just saying that it was a happy coincidence that you managed to be over here at my place yesterday morning, getting your proverbial cock sucked, when it happened . . . that's all. Right? (*Beat.*) The one day out of the year you're supposed to be downtown for us and you decide to skip out, come over, get some head . . . that's not bad.

Ben So?

Abby So . . . there's probably a lot of spouses out there right now who wish their dearly departed would've stopped to pick up a nice Frappaccino or dropped off that roll of film they were carrying around in their pocket . . . hell, maybe *paid* for a blowjob, even. Whatever it takes to stay alive . . . (*Beat.*) I'm saying you really dodged a bullet there . . .

Ben Plane. I dodged a 'plane'.

Abby Ooohh. Careful with the humour thing, remember?

Ben Yeah. (*Beat.*) That's a shitty thing to say about me . . .

Abby Even if it's true?

Ben Yes. Even then.

Abby Sorry. I'm an honest person . . . (*Laughs.*) Mostly.

Ben Yeah, make sure you slip that one in. 'Mostly'.

Abby I believe you just may be pointing a finger at me, Mr Harcourt . . .

Ben I just may be, Ms Prescott.

Abby Ahh. And what, in your mind, have I been dishonest about?

Ben Nothing . . . I mean, other than, oh . . . your entire life.

Ben sits back down on this, pulls out the cell phone again. He turns it on and sets it on one knee.

Abby I'm being dishonest?

Ben Just a little.

Abby About what?

Ben Come on . . .

Abby No, seriously, what're you . . . ?

Ben Which category . . . work, rest or play?

Abby You tell me.

Ben Well, umm . . . me. There's that topic.

Abby You?

Ben Yes. I think so, yes. / For three years . . .

Abby How? / What, that we're an *item*?

Ben Yeah. That.

Abby Oh, come on . . .

Ben What?

Abby People know that. Jesus, I mean . . . *lots* of people! Well, not your wife, maybe, but that's about it . . .

Ben That's . . . not true.

Abby She knows?

Ben No, Jesus . . . I mean people. People don't know.

Abby Ben, come on . . . I'm sure they do.

Ben I'm serious. We've been cautious.

Abby We have? / When?

Ben Yes! / What're you *talking* about? I'm always careful to . . .

Abby What, call on your cell phone? / Keep my keys hidden in the ficus tree at the office?

Ben . . . Yeah. / And other stuff.

Abby Shit, Ben, *please* . . .

Ben I'm not kidding!

Abby Neither am I!

Ben Hey, I've never told anybody about us. No one. Ever.

Abby I know that.

Ben I've been a steel trap this whole time.

Abby Of course you have . . .

Ben I have!

Abby I know, Ben. I'm *agreeing* with you . . .

Ben So then what?

Abby I have been.

Ben What?

Abby Indiscreet.

Ben You have . . . what? Told someone?

Abby Yes.

Ben Shit. I mean . . . why the fuck would you do that? Huh?

Abby . . . Because I used to be proud of the fact.

Ben Oh.

Abby Back whenever. (*Beat.*) Don't worry, I'm not a complete Kamikaze . . . it was family, not at the *office*. But people are not dumb, Ben, no matter how much you wish they were. We hire smart folks and I'm sure there's a few that've got us figured out . . .

Ben I didn't mean . . .

Abby Anyway, it was a long time ago. *Years* ago. I'm sure they've forgotten . . . / I know *I* have.

Ben I wasn't being . . . / Come on, you know what I'm saying.

Abby Of course I do. I've always known –

Ben Okay, then . . .

Abby – you like fucking the boss, but you don't want it getting around.

Ben Abby . . .

Abby Get it. I got it. (*Beat.*) But maybe you should ask the boss some time if she likes fucking you . . .

> *Ben looks over at this. Abby wanders over to the window and looks out. Comes slowly back into the room as Ben follows her with his eyes. After a moment, Abby's phone rings, then stops after three more rings. Silence as they look at one another.*

Ben . . . And what's that supposed to mean?

Abby Just a suggestion.

Ben Ask you if . . . what?

Abby . . . How I feel about the two of us.

Ben I know how you feel about us.

Abby You do?

Ben Of course, I . . . Yes, sure. I do.

Abby Oh.

Ben . . . Don't I?

Abby Sure you do.

Ben I mean . . .

Abby I'm sure you *think* you do, anyway.

Ben Alright, this is . . . I know what you're doing.

Abby What?

Ben I see what . . . I know this trick.

Abby I'm not tricking you.

Ben Yes, uh-huh, yes, you are . . . this is the 'make him feel insecure about his manhood' thing. / I know this game . . .

Abby Don't be insecure. / It's not a game, Ben . . .

Ben Yes, it is . . . the 'manhood' game. And I don't mean 'manhood', anyway. I'm saying, you know, like, my 'manliness'. Virility. That's what you're trying to attack . . .

Abby Am I?

Ben Yeah, you are, my *prowess* . . . and I'm not buying any of it.

Abby Fine.

Ben I'm not.

Abby Think what you want . . .

Ben What're you . . . Listen, you don't like having sex with me, you wouldn't have it. It's that simple. / You're that kind of woman.

Abby Nothing's that simple . . . / You think so?

Ben I *know* so. (*Beat.*) You don't like some assistant at work, they're outta there in twenty minutes. You don't fancy a *salt-shaker* in the cafeteria, it's changed. If you didn't want us coming over here, or sneaking off at conferences and me banging the shit outta you, we wouldn't be doing it . . .

Abby Really?

Ben Yeah, really. If anybody's *manhood's* in question, it's yours . . . / You're the fucking 'guy' in this relationship, let's not kid ourselves . . .

Abby Okay, Ben . . . / I said 'okay!'

Ben Ms Prescott sports the Hagar slacks around here . . .

Abby Well, *somebody's* got to!

Ben Yeah, but 'somebody' doesn't have to be an over-dominating cunt about it . . . (*Beat.*) Sorry, shit, I didn't mean . . . You know . . .

Abby Oh, I'm sure you meant that in the best possible way . . .

Ben No, I just . . .

Abby As you always say, Ben . . . whatever.

Abby heads back to the kitchen. Ben looks at his phone, shakes it, listens.

Ben . . . I don't have any sexual problems.

Abby I wasn't saying you did. Or implying it . . .

Ben Fine.

Abby But somehow, like usual, you were able to turn something about me into a thing about you . . .

Ben What? When . . . ?

Abby I said you should ask me if I like doing it with you. Not that you had a problem . . . per se.

Ben Why wouldn't you like doing it with me?

Abby That's not what I . . .

Ben We're great together, why wouldn't you . . . ? I do not get you! What the hell are we even . . .

Abby Don't worry, Ben, I like screwing you just fine.

Ben Oh.

Abby See, no worries . . .

Ben I didn't think so. That there was a problem, I mean . . .

Abby I didn't say there wasn't a problem. I don't mind the actual act. You and me. I'm fine with that part of it.

Ben Well . . . then I . . . What don't you like?

Abby The rest.

Ben What 'rest'? There is no other . . . (*Beat.*) You mean, like, oral?

Abby No! God, you're like a twelve-year-old . . .

Ben Well, I'm missing something . . .

Abby I know. Me too . . .

Ben No, I mean . . . you're just going in loops here, and I'm . . .

Abby Ben, come on, you're a goddamn grown-up! Stop it. (*Beat.*) I don't like what we've been doing . . .

Ben Oh. You're still talking about the, you know, secrecy and all that. The not telling people about us . . .

Abby No, not even that. I mean, I don't *love* it, not at all, but I'm whatever about it . . . I'm talking about the rest. Other stuff.

Ben Abby, *what*? Shit, I don't . . .

Abby Ben, God, you can be thick . . . it's sexual harassment, you know that.

Ben . . . No, it's not.

Abby Yes, it is. Yes. Very much so . . . we're a *Maury Povich Show*, waiting to happen.

Ben . . . That's not, no, it's *consensual* . . .

Abby How many times have you gone to those seminars and shit?! I mean . . . a million . . .

Ben I don't *listen* at those things . . . Do you?

Abby As a matter of fact, yeah, I do. I'm usually the one *giving* them, remember?

Ben That's true . . .

Abby And when I'm standing up there, going on about a 'hassle-free environment' and an 'empowered workspace' and all the while I'm fucking one of my employees, how do you think I feel? Huh?

Ben I don't know . . . clever?

Abby No, Ben, not 'clever' . . . I feel like shit. Like a fucking Judas and just plain awful. Alright? That's how . . . (*Beat.*) You don't think I've fretted over promoting you, or not promoting you or whatever the hell I see fit . . .? (*Beat.*) Every second of every day since we've been together I've worried about this. Us. Worried myself sick if we're talking in the hall too long or we kiss at a restaurant or I lean over and grab your knee under some conference table in *San Diego* – I may like it, usually feels great while we're doing it – but something inside me, up inside me somewhere, is screaming, 'You fucking idiot! You stupid needy bitch . . .' After everything I've worked for, the *pounds* of shit I've eaten to get where I am . . . to blow it all on a piece of ass . . .

Ben I'm a piece of ass?

Abby Sometimes, yeah, Ben . . . you are.

Ben Oh.

Abby I'm sorry, but . . .

Ben No, I mean, that's how you think of this?

Abby On occasion. (*Beat.*) At first, maybe, yes, I did.

Ben . . . Well, I'm fine with that. / Seriously, I am.

Abby . . . What? / You are?

Ben Absolutely. I feel the same way about you . . . Not that I only think of it in that way, but yeah, I've said that to myself a number of times . . . 'She may be the boss, but ol' Abby's simply one hell of a sweet fuck.'

Abby See?

Ben What?

Abby We can't escape it . . . you just did the same thing.

Ben What thing? / No . . .

Abby The 'boss' thing. You relate to us in terms of who we are at work, our positions . . . / You just did!

Ben 'Listen, sister, the only position I relate to you in is when you're face down on this rug, faux or not . . .' / No . . . I'm playing!

Abby Oh, really? / You sure it's not a 'control issue'?

Ben Yes! (*Beat.*) I don't care if you're my project director or a waitress, the corner deli . . . I like you for you.

Abby . . . Then why do we always do it from behind?

Ben . . . We don't.

Abby *Always*. From the first day since. All fours, face down, never looking me in the eye.

Ben I'm . . . That's not fair. No. And I've done lots of other . . .

Abby You go down on me occasionally, that's true . . . because you think you're good at it. / You're not, by the way, for the record. Good. You're okay, not terrible, but by no means outstanding . . .

Ben No, I enjoy . . . / Wow, let 'er rip while we're . . .

Abby And you'll let me give you head. Which I'm free to do any which way I like . . . standing, sitting, on a train, in a plane . . .

Ben We've never . . .

Abby On a boat, with a goat . . . it's like I'm fucking Dr Seuss!

Ben I don't force you to do that! Don't say that I'm . . .

Abby Even underwater in your hot tub . . . back when we were adventurous and you snuck me up to Westchester when the family was away . . .

Ben Abby . . . this is so out of whack that I can't even . . .

Abby But you never even *glance* at me, Ben, when we're making love. Not ever. (*Beat.*) Why is that?

Ben . . . So, is this something . . . What, you've just been laying in wait for the right . . . ?

Abby As a matter of fact, yes. It is.

Ben Okay. Well . . . umm . . . let's see . . .

Abby You don't think it's maybe just a little bit of 'I'm gonna let the ol' gal have it for getting that promotion over me'? Not just a *touch* of that?

Ben No. I don't.

Abby Sure? I mean, you barely used to acknowledge me when you first started at our office . . . not even a smile in the morning, we're on the elevator together. / We had that whole competitive thing going right off the bat, don't say we didn't . . .

Ben I was new, that's no big . . . / Maybe, yeah, maybe so, but . . .

Abby But then I get a boost, right, I snag the position we've both been gunning for and *bang*, like, a month later, you're suddenly jockeying for private dinners out and discussions after work . . .

Ben You're my boss! What the hell . . .

Abby I'm just saying, your timing, like yesterday, is impeccable . . .

Ben Hey, we started working together . . . I fell for you, it's not a crime . . .

Abby Ahh, actually, in some states it is . . . you're married.

Ben Yeah, well . . .

Abby And then we got together – on that retreat the first time, remember? Up in Connecticut – and that was pretty much the last moment you looked me fully in the face. Three years ago . . .

Ben This is crazy . . .

Abby I know. I know it is . . .

Ben I want to be with you . . . together, with *you*, for the rest of my life, now if that's –

Abby I'm not talking about that, I'm . . .

Ben – if you wanna find some way to *ruin* this, that's fine. Go ahead.

> *Abby stops for a moment and studies Ben. Watches to see if his body betrays him at all. It doesn't.*

Abby . . . It just makes a girl wonder, that's all.

Ben Fine. If you wanna . . . fine. 'Missionary' it is . . . fuck. (*Beat.*) Anyway, it's probably just guilt or whatever. The 'doggie-style' thing . . .

Abby Guilt? / Not Oedipal, I hope . . .

Ben Yeah, you know . . . / NO! I mean about cheating and stuff . . . Maybe it's just hard to look you in the face or, God, I dunno.

Abby Hell, Ben, I feel guilty. Every moment. But I still wouldn't mind making *eye contact* once a week . . .

Ben It just hurts sometimes. That's all . . .

Abby Then don't do it. It's a pretty simple equation . . .

Ben Abby . . .

Abby Seriously.

Ben Why're we even . . . ?

Abby I mean it. If you feel so 'not good', then stop putting your thing in me and go the hell away . . . / Or at least switch your phone on and take your wife's call . . .

Ben That's not what I'm . . . / Aww, screw this . . .

Abby Let 'em know you're alive, do that much! / Quit hiding out in my loft and do the '*right*' thing, I mean, shit!!

Ben I don't want that! / I want you!

Abby . . . Oh.

Ben I *want* you, Abby . . . that's what I want.

> *They both come to a stop and stare at each other, having let out far more than they expected. Silence. The sound of sirens out there somewhere.*

Abby . . . Then why don't you say that every few days, just so I'm in on it. Okay?

Ben Yeah, sorry, I should. (*Beat.*) I do want you, though . . . I do.

Abby . . . I'm glad.

Ben And I don't expect anything for it or care who knows it or will *ever* use it against you . . . I just – want – you. That's all. (*Beat.*) . . . By the way, I enjoy having sex from behind. It feels nice and, like, intimate. I love being with you like that. I do . . .

Abby Thank you, Ben. That's very . . . Thanks. (*Beat.*) It's funny, comical almost . . . almost comical the things you can imagine while you're being fucked that way. Face down. Turned away from a person. It is to me, anyway. The ideas, or images or, you know, just *stuff* . . . that goes through your head if you do it that way for too long. Ha! Wow, it's . . . I don't know. Just funny . . .

Ben What do you mean? Like . . . like what?

Abby Oh, just things. Things that you'd never expect, or be prepared for or anything, visions that will just suddenly appear as you're kneeling there. Doing it. Having it done *to* you. 'Cause that's how it feels when you make love that way all the time, like it's being done to you. That it really doesn't matter to the person . . . back there . . . who 'it' is. Just that it – meaning, a backside – is there and available and willing. And so a lot of the time when you're going at it my mind has just drifted off and I'll think of such crazy thoughts . . . sometimes fantasies, like it's somebody else, a lover I've taken, or that I'm being attacked, jumped in an alleyway by some person . . . or I'll just make lists, 'to do' lists for work or shopping or whatnot. I can remember figuring out all my Christmas ideas one night in Orlando at the Hyatt there, during one of our little . . . on the carpet, as I recall. Do you remember that night? We had those adjoining suites . . . That was a nice conference. In fact, that might've been where I first noticed your particular bent for . . . well, you know. My back porch . . .

Ben Abby . . . why don't we just . . .

Abby But most of the time I just imagine that it's your wife. Lately that's the thought that I can't seem to get out of my head. That it's your sweet little Mrs from the suburbs behind me with one of those, umm, things – those, like, *strappy* things that you buy at sex shops – and she's just going to town on me. Banging away for hours because of what I've done to her life and you know what? I let her. I let her do it because somewhere inside I feel like I probably deserve it, it's true . . . And when I think about it, when I stop and really take it in for a moment, it doesn't actually feel that much different that when we do it. Honestly. I mean, in some ways, who better? She knows what you do it like, the speed, rhythm, all that. Unless you do it with her all pretty and tender and who knows what. Do you? No, probably not . . . she's probably read the ol' *mattress tag* more times than even me, God bless 'er. (*Beat.*) I dunno. Maybe that's what Hell is, in the end. All of your wrongful shit played out there in front of you while you're being pumped from behind by someone you've hurt. That you've screwed over in life. Or worse, worse still . . . some person who doesn't really love you any more. No one to ever look at again, make contact with. Just you being fucked as your life splashes out across this big head board in the devil's bedroom. Maybe. Even if that's not it, even if Hell is all fire and sulphur and that sort of deal . . . it couldn't be much worse than that.

Ben . . . No, I s'pose not.

Ben nods at this, aware that she's speaking a bit of truth. After a moment, Abby sits nearby, getting off her feet. They stare at one another. Another distant siren.

Abby So . . . what do you think they'll say about you?

Ben Huh?

Abby You know, at the wake or . . . whatever it is that your people do. I mean, between the potato salads and cold meats, what kind of speeches do you think your loved ones're gonna make?

Ben About me?

Abby Yes.

Ben . . . I dunno.

Abby Oh, come on . . .

Ben Seriously, no, I'm not gonna do that.

Abby We're just imagining . . .

Ben Yeah, but it's creepy. That is spooky shit and I don't wanna think about it . . .

Abby What do you care, you're *dead* . . . (*Smiles.*) I bet they get you a nice big stone. With the metal plaque and what-not. You said your wife's good at that kind of thing . . .

Ben No, I didn't . . .

Abby Yes, you said . . . / Still . . .

Ben I said 'decorating'. / Matching up *towels* and wallpaper and shit, not funerals . . .

Abby Same idea, just . . . permanent.

Ben Whatever.

Abby Hell, maybe the company'll pay for it. Least they can do . . .

Ben Right.

Abby After losing one so young and gifted . . .

Ben Okay, okay . . .

Abby Probably get you one of those kind with an angel perched up on it . . . maybe a little flame thing, even. That'd be cute . . . / It's probably a tax write-off, too.

Ben You know, Abby, you're . . . / Exactly. Now *that* I believe . . .

Abby What'll it say? Hmm? Your little marker, do you think?

Ben What do you mean?

Abby Your epitaph. I mean, if you could write it. I'm sure it'll have the 'loving husband, father' bullshit, no doubt, but if it was you out there with the chisel . . . what would you put?

Ben starts to say something, then stops. Considers. Then:

Ben 'He was okay.' / Yeah . . .

Abby '*Okay*'? / Why on earth would you . . .?

Ben Because 'okay' is not such a bad thing. It's pretty fucking underrated, actually . . .

Abby Your big chance to sound good and you go with 'okay'. Wow . . .

Ben Let me tell you something, there's a shitload of people out there, right now, who would like to be just 'okay'. Would *love* it. It's . . . I'm sick of the ups and downs, you know, greatest guy on earth when the going's good and a son-of-a-bitch when I run through a yellow light. You grab the last thing of orange juice in Waldbaum's and somebody hates you for the next six hours . . . The wife wonders how the fuck she ever got mixed up with a prick like you when, in college, you were the guy whose smile used to make her cry herself to sleep. Just you *smiling* at her could do that, she wanted you so badly . . . So, you know, fuck it. 'He was okay' sounds pretty damn good to me . . . I never needed to make a scene, stand out or any shit like that. I didn't. I may be lucky and get by on my . . . whatever, it's true, but 'okay' was about as much as I was ever shooting for . . .

Abby Well, Ben, if it's any consolation . . . you're 'okay' by me. I mean that. / More than okay . . .

Ben Thanks. / I appreciate that . . .

Ben reaches over and kisses Abby lightly on the cheek. A look between them, something almost soft, for a moment.

Ben Thanks . . . (*Beat.*) That's not what I meant before, anyway . . .

Abby About what? / No . . .

Ben You know . . . / The 'steel trap' thing . . .

Abby Oh. Then what were you saying?

Ben I'm saying that . . . I don't know. I don't know what I'm saying exactly, but . . . not that.

Abby Okay, good, just so long as it's clear as mud.

Ben I was never saying don't tell anyone. You know I wouldn't tell you that . . . I just . . . We had to be adult about this.

Abby 'Adult'?

Ben You know, grown-up . . . I mean . . .

Abby I'm in my forties. I think that qualifies . . .

Ben I don't mean . . . Christ, you pounce on every word!

Abby Well . . .

Ben I didn't not tell people because I was embarrassed or trying to lead two lives or whatnot . . . I was thinking of us. The overall situation.

Abby . . . Okay. If that's what it was, then okay.

Ben It was. We had to take it easy before, that's all . . .

Abby I get it. Alright.

Ben But now it's . . .

Abby . . . fine. Right? Because you're *passed on* . . .

Ben Exactly . . . (*Almost a smile.*) I am.

Abby You and the six thousand other . . . heroes.

Ben Come on.

Abby Well, I'm sure a few of them are, anyway.

Ben Don't bring that up again, okay, not the . . .

Abby What?

Ben The 'hero' thing. I feel shitty enough.

Abby Yeah? Really? (*Beat.*) I'm not sure you do. Not as shitty as they feel, anyway . . .

Ben Who?

Abby Whomever. The victims. Their families. No, I think you're down the list a bit, Ben . . . *way* the heck down there.

Ben Abby, please, I mean . . . they're missing.

Abby Dead.

Ben Whatever.

Abby Exactly. Whatever. (*Beat.*) That's the position this puts me in . . . Six thousand people are dead, *killed*, some of them *our* associates, and my entire response is, 'Oh well, whatever . . . at least now we can sneak off to the *Bahamas.*' (*Harsh laugh.*) That's not very nice . . .

Ben I'm not . . . who says you can't mourn? Huh?

Abby Ben . . .

Ben I didn't say a word about that . . .

Abby It's your whole demeanour about the . . .

Ben Go down and help sift debris if you want to, or keep a candlelight vigil, I don't care . . . fuck! (*Beat.*) How did we even get on this?

Abby I think I accidentally started to feel something for a moment. Sorry . . .

Ben Come on, that's . . . bullshit. That's total . . .

Abby Won't happen again. I promise.

Ben Fuck, Abby, that's unfair. (*Beat.*) I know a lot more people that work down there than you do. *Tons* more.

Abby As in, 'tons' of rubble?

Ben STOP! Will you? God . . . (*Beat.*) I used to work out of that office, if you recall. I did. For years. I mean, took my calls outta there, anyhow. And so, yeah, I got a bunch of faces in my head right now . . . Why the hell do you think I've been sitting here like a fucking pothead on the edge of the loveseat, staring into space for a day? Huh?

Abby I don't know.

Ben Well, that's why. Because of . . . you know, the
weight of this thing . . .

Abby Oh.

Ben Alright? I mean, guys I've talked to, had *coffee*
with . . . it's mind-boggling. It really is . . .

Abby So . . . all this time, you've been thinking about
these people that you met down there over the years.
Like, in the elevator, or at some little sandwich place . . .
people like that?

Ben Of course!

Abby . . . Okay. (*Beat.*) I thought maybe you were
thinking about us –

Ben No. I mean, yeah, I was, yes, but . . .

Abby – and the family you're ditching . . . maybe all the
hope they're probably pinning on the fact that you don't
really work in that office any more, I mean, the *prayers*
they're sending out for you right now . . . I figured you
were taking all *that* in! Shit, silly me . . .

Ben Abby . . . you just asked me how I . . .

Abby Maybe you should've had one of the guys from
maintenance bring you over some fucking cheese . . .

Ben That is so . . .

Abby I'm serious!

Ben The guys from maintenance are probably all *dead*!

Abby Oh, I'm sure some of them were cheating on their
wives, you just need to call around!

*Suddenly, Abby's buzzer rings. She and Ben freeze as it
rings again. They look at one another. He gestures to*

her and she approaches the front door. She hesitates but goes out. Ben waits until she returns.

Abby It's my neighbour . . .

Ben Oh.

Abby One floor down, actually.

Ben Okay . . .

Abby Her kids needs milk.

Ben Umm . . .

Abby The stores are out. That's what she says . . .

Ben Alright, so, we could, ah . . .

Abby Would you mind running up to D'Agostino's? (*Smiles*) . . . Kidding. I have the rest of that gallon.

Abby grabs the milk out of the fridge and heads back to the door. Opens it and disappears for a moment. Ben stays hidden. Abby returns and locks the door.

Abby Her husband works down there . . .

Ben . . . He does?

Abby Yes. I think so. I mean, I don't know *right* down there, but somewhere in the area . . .

Ben Oh. (*Beat.*) Did she say if . . . ?

Abby No. And I didn't ask. She wanted milk and I gave it to her. (*Beat.*) Is that okay?

Ben Of course.

Abby Good.

Ben . . . I don't even like two-percent.

Abby So it's not some grand gesture, then. It's *milk*. She needs it. That's enough . . .

Ben Sure . . .

*Abby smiles sadly at Ben and goes down the hall
toward the bathroom. Water runs. Ben goes to a chair
and sits. Plays with his phone. Turns it on. It rings
almost immediately. He shuts it off and waits. Abby
re-enters.*

Abby . . . What was that?

Ben What?

Abby Just now. Did I hear your –

Ben What?

Abby – phone.

Ben No.

Abby I didn't?

Ben Uh-uh. I was, you know, fiddling with it, but it
didn't ring. / I mean, the message thing went off, but . . .

Abby Oh. / And who was it?

Ben I don't know. I didn't see . . . or check, I mean.

Abby Not curious?

Ben No, I'll . . . I can find out later. / Check 'em at some
other . . .

Abby . . . sure. / Yep. (*Beat.*) Maybe when I go out to get
you more cheese or something. When it's *safe* . . .

Ben Oh shit . . .

Abby That'd be a good time to do it.

Ben Okay, I know that means something. Obviously that
means something or you wouldn't have said it . . . so, go
ahead.

Abby I'm saying, pretty straightforwardly, that in the three years that we've been together I can't recall you taking a phone call or listening to a message in front of me. I can't. / Not a personal one, anyway . . .

Ben I have, too . . . / That's not . . .

Abby Yes, it is. It's completely true.

Ben No, I've . . . no . . .

Abby Now, why do you think that is? (*Beat.*) Huh?

Ben Because I don't . . . / Maybe I didn't wanna hurt you.

Abby What? / Hurt me? How?

Ben You know –

Abby No . . .

Ben – make you listen in on that part of my life. The kids and, you know, the way we talk to each other, and all that kind of thing.

Abby Oh.

Ben I've been . . . sparing you that.

Abby Please . . .

Ben I have . . .

Abby Well, don't, alright? Do me a favour . . . / I want the whole 'you' or not at all.

Ben Fine. / What, you wanna hear every little . . . ?

Abby No, not 'every,' just once! One time where you stand in front of me so I know what's coming out of your phone now is the same shit you're telling me ten minutes later . . .

Ben Oh God . . .

Abby That'd be a real treat . . .

Ben I mean, you're just ranting here, seriously . . .

Abby I am not ranting!

Ben Fuck, listen to yourself!

Abby I can do ranting, believe me, I can, but this is not it . . . THIS IS NOT 'RANTING'!

Ben All over a goddamn phone call . . .

Abby It's not the call, Ben. It's not that . . .

Ben Then what?

Abby It's trust! And openness! Your wanting to share everything with me . . . it's having the *desire* to do that! I'd probably listen to five minutes of your family drivel and pass out from boredom, but it's in the asking . . .

Ben I'm sorry . . . I didn't know.

Abby . . . And that's bullshit right there, that's what that is. It is because I've said this a thousand times, almost literally a thousand. No secrets. / You can keep 'em from her but not from me, otherwise I might as well *be* her! Don't you get that?

Ben It's not a *secret* . . . / It's just a private phone call . . .

Abby 'Private' makes it secret! / I don't care!!

Ben With a CHILD! / But all I'm doing is . . .

Abby Doesn't matter! It does not matter . . . because once you slip into the bathroom or turn on the fan or step back out on to the sidewalk, you might as well be . . . I dunno . . . Guy Burgess.

Ben Who?

Abby Nothing . . . shit . . . it's not . . .

Ben The guy who wrote *Clockwork Orange*? / What the *hell* does he have to do with . . .?

Abby No . . . / That's Anthony Burgess! Your lit course didn't stick so good, did it?

Ben Well, I got the last name right, I just didn't . . .

Abby Guy Burgess was a spy, an English spy who went over to the Soviets . . . him and some friends. In the fifties.

Ben Okay, I'm lost, but whatever . . .

Abby Jesus, Ben, I'm saying it *still* applies if you're just reading to your daughters about *The Gingerbread Man*! You sneak off and make a call, always keep me out . . . The mind's gonna wander.

Ben I'm sorry. I thought it was the best thing . . .

Abby Obviously . . .

Ben I did! I figured you didn't need to be constantly reminded of the situation . . .

Abby I've never *known* what the 'situation' was because of the way you live your life!

Ben Why is it some federal thing if I wanna make a call in my . . . in the quiet of my own . . .

Abby That's okay, *calling's* okay, but you can't . . .

Ben I'm a private person, so what?!

Abby Well then, don't invite somebody in and ask them to hand over their life if you can't do the same fucking thing!

Ben Good God! And what 'life' am I asking for, huh?

Abby Ben . . .

Ben No, I mean it, let's not get completely off the . . .

Abby Look at us! Look at the current state of things and tell me I don't need to give up my life . . .

Ben What're you even . . .?

Abby Okay, no, you haven't said, 'Abby, forget about your job. Let's run away . . .' No, I grant you that.

Ben . . . Good, because . . . / Fuck, you are really on a tear, aren't you?! You really, *really* are . . .

Abby Because that would require some actual *commitment*! / Ben, what're we *really* talking about here? You know, we keep dancing around it, but let's say it, let's just put the thing out there and see what we've got.

Ben Whatever. If you need to . . . go ahead.

Abby Alright . . . (*Beat.*) This 'meal ticket' of ours . . . tell me what that is exactly.

Ben You know what it's . . .

Abby Just say it. For me. / Please . . .

Ben This is stupid . . . / Fine. I'll . . . fine. (*Beat.*) I think that we can do it this time. / Be together.

Abby Do what? / We *are* together . . .

Ben I mean always . . . as a couple.

Abby You mean *run* away. Just say that's what . . .

Ben Not *run*! We don't have to . . . I mean, we can't even get out of town right now, so it's not exactly 'running' . . .

Abby You know what I mean.

Ben Yeah . . . (*Beat.*) Okay, so, yes, leave. Escape. Get away from this city and be with each other for the rest of our lives.

Abby Or, as they used to call it . . . 'run'.

Ben . . . Yeah. We could run.

Abby Good. You said it. Just so it's been said . . .

Ben Don't you want to?

Abby More than anything . . . / Since the day I met you . . .

Ben So do I! / Well, now we can . . .

Abby We could've before. *Any* day before this, we could have . . .

Ben But now we can do it clean, you know, without any kind of hassle or, whatever . . . strings on us . . .

Abby Was that the problem? Strings?

Ben Of course! Jesus . . . my wife, the kids, a fucking *mortgage* . . . All the shit that would've killed us, this thing we have.

Abby Paying child support would've 'killed' us?

Ben No, but, I just mean that . . .

Abby We've lied to everyone we know, every minute of our time together for this long . . . because of a fucking *house payment*? Tell me that's not true . . .

Ben She would've buried me on a divorce, you know that!

Abby So what? I would've uncovered you . . .

Ben No, no . . . I don't want that . . .

Abby What, then, Ben? *What* do you want?

Ben . . . You. I've told you that.

Abby Just so long as you don't have to make a scene –

Ben No, but I . . . no . . .

Abby – as long as it can be done without causing a stink. Without you having to *sully* yourself . . .

Ben That's not what I'm –

Abby Tell the truth, Ben!

Ben Maybe I was thinking of the kids! Okay?! / I'm not using them!

Abby No, don't use them to . . . / Don't do that!

Ben You don't know what it's like, to see their faces . . . to, to, to see them *waiting* and . . .

Abby No, I don't, but . . .

Ben You have no fucking *idea*!

Abby Ben, I know I don't, but I still . . .

Ben Maybe if you'd stop for a second, quit chewing your way up the corporate rungs there like a plague of fucking *locusts* and *have* yourself one . . . then, just possibly, you'll know! / . . . Okay, then.

Abby starts to retort but just shakes her head, turns away. Ben doesn't pursue her on this, having said more than he wished to.

Abby . . . Alright. / I accept that. (*Beat.*) 'S that true?

Ben What?

Abby . . . That you did it for them? Is it? Tell me . . .

Ben thinks for a moment before he speaks. He catches himself once before saying anything. Abby studies him.

Ben . . . No. not completely. Or about her . . . or you or anybody else.

Abby Careful, Ben, I'm smelling a waft of truth over here . . .

Ben It's true. (*Beat.*) I was protecting me . . . How's that?

Abby I like that just fine.

Ben Yeah?

Abby If you're going to come clean, I like it a lot . . .

Ben I wanted this to work out, I did. For *every*body, yes, but most of all . . . for me. (*Beat.*) There, better? Clean . . .

Abby We could've worked anything out. At any point.

Ben No, we couldn't . . . I don't think we could.

Abby Why?

Ben Because I wasn't strong enough . . . (*Beat.*) But now I am. / I mean it, now I'm . . . ready.

Abby Yeah? / You're sure . . . ?

Ben So totally sure . . .

Abby 'Kay. (*Beat.*) I'm glad.

Ben Me too.

Abby And what you're asking – I'm just saying it so that there's no question what we're up to here – what you want is for us to hide out in my house until it's safe, right? I mean, till the city gets itself back in gear and then we would . . . .

Ben Just, like, until the roads are open, you know, until we can drive ourselves out of . . .

Abby Right, right, that's what I mean . . . . Stay here until we can get in the Saab and take off. Drive to another state, an airport somewhere, and slip away . . . while everybody else – not just your family, but friends, the company – all the people around you, really, can have this, just, *major* outpouring of grief in your honour . . . something like that?

Ben . . . Yeah. That's the *Reader's Digest* version, but yes . . .

Abby Okay, that's what I thought.

Ben It's sooo easy . . . really . . .

Abby . . . And my job, I should just, what? Call in with a *migraine* for a few weeks, or . . . ?

Ben I think so. I mean, otherwise, you're giving up a lot of sick days. But if you use those first, then you can . . .

Abby Eventually, though, once I do the whole 'I'm too devastated to come back to work' thing . . . then what?

Ben You quit, right? Isn't that what we . . . ?

Abby I quit. Just up and resign . . .

Ben . . . It's what we already discussed. Last night.

Abby I know, I guess I just never really heard the whole thing before, not laid out like this. (*Beat.*) So, I give up my position . . .

Ben Yes. I think a transfer's 'iffy' because people would still be flying back and forth from here, there's just that small chance of crossing paths with folks we know, so that's not an option. I mean, I don't wanna be like one of those Japanese soldiers they used to pull outta the bush on *Tarawa* or someplace forty years later, just because I bump into the wrong person in some Arby's near the Denver office. Right? (*Beat.*) But you can take a similar position with another company – you were considering that place in Flagstaff, like, what, a year ago? And we set up house. I get myself a licence, a credit card or two, the whole deal . . . (*Beat.*) Get back into *sales* even, shit, I don't care, whatever it takes.

Abby . . . Like the Witness Protection Program or something. Right?

Ben Sorta.

Abby Huh. (*Beat.*) And my seniority with work now? My pension plans and all the things I've worked toward, I should just . . .

Ben I know, Abby, I'm aware of the cost here . . . We're both giving up a lot.

Abby What're you giving up again? Just remind me . . .

Ben My family! Shit, I mean . . .

Abby I thought you wanted to give them up . . .

Ben I mean, I do, I do want to, but . . . not the girls. Not that. / Because! Jesus, I want to get out of all the other . . . you know . . .

Abby Then why do it? / Ah, yes, the 'other' stuff . . .

> *Ben sits up at this, eager to make his point. Abby watches him.*

Ben You think I *like* the idea of those little girls growing up without a father? Huh?! Well, I don't . . . but it's a hell of a lot better this way, letting 'em think whatever happened, okay, rather than dragging them through court for a year and fighting over who gets which *Barbie*, and for how long, and at which designated location! (*Beat.*) This is better . . . as hard and horrible as it's gonna be, it's still better.

Abby You'll never be able to see them. You understand that, don't you? Not *ever* again.

Ben . . . Yes.

Abby No Disney, no proms, no walking down the aisle . . .

Ben I GET IT! Fuck . . . you think I didn't consider all that? Weigh it in? / Well, I did . . .

Abby I'm just saying . . . / Alright, then. Okay. (*Beat.*)
Plus, you die a hero . . . right?

Ben Shit, Abby, that's not fair! Fuck!! (*Beat.*) It is the
best thing for all of us . . . / YES! And it fell right in our
laps . . .

Abby You're sure? / I know, but . . .

Ben It absolutely is! This way, we completely dodge
around all the shit that I'd have to wade through . . .
all the, you know . . .

Abby Yeah, that messy shit, like . . . sitting your wife
down and telling her honestly what you want. 'Shit' like
that?

Ben Fuck, fine . . . if this is gonna turn into one of your . . .

Abby I'm just asking! Is that what it basically comes
down to . . .? I can cash in my life and go on the *lam*
with you – because this is basically illegal, fyi, it is – I do
that for you just so you can miss out on the discomfort
of having to break it to your one-time *prom queen* that
she doesn't turn you on any more?

Ben . . . Yes. / I'm asking you to do that . . .

Abby Okay. / Just so we've said it –

Ben That's what I'm asking for.

Abby – just so *truth* reared its ugly head here one time
today.

Ben I am begging you to walk away . . . to leave a job
that I've heard you bitch and moan about for the three
years we've been together. To just pick up and leave this
co-op that you tell me you hate 'cause it's in the wrong
section of town now . . . I'm asking you to show me you
love me by dumping the lifestyle that I hear you crying

about at, like, two-thirty in the morning when I'm lucky enough to be around you at two-thirty in the morning, which is maybe *once* a month! I am asking you to throw this mediocre, less-than-desirable single life of yours out the fucking window and make a dash for the border with me. (*Beat.*) Do it, Abby . . . we can do this.

Abby I know we *can* . . . (*Beat.*) And do you love me?

Ben Abby . . . of course. You know that, I . . . Yeah.

Abby That's really not the same as just saying it.

Ben I do! Abby, please . . .

Abby Then – say – it.

Ben Shit . . . I love you. There.

Abby Wow, that makes me feel all tingly inside . . . / And I didn't even have to use the *bamboo shoots* . . .

Ben Come on . . . / Don't make this some . . .

Abby Well, it didn't exactly *flow* out of you!

> *Ben is suddenly up and crosses to Abby. He takes her into his arms and holds her. She starts to resist but he is too strong. She slowly melts into the hug that leads to a hungry, naked kiss. She begins to cry. A long silence between them.*

Ben . . . I do. Love you. (*Beat.*) Better?

Abby Much.

Ben Good.

Abby Very . . .

Ben I agree. And that's what all this is about . . .

Abby What?

Ben Making things very good. For us.

A smile, finally, between them. Ben gives Abby a last little squeeze and then moves away, dusting his clothes off and heading toward the bathroom door.

I think I'm gonna take a shower and then we can start to . . .

Abby Ben.

Ben . . . Yeah?

Abby Let me ask you something . . .

Ben What, honey?

Abby Just a theoretical thing, so don't get all . . .

Ben No, go ahead. What?

Abby You're asking me to do this . . . all these things for us . . .

Ben Yeah . . .

Abby I'm just . . . would you do the same for me?

Ben What do you mean?

Abby In *theory* . . . would you make the same kind of gesture for me. If I asked you.

Ben . . . Of course. Yes.

Abby Even though you couldn't do it before this . . .

Ben We've talked about that . . . / It's different now.

Abby I know, but . . . / That's what I'm saying. Now that this whole . . . has happened, you've pulled your, you know, *Lazarus* thing . . . would you do it for me?

Ben Obviously, yeah . . . I'd do anything for you.

Abby Anything?

Ben Yes, Abby . . . I would. (*Beat.*) Why're you so . . .?

Abby Then make the call.

Ben stops halfway out of the room. Turns slowly to face Abby. She doesn't waver.

Ben . . . What?

Abby The call you were going to make. Yesterday, before all this . . .

Ben Huh?

Abby I cannot do this. This 'ride the rails' thing with you . . . (*Beat.*) If we're going to make it, you and me, I mean . . . then you need to call your wife and kids and let them know what's going on. Tell them the truth . . .

Ben Oh. So . . . this was all a . . . what, trick? Some kind of –

Abby No, not a *trick*, I just can't . . .

Ben – get me to go out on a limb with the 'love ya' thing and then push me off the fucking branch?!

Abby I'm just saying I can't do what you're asking me!

Ben Fine . . . fuck, fine, we'll just . . .

Abby I don't wanna carry all that shit around, I'm not willing to do that!!

Ben Shit, SHIT! Shit on you for doing this . . .

Abby I'm not 'doing' anything, Ben, I'm asking you to . . .

Ben You know I can't! I cannot do that!! / No, no, NO!

Abby Why?! / WHY NOT?!

Ben . . . Because it ruins it. It ruins the ending . . .

Abby takes this in, processing.

Abby This is not a movie, Ben.

Ben I'm not saying that.

Abby You can't dictate how life is supposed to . . .

Ben Yeah, I could . . . in this *one* instance, I could've!
(*Beat.*) We had no chance here . . . a day ago, we were
just another two people fucking each other and
pretending that we had something 'special'. Now we've
got a chance to actually make it that. Special . . .

Abby It wasn't special?

Ben It was an *affair*, Abby, fuck, can't we just be . . . ?

Abby It was special to me . . .

Ben Of course it was 'special', that's the wrong word. I just
mean that it was common. It happens. But this thing . . .
this disaster . . . makes what we're doing . . . possible.

Abby I see . . . now I see . . .

Ben All we have to do is walk away, Abby! Not run . . .
just walk. Walk off into the sunset.

Abby . . . Alright. Okay. Duly noted. (*Beat.*) But after
you make that call.

Ben Shit, Abby . . . don't ask me to . . .

Abby I *need* you to do that for me. / Will you? Ben?

Ben . . . I can't . . . / Oh God . . .

Abby Please . . . Ben, please . . . for me . . . do it for me.
Please.

Abby stops talking but continues staring at Ben.
Finally, Ben folds. Nods.

Ben . . . Yeah. (*Beat.*) Okay . . .

Abby Thank you.

Ben I will. (*Beat.*) You, umm, you want me to . . . what, make the call that I was gonna make yesterday, right? The call I said I was going to make before this . . . all this . . . whatever.

Abby That's what I want. Yes.

Ben Alright, Abby, I'll do that . . .

Ben crosses back to the couch and sits, rubbing his eyes. Pulls his cell phone out of his pocket and switches it on. Abby starts across the room.

Abby . . . I'll give you your privacy.

Ben No, you don't have to.

Abby It's okay, you should have time to . . . / It's fine . . .

Ben I want you to hear this, Abby. / ABBY!

She stops and looks at him.

You need to hear this . . . Go ahead, take a seat.

Abby crosses back toward the kitchen and sits on the edge of a stool near the counter. Ben takes a deep breath, then dials a number and waits. After a moment, Abby's phone begins to ring. She looks up, startled, and mimes to Ben, 'What should I do?' She starts to panic but Ben motions for her to take the call.

Abby Hello?

Ben . . . Hi.

Abby Ben? Why're you . . .?

Ben Just listen. Okay? Just . . . listen to me. (*Beat.*) So . . . this was the call I was going to make yesterday.

Abby . . . No, no, I don't want you to *pretend* with me, I want you to call them and . . .

Ben Abby, shut the fuck up and listen! I was going to call *you* yesterday, not them. I was gonna make this call on my way to work, and then I thought, what the hell, it's only a few blocks over, I'll stop in and talk to her. Tell her face to face. Be brave, like she's always asking me to be . . . She deserves that. (*Beat.*) I wasn't gonna phone home, Abby, I can't do that. You can call my wife, spill your guts if you want to, but I'll never be able to . . . can't do that. (*Beat.*) That's why all . . . *this* . . . suddenly seemed so logical, like the only thing possible. And I wanted it. God, I did! But now . . . look, I think you're great, and we've had, umm, the most amazing . . . whatever. But if you want reality and a clean break and all that shit you'd see on some *Movie of the Week*, then you've got the wrong guy . . .

Abby Ben . . . don't . . .

Ben I promised you I'd make a call and this is it. I'm calling to tell you I can't do this any more, I'm tired of dodging and hiding and all the, just, bad shit I've done so effortlessly since we met. If you'd taken this . . . meal ticket . . . of ours, then great. I'd've worked in a fucking *lumber yard* the rest of my days to be with you, but if you wanna make me come clean about what I've done, purge all my sins for some un-fucking-fathomable reason . . . it's just ain't gonna happen. And if I'm publicly forced to choose between those little girls' hearts and your *thighs* . . . well, then, there's just not much question . . . (*Beat.*) I was not made to be some sideshow on *Oprah* . . . Sorry, Abby, I'm really very . . . I don't know. Just sorry. G'bye.

> Ben clicks off the call. After a moment, his cell begins ringing and continues while they sit staring at one

another. Abby slowly hangs up. Ben finally snaps his cell shut and pockets it.

Abby . . . Goodbye. So, you were never going to call your . . . ? (*Beat.*) And my little 'pick-me-up' to encourage you, that was . . . ? Hmm, what? A last suck for good luck?

Abby slowly goes over to her things and begins to suit up. Coat, scarf, etc.

Ben . . . What're you doing?

Abby Going to get some cheese . . . Kidding . . . I'm gonna walk over to our office, I guess, find out what's happened down there . . . see if I can . . . something . . .

She starts to cross out of the room but stops near Ben.

Just tell me the company line before I go. 'Kay? Are you gonna stick with the 'hero' thing – went up in the fire and all that – or will you miraculously wake up in some alley and stagger back to your desk tomorrow? We should get our stories straight . . .

Ben I don't . . . know . . . Abby, I don't know what to . . . do . . .

Abby You call your family or you don't. You run for the hills or you don't. You come back in and work on the AmTel Account with us or not. Your life's in front of you, right now, Ben . . . but *you* have to choose. (*Waits a moment.*) See, it's not so easy when it's real, is it? But that's the price . . . (*Beat.*) You already made one choice – me – so you can leave the keys on the counter or in your *ficcus tree* or wherever . . . and if I see you back at work, that'll be great. It will be.

Abby hesitates, moves toward the door. Has one more thought.

You can't stay here. Uh-uh. I'm not gonna rat you out, whatever you decide, I won't do that. I'll show you some mercy . . . more than you've ever shown me, anyway.

Ben . . . Don't do this . . .

Abby But I'm not gonna give you any cash or maps or, you know, *waterproof matches*. I'm not Harriet Tubman and I just don't feel like helping. So, you'll have to do whatever – you can't use your ATM card out there or any of that other shit, either, I mean, not if you really wanna disappear – but if you're going to start over, then – do – it. Right now. Today. (*Beat.*) Otherwise, wash your face and go home. See your children, tell them you love them . . . And your wife, too. Because you do, you know. Love her. You must, or you'd already be at that lumber yard in the Bahamas . . . with me.

Ben Abby, I'm not . . . It's only because I'm . . . I'm just a little lost right now . . .

Abby Yeah, me too, Ben . . .

Abby pulls her scarf up around her mouth and opens the front door. Rattles her keys.

I am, too.

Ben Couldn't we just . . . ?

Abby closes the door behind her and the lock slides shut, cutting Ben off in mid-sentence. A kind of quiet falls over the room. After a long moment, Ben sits back on a couch and pulls his cell phone out of his pocket, turning it on. It rings almost immediately. Ben stares at it, turning it over in his hands. It rings and rings.

Silence. Darkness.

THIS IS HOW IT GOES

This Is How It Goes was first produced by the Public Theater, New York, on 27 March 2005 with the following cast:

Man Ben Stiller
Woman Amanda Peet
Cody Jeffrey Wright

Director George C. Wolfe,

The British premiere opened at the Donmar Warehouse, London, on 26 May 2005 with the following cast:

Man Ben Chaplin
Woman Megan Dodds
Cody Idris Elba

Director Moisés Kaufman
Designer Tim Hatley
Lighting Designer Paul Pyant
Sound Designer Fergus O'Hare

Characters

Man
Woman
Cody

Silence. Darkness.

A Man walks on stage. Let's give him a little light.
There, that's better. Now what? Wait – I think he's going
to say something. Yes, he is. Good.

Man . . . Okay. This is how it goes. I mean, went. This
is the way it all played out. Or, is going to . . . right now.
Doesn't matter, you'll figure it out. I think. No, you
will . . . sure you will! No problem. (*Beat.*) What you
need to know for now, I mean *right* at this moment, is
that there was a girl. Course, there always is, isn't there?
I mean, unless there isn't. Then there's not . . . but that's
pretty self-explanatory. In this one, there's a girl. There's
definitely a girl.

Another light up. We need it – a Woman has just
appeared. Sitting all alone. For now. The Man glances
at her.

Huh. I think I'm gonna go talk to her, because . . . well,
girls are nice. Basically. And that would be enough, but
I need to, *talk* with her, I mean. To get this started. Or
keep it going . . . or whatever. You know what I'm saying!
Sort of. And which is okay, because *I* only sort of know,
too, at this point. (*Beat.*) Geez, I think I might end up
being an unreliable narrator . . .

The Man starts to approach the Woman, who is seated
on a bench. Moves next to her.

. . . Hello.

*The Woman doesn't react and the Man snaps his
fingers, jumping back to his light spot. What's up?
Let's find out.*

Just one other thing . . . I know her already. From before.
Like, before *now*. From school. Okay, good. I just wanted
you to know.

*The Man moves back over to the Woman. Taps her on
the shoulder.*

. . . Hello.

*The Woman turns, looks at him. It takes a moment,
then she reacts. A lot. She even stands up.*

Woman Yes? (*Beat.*) Oh my God . . . oh-my-God! Hey,
hello. Hi!

Man Hello. Again.

Woman Yeah, *again*! Way-way-back again. Wow. Hi!

*Out of nowhere, a hug. Nice. Now we're getting
somewhere. The Man hugs her right back. Of course.*

Man I just . . . saw you. Saw you sitting there and
thought, 'Hey.' I mean, more than that, more than just
'Hey,' but that was first. 'Hey.' You know? 'I know her.'

Woman Well, good. God, I hope it was more than that!

Man No, it was, yeah, it totally was!

Woman Good, because I can't believe it! I can't believe
you're just . . . I mean, standing there. *Right* outside of . . .

Man . . . Sears. I know, funny, right?

Woman No, more than! It's weird . . . after, what, like,
ten years? To see . . .

Man It's twelve. Yeah. Almost twelve years.

The Woman looks at him again. We might need more light now – some 'Sears' light. She gives him another hug.

Woman Wow. Really? It's just . . . wow. Weird.

They stand looking at one another for a moment, then talk again.

Man . . . I mean . . . it's okay, though, isn't it? To meet again.

Woman Oh, God, of course, yes. It's good! It is. It's fantastic, but, you know . . . yeah. It is weird.

Man Yes. It definitely has a 'weird' flavour. There's a little *weirdness* sprinkled in there . . .

They stop again for a second, looking at one another. That's okay – give 'em some time.

Woman . . . You look so . . . I dunno.

Man Different?

Woman No, not so much different, 'cause I could recognize you, like, almost instantly. But you're, I dunno . . .

Man What?

Woman Kind of . . . I mean, you were a lot . . .

Man I was bigger.

Woman . . . Yes. You were a bigger guy then. In high school.

Man I know. I was, wasn't I? Yep. *Big* boy back then!

They laugh – what the hell, let's have another hug.

I did some . . . well, I did ROTC in college, and that was cool. And then, I dunno, I just sort've stopped acting like 7–11 was my *kitchen*!

Woman Right . . . right! You always used to, at lunch, you'd walk down and get those hot dogs, the . . .

Man Two-for-a-dollar ones, exactly! I was, like, you know . . . that little kid at the movies, remember? The commercial at the drive-in . . . (*He demonstrates.*) 'Two-fisted style!'

Woman I remember that . . . yes!

Man Yeah, it was always right after the dancing-candy and soda-pop one . . . (*Beat.*) I mean . . . I think we even went to the movies once, there at the outdoor place that one time. Didn't we?

Woman . . . Did we?

Man Yeah, I think. Remember? Over at the . . . with the paddlewheel ship out front – what was that called? The . . .

Woman . . . Showboat?

Man Yes! That's it . . . some crazy double feature that we all went to. This *group* of us. You don't recall that?

Woman Umm, no, I do . . . I think I do.

The Woman stops, working to remember this. The Man steps away for a minute. Toward us.

Man . . . I don't think she does. Not really. I mean, she may say she can, remember us going there, but I don't believe it. Girls generally go on more dates and stuff than us guys do at that age, sixteen or so, and that's probably why it's harder to dredge up specific memories. That might be it. 'Cause it really is like yesterday for me. Seriously. It is . . .

The Man walks back over to her – she's still thinking. Looks kind of cute while she does this.

148

Woman Yeah, I think I do, actually. Yes. It was, like, a *comedy* or some . . . wasn't it?

Man Ahh, no. It was *Dances with Wolves*, I think.

Woman Oh. (*Beat.*) Well, that had some funny parts . . . didn't it?

Man A couple. Maybe the other one was a comedy, I don't remember.

Woman Yeah, that could be it.

Man Right, sure . . . (*Beat.*) So, is that place still open?

Woman What . . . The Showboat?

Man Yeah.

Woman Oh, no . . . no way! There's, like, a *mall* there now, or something. Strip mall – where they have stores, but you walk outside. Is that what they call 'em?

Man Uh-huh. I think so . . . I mean, sometimes they come up with a fancier name – Oakbrook Commons or whatnot – but yeah . . .

Woman Huh. Well, that was, maybe, eight years ago they did that. Put in the strip there. (*Beat.*) How long since you've been back?

Man Oh, you know . . .

Woman Umm, no, not really.

Man No, I mean, I wasn't finished . . . sorry. I guess, around, ahh, maybe five years. Well, one time about three months ago, just out at the airport – missed a connection so I was there for a couple hours – but five years, more or less.

Woman . . . Wow. (*Smiles.*) Hmmm.

Man What? What's so funny?

Woman That was a *lot* of answer for, you know, that one question.

Man Sorry! God, yeah, I can go on a little bit . . .

Woman No, don't be . . .

Man I guess I'm kinda *thorough* . . . it's the law school in me.

Woman Oh . . . great! So, you're, I mean . . . is that your job? 'Lawyer'?

Man No . . . 'fraid not. That's my ex-job. *Ex*-lawyer. *Ex*-husband, *ex*-military. (*Beat.*) I'm great at 'used to be'.

The Woman laughs at this. An easy laugh. She's loosening up a bit. That's nice.

Woman That's funny . . . I remember now. You were always pretty funny.

Man Yeah? Good. Glad you thought that.

Woman Oh, yeah . . . everybody thought you were funny.

Man Yep . . . that's me. *Mr* Comedy. (*Beat.*) Anyhow, sorry about going on like that before . . . blah-blah-blah!

Woman No, I wasn't saying . . . I mean, it's nice.

Man Yeah?

Woman To talk, I mean. About, you know . . . whatever. Just have a five-minute *conversation* with a person . . .

Man Why, is your husband a mute?

The Woman looks at him strangely for a moment, without speaking. The Man clears his throat.

God, I hope not! I was kidding. I saw your ring, *noticed* it, and . . . that's all. (*Beat.*) He *can* speak, can't he?

Woman . . . Rumour has it. Not to *me*, of course, but I know he must. Every so often . . .

Man Ahh. One of those, huh?

Woman Yep. He's a guy. *Classic* guy . . .

Man Ouch. From all of us.

Woman No, sorry, I didn't mean . . . Gosh, listen to me! Listen to me go on like one of those people that you run into . . . at, like . . .

Man . . . Sears.

Woman Exactly!

The Woman laughs again – it's a good sound. Then another hug.

Man People're gonna start to talk . . .

Woman That's okay. Let 'em! Haven't seen you in ten years, so let them say stuff if they want to . . .

Man Twelve. It was twelve years.

Woman Right. Even better . . .

The Woman lets this thought hang, glancing at her watch. She reacts.

Woman Oh, damn . . . can you hold on a sec? I need to . . . I'm getting a couple keys cut, I need to grab them before five. Just one minute . . .

Before the Man can respond, the Woman scurries off. Just disappears. Let's leave the lights up for a bit. I think she'll be back – I think we can trust her.

Man How great is that? Huh? I came in here for the *baseball card shop* and I run into her. That's pretty damn nice, I mean . . . Am I being too obvious? 'Cause I really liked her back in school, junior year – hell, even as a senior, she was in my Honors English class. And Civics, too, I think. Yeah. God, she was something else . . . (*Remembering.*) I used to sit there and watch her, watch her lips moving as she read along with the teacher when we were doing *The Scarlet Letter.* (*Beat.*) I know she's married and all, probably got kids, even, but . . . hey, I'm just saying. Whatever. 'S just a little history.

And then the Woman returns. I told you she would. A small envelope of keys in one hand.

Woman . . . Hi. Sorry about that.

Man Not a problem. (*Points.*) You lock yourself out or something?

Woman What, these? No . . . it's for a, we have an apartment. Over the garage. A *garage* apartment . . . you know what I mean?

Man Umm . . . like, an apartment that's above your garage?

Woman Sorry! Yes . . . now look who's being thorough! And *obvious* . . .

Man Right! Thought I was bad . . .

Woman Uh-huh. Forgive me . . . comes from being around a two-year-old.

Man Yours?

Woman Of course . . . a boy.

Man No, I didn't mean like you *stole* him or anything, just . . . you could be a teacher, for all I know.

Woman Well, that's true. I'm not, but I could be . . . could've been a *lot* of things, but I'm the mother of a great little two-year-old.

Man . . . Plus, a wife.

Woman Yeah. That, too.

Man *And* married a mute! Not many people can claim that . . .

That laugh again from the Woman. The Man laughs, too. Lots of laughs from these two.

Woman No, not very loudly, anyway . . . (*Beat.*) Get it? If I was mute, I couldn't . . .

Man I never said you were mute.

Woman That's true. Sorry.

Man I said you married a mute . . . as far as I'm concerned, you're perfect.

Big pause right here – some cards have just been thrown on the table. The Woman is about to respond, thinks better of it, then looks in the little envelope and counts her keys.

Woman Anyway . . . we've got this thing, this *space* over the garage and we fixed it up. To rent.

Man . . . Nice. Yeah, I'm looking for a place myself. A 'garage apartment', huh?

Woman Uh-huh. He calls it a *guest house*, but it's really just . . . anyway, it's nice.

Man Sounds good. I mean . . . complicated.

Woman Yeah, my husband just up and . . . hey, whatever. It'll be fine. (*Beat.*) So, it was great to see you.

Man You, too. Seriously.

Woman Yeah, definitely. It definitely was . . .

Man Okay. O-kay. (*Beat.*) So, maybe I'll see you at the *strip mall*, or . . .

Woman . . . I'm hardly ever over that way.

Man I was kidding.

Woman Oh. Alright. Because . . . no, I just thought that'd be nice. To see you again. At the Wal-Mart there, or . . .

Man Shoe Carnival . . .

Woman Exactly! That would make me happy. To do that. And there's one of those over there, too, so . . .

Man Well, we're damn near *obligated*, then, aren't we? (*Laughs.*) I mean, we could . . . we can make that happen, I suppose. A strip-mall *rendezvous*. (*Beat.*) I'm generally pretty free in the daytime . . .

Woman So, later would be bad? Just so I know, because . . .

Man No, I was gonna say, followed by evenings *full* of nothing to do. My nights, of course, are absolutely open . . .

An ease with one another is starting to build. It feels nice, even from way over here. Comfortable.

Woman I can always get a sitter. If I need to. My mom or whomever . . .

Man No, we don't have to make it too late . . . whatever works for you.

Woman Or my husband could watch him. Cody.

Man That's cute. Isn't that a really popular kid's name? Cody.

Woman I guess so, but no, that's, no . . . my son's name is Ralph. Cody's his dad. That's *his* name . . .

Man Ralph. Huh.

Woman Yeah, I know. (*Beat.*) It's his dad's name. *Middle* name, really. One of those family thingies, you know . . .

Man . . . in which you had no say.

Woman You must be a great lawyer.

Man *Ex*-lawyer.

Woman Right . . .

Man . . . and I was just fair at it. Just average. (*Beat.*) The 'Ralph' thing was kinda easy.

Woman Really?

Man Yeah . . . I mean, with a dad named Cody.

Woman Well, what can you expect from a *mute*, right?

This time it's the man who laughs first. Quite happily. I'm starting to have high hopes for these two.

Man . . . I knew a Cody in school. Our school. That guy who ran track . . . the runner.

Woman Me, too. I mean . . . still do.

The Man stops in his tracks – well, he's not really moving, but if he was he'd be stopped in his tracks. He processes.

Man . . . Oh. That's right, I remember you guys were . . . So, you married Cody Phipps?

Woman That's me . . .

Man 'Belinda *Phipps*.' Huh. Geez.

Woman Wow . . . you pronounce it like a death sentence.

Man Is it?

Woman Umm, no, not really . . . it's probably pretty regular. As marriages go.

Man Great . . .

Woman I didn't say it was that. No, it's just . . .

Man . . . regular.

Woman Yep.

Man Cody Phipps. That's . . . wild.

Woman Why? (*A bit defensive.*) How so?

Man Just, you know . . . I dunno. Well, he was a talker, for one thing. In, like, gym . . . you couldn't shut the guy up! So, when you said . . .

Woman Yeah, well, he got a lot quieter . . .

Man Huh. I guess we all do, though. People tend to, in life . . .

Woman Uh-huh. He got a *lot* a lot quieter.

Man I see. (*Checks watch.*) Hey, you know what? I need to, umm . . .

Woman God, I'm sorry, *listen* to me . . . Who cares, right?

Man No, it's not that, promise. (*Beat.*) I have to meet with a realtor in a half-hour, so I need . . .

Woman 'Kay. Anyway . . . great to see you.

Man You, too. Honestly. You look . . .

Woman Don't say it! It'll never be right.

Man Alright. But you do . . . seriously.

Woman Thank you. You, too.

Man . . . So, Shoe Carnival it is, then?

Woman Absolutely! When?

Man Any time.

Woman Ahhh, this week. (*Beat.*) Ralph needs some sandals. Me, too, actually.

Man Got it. How about tomorrow, one-thirty?

Woman Great! Okay then . . . Bye.

Man Bye. And say 'Hi' to, you know . . .

Woman 'Flying' Cody Phipps . . .

Man Yep. That's the guy!

Woman I will. See you . . .

Man Goodbye. *Mrs* Phipps . . .

> *A last hug – and it's a nice one. The Woman is gone and those Sears lights fade. The Man wanders back to his first spot.*

Cody Phipps. Holy shit . . . I mean, you know, come on. Come *on*! I can't believe she went and . . . no, I guess you can believe whatever happens in life – there's actually very little that is *un*believable . . . but that's way out there. Cody Phipps. Not that he wasn't, you know, popular and stuff, or good-looking, I guess, in that *Greek god* sorta way. Special, that's what he was . . . and that dude could run! Damn, could he . . . he was amazing. Not fast, not so much that, like a lotta those guys are . . . he didn't *sprint* or anything. No, Cody did all the distances. He would kill you in the long-haul, just totally wear you down, then fly right past you . . . Eight hundred, twelve hundred. The fifteen. Cross-country in the fall, which sorta pissed people off because he was great at football, too, but nothing he liked more than running.

The lights change to some sort of restaurant. Now there's a table and some chairs – I didn't even notice that before.

Why don't we just go meet the guy? Save a little time. You know, I could talk all night about Cody Phipps – longer about Belinda – but if we were to meet him, just take a second and get acquainted – I think it'd give you a real sense of the *dynamics* we've got going here. Okay? Cool . . .

The Man moves over to one of the chairs, sits. Not long after Belinda walks in, looking nice. Even better than before. She waves at the Man, smiling, and crosses to him. They kiss on the cheek and she takes a seat.

Woman Hi there . . . sorry we're late!

Man Hey! (*Checks.*) Sandals look nice . . .

Woman Yeah, you got a great eye . . .

Man Thanks. So, is Cody . . . ?

Woman He's parking the car . . . he doesn't like it to be next to anybody else. You know? Thinks everybody's out to scratch his paint . . .

Man Right!

And as if by magic another man appears – stands for a moment, looking around the restaurant. Spots them and wanders over. He takes his time. By the way, he's a black guy.

Woman Cody . . . (*Waves.*) Honey!

Cody Hey, how's it going?

Man Good. (*Offers his hand.*)

Cody Cool.

Man Yep.

A smile for both men. Cody plops down in a chair and puts a confident arm around Belinda. The marrieds sit together.

Woman Glad the timing all worked out for us to . . . I think this could be, you know, terrific. If you moved in.

Man Thanks, yeah, I'm definitely interested.

Woman Good. (*to Cody*) See, I told you he looks different. Doesn't he?

Cody I guess. I don't really remember you that much. I mean, from class.

Man Thanks.

Cody No, man, no offence, I just don't. Not anybody from then, really, even though we still live here . . .

Man That's alright. 'S the privilege of being rich . . .

Cody smiles at this – an easy smile. He doesn't mind being called that. Some things he doesn't like, but this is okay.

Cody Nah, hey, we're not rich . . . we're *stinking* rich! (*Grins.*) Kidding. We just, you know . . . take advantage of the ignorant middle class, that's all! 'S true . . . take away all the *Ralph Lauren* and shit, they'd only be hardware stores.

Woman . . . Comfortable. That's what we are.

Man Huh. Anyhow, I do look different.

Woman You really do.

Cody You're not so fat, right?

Silence. Then the Man bursts out laughing – the Woman turns white. Whiter than she already is.

Woman Cody . . .

Cody What? That's it, isn't it? What's the matter with the truth?

Man No, you're right, that's pretty much it. I was fatter.

Cody 'S my point. No big deal.

Man Very true. (*To the Woman.*) I thought you said the guy didn't talk much.

Another silence. The Man means it as a joke, but it obviously stings. The marrieds glance at one another.

Cody You say that?

Woman I just meant that . . . we were talking about school and all, and I . . .

Cody Shit. (*To the Man.*) I talk. I just don't *over*-talk . . .

Man Got it. See, now, this is the Cody I remember. He always had *plenty* to say . . .

Cody Still do, man. I always do. Just say it in my own time . . .

On that, Cody raises a hand to try and catch the eye of a passing waitress (unseen). She doesn't even pause. Cody nods his head, turns back to the others.

Somebody else might as well try it, 'cause she ain't coming over here for *me*. (*Beat.*) Doesn't matter how many shops I open in the area, I'm flat outta luck when it comes to gettin' some *service* . . .

Woman Honey, I don't think she saw you.

Cody Course she did. She totally saw me. My hand in the air, like a *schoolboy* or something . . .

Man Nah . . . I think this place always had bad service.

Cody Yeah? When'd you eat here last?

Man Good point. A *decade* or so . . .

Woman It's okay, I can . . .

The Woman starts to stand, gets to her feet even, before Cody places a hand on her wrist. A firm hand.

Cody Just sit. You don't have to do that, go begging . . .

Woman I'm not, I'm just going to . . .

Cody *Sit.* Jesus, just when she comes by again, keep an eye out. Okay?

Woman Sure. (*Tries to smile.*) So . . . should we talk about the rent, maybe?

The Woman sits again. Settles herself. A quick glance over at the Man. Cody is still watching the waitress.

Man I can go grab us something at the counter, if you guys want . . .

Cody No need. She'll be back . . . (*Smiles.*) That's the thing about women, they always come back.

Man That's a lovely sentiment . . .

Cody I wasn't being sentimental. It's true, is all. They usually come back.

Man Like Lassie, you mean?

Cody Huh?

Man Lassie. She was famous for getting home. Returning. And she was a woman. Or female dog, anyway . . .

Cody . . . A bitch.

Man Well, yeah, technically.

Woman Sweetie . . .

Cody What? That's what they're called.

Woman I know, but . . . people are . . .

Cody It's just a word. What's wrong with that? Words only have power if you let 'em . . .

> *Cody is about to continue, but the waitress is moving past again. Cody practically has to snap his fingers to get her attention. Still misses her.*

Cody Shit . . . (*Beat.*) I guess this is why they call her a *wait*ress.

Man Right . . . I think you made a friend.

Cody Just trying to get some fuckin' *water.*

Woman . . . That's all Cody ever drinks, is water. He's like *Jonah.*

Man Yeah? You mean the guy with the *whale?*

Cody Pretty much. 'S good stuff. 'Pure. Clean. Feeds the machine.' That's what my dad told me, anyway –

Man – and it rhymes, which is cool.

Cody You're kind of a smart ass, aren't ya? Like, a *jokester.*

Man Just a little bit.

Cody I think I do remember you now. We had PE together or something . . . Traded a few rookie cards.

Man Yep. That's right.

*A silence seeps into the proceedings. Smiles between
the Man and Woman. Cody looks around for the
waitress.*

Man . . . So, Cody, you still a runner?

Cody Yep. Every day.

Man Great.

Woman Ten miles . . .

Cody Not always. Sometimes I gotta get into the office
early, but usually I can burn up ten by breakfast.

Man Wow. That's . . . I mean, I started jogging a little,
in the service, but you know, like, two, maybe two and
a half's all.

Cody Hardly break a sweat like that! Not even burning
calories till around forty-five minutes . . .

Man Yeah, but I just do it for fun.

Cody *Fun?*

Man Sort of. Got hooked on it . . . (*Beat.*) We should go
sometime.

Cody . . . I don't do nothing for fun.

Woman Cody, come on . . . (*To the Man.*) That is not
true. He's . . .

Cody What? What do I do that's fun . . . or 'for' fun?

Woman Umm . . . oh, you know. Just stuff. All people
have fun.

Man I do.

Cody Well, then, we're different people, aren't we?

Man That is true.

Woman Ahhh . . . you help out at the school. With track. That's fun, isn't it?

Cody Yeah, but it's . . . no. It's helping out. I mean, yes, I *like* it, but I don't do it for fun. I coach a few runners, that's not, like, some big *hobby* or anything . . .

Man That's great. Give a little back . . .

Cody That would imply that they gave me something in the first place.

Man Touché.

The two men look at one another – a smile between them. It's one of those 'guy' things; better just leave it be. Cody seems happy to pursue this subject when the waitress moves by – all three of them shoot their hands in the air. They drop, one by one. Silence.

Man . . . She seems very sweet.

Woman Right! (*Laughs.*) A lovely young woman.

Cody Yeah, delightful.

The Man smiles at this and stands up. Cody looks up at him, then around the restaurant. The Woman watches.

Man . . . Lemme just run up front, it'll be faster.

Cody Give 'em hell . . .

Man Yep, that's me. The hellraiser . . . (*Gestures.*) If my head was shaved, you could see the *pins* and everything! (*Beat.*) You know, the movie with the guy who's all . . . I'll be right back.

The Man smiles and moves back into his original light. Looks out at us, with maybe a quick look back at the marrieds.

Is it me, or does he seem a little pissed off? I totally get that vibe from him. Pissed right off about something. (*Beat.*) He didn't always used to be that way, not when I knew him, anyhow. Not that we were, like, tight or anything. Best buds. But I knew him enough . . . enough to say that much about him, and he never seemed so keyed up like this. I mean, maybe after his mom left, for a while there he was kinda . . . you know. How you get when that sort of thing happens. You're just cruising along and then, wham! Life gets, like, all shitty. Matter of minutes . . . I think that happened to him. And, thing is, she'd do it about every other *month*. Plus there's the whole race thing – which I *totally* understood since he was the only black kid around for, like, a *hundred* miles or so – not that he made a huge deal about it at school, but, yeah, he pulled that card out a couple times back then. School lunch line, picking teams for gym, when some girl or other wouldn't go out with him. That sort of thing. A few of the kids used to call it the ol' Ace of Spades. I mean, not to his face, God no, you kidding? Cody was, well, you know . . . kinda *fierce*, so no. They'd say it when we were alone, just one or two of the guys. Say, like, 'Hey, look, Cody just whipped out the Ace a' Spades.' And that's when somebody'd say, 'You just gotta call a spade a spade.' (*Smiles.*) They were just joking, but it was pretty funny. At the time . . .

> *On a counter are three drinks – Coke, lemonade and water. Man moves toward them.*

I'm gonna head back over there . . . these drinks wouldn't take all that long to get, right?

> *The Man nods to us, then turns and moves back to his chair. Carrying the tray as he arrives. Takes a drink.*

See? I was right. Speedy.

Woman That's great. Thanks . . .

The Man and Woman take drinks from their respective glasses. Cody sips at his water, studying Belinda.

Anyway . . .

Cody Why'd you get lemonade?

Man . . . Huh?

Cody *Lemonade.* How did you know that's Belinda's favourite drink?

Man Oh, I . . . umm . . .

Cody Funny that you'd know to do that.

Man No, I'm, I saw her . . . she's . . .

Woman . . . from the other day. When we met at the shoe place. I told you. We went to the . . . Remember?

Cody Not really.

Woman Yes, I *showed* you. (*Points.*) These. And Ralph's little . . . ?

Cody Oh, yeah. Right. And?

Woman We went to the food court after and had some lunch. I ordered a . . . you know –

Cody – lemonade. Huh. (*To the Man.*) Good memory. (*Beat.*) So . . . what brings you back to town?

Man Umm, this and that. Stuff. How's that for vague?

Cody Pretty good. You nailed it. So?

Woman Cody, if he doesn't want to . . .

Man No, I'll talk about it, there's . . . not much to talk about in that sense, really. I'm just moving back. I miss it.

Cody . . . Yeah? You miss *this* place?

Man I do.

Cody Huh.

Woman That's nice. To miss the town where you grew up . . . People don't care enough about their roots.

Man I agree. It's easy to forget what's important. Where you come from.

Woman I know, it really is. *Roots* . . .

Cody What do you mean by that?

Man I think she's saying you should move back to Africa . . .

> *Big silence on this one. Remember how I said that there are certain things Cody doesn't like? This would be one of them.*

Cody . . . Man, that is not cool.

Man It's a *joke*. (*Beat.*) I mean, come on, I was just. . . .

Woman Cody, I don't think he meant to . . .

Cody No, hey, whatever. Come to meet a guy, allow him to move into my *home* and he insults me, that's fine. If you don't mind that, honey, then that's fine . . .

Woman I think we're all just a little nervous.

Cody I'm not nervous, why would I be nervous? Hmm?

Woman I dunno, maybe . . . you know.

Cody No. I don't know. I've got this nice new studio over my garage and I'm looking for a tenant. Not some asshole.

Man Cody, honestly . . . It was just a . . . She said 'roots' and it popped into my head. The show, that's all. With the dad from *Good Times* and, you know . . . There was no disrespect meant.

Cody Fine.

Woman It's okay.

Cody Hey. (*Looks at Woman.*) Don't you do that. Don't apologise for me, or go saying that something is okay. Got that? Do not. I said it was 'fine', not that it was 'okay'. *Big*, big difference . . .

Woman . . . Sorry.

Man What's the difference?

Cody What?

Man You just said something about the difference between 'fine' and 'okay', and I'm trying to think what it is.

Cody Dude, just leave it.

Man Alright. Just trying to . . .

Woman . . . I don't really get it either.

Cody You know what 'okay' means, means that it's okay. It's all alright. And 'fine' is something else. Says, 'Yeah, I'll let it go.' *I'm* letting it go. Fine. But it is not okay.

> *They all take long, uncomfortable sips from their beverages. Waitress passes again. Oblivious. Doesn't see Cody's hand.*

. . . And that shit is not 'okay', either! What is it with her?

Woman She's probably trying to cover too many tables. I used to work here back whenever, in school. (*To the men.*) Do you remember that?

Man Depends. Do you remember me sitting in that corner booth there, almost every day after class?

Woman . . . I do. With your homework.

Man Yep!

Woman It was always quiet then, around four or so, before the dinner rush . . . and you'd be over there reading and sipping on a drink.

Man Uh-huh. And probably a basket of cheese fries, too! I was a *porker* in those days . . . God.

Cody Yep. You were a tubby sort of guy back then, weren't you?

Man Oh yeah.

Cody And with the wise mouth, too.

Man You are correct.

Cody Surprised you didn't get picked on more . . . beat up and shit.

Man I got my share, don't worry. There was plenty of that . . .

Woman That's awful.

Man Nah, made me a better person. It's what I told myself, anyway, laying there in *traction* . . .

Woman Oh my God. (*Beat.*) Really?

Cody No, that's bullshit.

Man Course it is. But I did get a few bumps in my day, the occasional *undies* up the flagpole.

Cody laughs at this, the first time we've heard that. It seems out of place, almost frightening.

. . . Well, now I know who was behind *that*!

Cody No, man, sorry, but, I can remember it. Seriously.

Seeing your *big ass drawers* flapping up there, all the way down by the track! Certain times . . . that was funny.

Cody laughs half-heartedly again, but it's passed now. Over.

Anyway, whatever. So what's the deal? You want the place or not?

Man Umm . . .

Woman Honey, he'd probably like to see it first. (*To the Man.*) Right?

Man Yeah, that'd be . . .

Cody Why? I mean, it's new. All the stuff in there is *new*, so what's the problem?

Man Nothing, no, just that it's, you know . . . furnished.

Cody So?

Man So, I'd like to see if my things'll go with . . . I dunno. The *carpet* . . .

Cody Oh. Okay, fine, if you're like *that* about it, all *particular*, then okay. Do it. Check it out.

Man Thanks.

Woman It's pretty nice. We did it all in neutrals. You know, with whites and creams and that sort of . . .

Man Great. I'll take a look. And it's how much . . . six-fifty?

Cody Yep. (*Beat.*) I was planning to knock it down if somebody wanted to do a little yard work for me . . .

Woman Cody, we never . . .

Cody I know, I know, I'm joking! I can *joke*, too, can't I?

Man Yeah. No, I'd make a hell of an indentured servant.

Cody I'm not talking about no servant. If you do some gardening, you get paid. That's all. (*To the Woman.*) Did the same thing with that one student, the exchange student. Remember?

The Woman nods, then takes a sip. Quiet for a moment. That's okay, they all need a breather.

Man Sure. I know, I get it. And I'm not above that . . .

Cody Good.

Woman Well, that's really nice . . . we can set a time to take a look later.

Man Perfect. I'd like that.

Cody . . . And why're you here again? Back in town, I mean?

Man Just, you know . . . getting back to basics. Simplifying. (*Beat.*) Wasn't so big on the corporate thing, all the wheeling 'n' dealing I had to do, that sort a' stuff. I'm no lawyer, that's what I found out. Course, I had to go to law school and take on about seventy *thousand* in loans to figure it out, but, hey!

They all chuckle at this – kind of vacant, but they're trying.

Anyhow, I'm cutting back, gonna do some writing that I always wanted to do, and . . .

Woman That sounds exciting . . .

Cody Sort of like that Grisham, huh?

Man What, you mean . . . John Grisham?

Cody Yeah, he did that, right? Stopped being a lawyer and became a writer.

Man Uh-huh. Yes, like that.

Cody Well, that's cool . . . lawyers are pretty good at making shit up. I know *mine* are! (*Laughs.*) Guess you have to do something since you're outta *work* . . .

Man Yep. Might have to sell a bit of my card collection for cash, but . . .

Cody . . . Seriously?

Man Kind of. Thought I'd . . .

Cody You still got that Jackie Robinson you took off me? Huh?

Man Hey, I didn't 'take' it off you, you traded it . . .

Cody Yeah, but . . .

Man Fair and square. (*To the* Woman.) Guy is still sore about that!

Cody 'S my favourite card.

Man Then you should've kept it . . .

Cody Right.

Man . . . or got yourself another one. Off the internet or something.

Cody Nah, I'll wait. Rather get my own back.

Woman What is it . . . a baseball card?

Man Uh-huh. It's one he gave me back in school. For a favour.

Woman Wow . . . that doesn't sound like Cody. Asking *help* from somebody . . .

Cody Yeah, well, I needed it. (*Beat.*) It was a sweet card, too. Rare.

Man I know. 'Fifty-two Topps.

Cody Mint condition. (*To the Woman.*) You know why there are so few Robinson cards from that time?

Woman Uh-uh. Why?

Cody Because people destroyed 'em. Dads, their kids, folks would get them – white folks, that is – find them in their gum pack and rip the fuck out of 'em because the dude was a black man, this uppity black who somehow snuck his way onto a ball team . . . That is why. Guys across America were tearing his picture up to show that they did not like it. Rookie of the Year, MVP, they still didn't give a shit. And that's why it's so damn scarce . . .

Woman . . . And that's why you want it?

Cody You don't get it. (*To the Man.*) She doesn't get shit like this. Never has . . .

Man That's okay. (*To the Woman.*) It's not just that, anyway. This one had a flaw in it. 'S a misprint that –

Cody Whatever. (*Beat.*) You serious about it, I'll swing a deal with you.

Man Maybe.

Cody and the Man share a brief look. Cody stands, stretches, then puts out a hand.

Cody I gotta go, need to shoot past the store over on Tamarack. Replaced a manager, so . . .

The Man stands, along with the Woman. Cody and his wife hold a look between them for a moment.

Good to see you. And, look, you two work out a time to check the place and make a decision or not on the, you know, *carpet* . . . (*Shakes hands.*) See ya.

Man Yeah, you too.

Cody (*to Woman*) Kiss the kids for me . . .

Woman Bye, sweetie. (*They kiss.*) Talk to you later.

Cody looks around the restaurant and moves off.
Exits.

Man . . . Well.

Woman Yeah. 'Calgon, take me away,' huh?

Man Exactly! (*Beat.*) And if the good folks at Calgon don't show up, I'd be happy to give you a lift somewhere . . .

Woman Thank you. (*Smiles.*) Might take you up on that.

Man Any time. Except Mondays . . . I have *yoga*. (*Beat.*) Kidding.

Woman Ha! (*Laughs.*) You're funny . . .

Man Thanks. (*Beat.*) . . . That was . . . not exactly what I was expecting. Got a little hot there for a minute . . .

Woman Yeah. I know.

Man Yep. (*Beat.*) So . . . 'kids', huh? You didn't say that before. *Kids.* How come?

Woman Oh, you know . . . because.

Man No, why?

Woman . . . Because he hates me. Cody *Junior*. He's *six* and he pretty much hates me. (*Beat.*) I'm just going to run to the ladies' room . . .

The Woman tries to smile but just misses pulling it off.
She grabs her bag and heads to the counter. The Man
is alone.

Man . . . And so, that's how I got into the apartment over the garage. I mean, we ate, the two of us, and I may've walked her out to her car . . . but it basically happened that way. Cody all tense and whatever, and me just trying to stay out of the way. Her, too. Belinda, I mean. Yeah, I get the feeling that she needs to stay out of the way a lot. Or, as she said earlier: a *lot* a lot. Yeah . . .

Lights need to pop up now on another playing area –
turns out we're going to need a few. This one should
be some kind of nice sitting-room area. Just a few
pieces to suggest it. We'll fake the rest.

Now, I'm not going to be in this next bit, I mean, I will in *spirit* or whatever, because I'll be talked about, things like that, but I won't actually be there. But this part right now is pretty important to the rest, so do pay attention. 'Kay? (*Beat.*) If you don't, you'll never find out how Belinda ends up with the black guy . . . eye, I mean 'black *eye*!' Geez, That's a Freudian slip, huh? (*Chuckles.*) Now, like I said, I wasn't there, so I didn't see it – but *you* get to see it all if you pay attention. (*Beat.*) So . . . this is how it goes. This part. Okay, I'll shut up now . . .

The Man smiles and backs off, disappearing just as the
Woman enters. Plops on to the couch after putting a
baby monitor down on the coffee table. Sorry – yeah,
we'll need a coffee table, too. She has a magazine and
a diet cola with her.

Woman . . . Hello. (*Beat.*) I'm in here!

Cody (*offstage*) Why? Why're you in there?

Woman I just . . . because.

Cody enters, drenched in sweat from working out.
Nike shirt, shorts. Maybe even wearing sunglasses.
He looks pretty cool.

Cody 'Cause why? Huh? Why do you always hole up in this room, way the other side of the house?

Woman Cody, I like it in here. It's sunny during the morning, and I can relax a minute when the baby's asleep . . .

Cody Hey, he's not a baby, okay? Kid is two years old . . . You *treat* him like a baby, but he's not.

Woman Listen, he needs to . . .

Cody No, you listen. What he doesn't need is taking a nap at eight in the morning! Alright? He just got up, like, hour and a half ago. And you give 'em breakfast and back to bed he goes . . . That's wrong.

Woman He's tired. He's . . .

Cody No, you're lazy, that's what it is.

Woman 'Lazy'?

Cody You heard me. Yeah. You get Cody Junior off to school – great – and put a little food down Ralph and then that's it for the day, far as you think . . .

Woman That is not . . .

Cody Bullshit! Bull–shit. I know it is.

Woman Cody, our son is tired, do you mind? I know *you* don't get that way, since you run every day and never come to bed before, say, *two* in the morning . . . but other people, we sleep. He's a child. A growing boy and he needs a nap whenever he feels like it. Right now, an hour from now . . . whenever.

Cody shakes his head and pulls off his shirt, flexing. Does a few stretches. Yes, he's in good shape.

Cody That shit is abuse . . .

Woman What?! I mean, why would you even say . . . ?

Cody It is! You ever hear of *raising* children? Huh? *You* raise them, they don't do it themselves . . . You're the parent, you set the rules, make the choices. Not the kid.

Woman And when was the last time you took part in that? 'Raising' him. Hmm?

Cody Don't start that crap . . . *I* work.

Woman Oh, please . . .

Cody What?! I do, 's more than you can say.

Woman Cody! I mean . . .

Cody Hey, truth hurts.

Woman (*to herself*) God . . . this is like a Thomas Hardy novel or something.

Cody The fuck does that mean?

Woman . . . That's kinda *Victorian*, don't you think? 'I work.' Come on! We both work, I just happen to work *here*. In this house of yours. I mean, your *father's* . . .

Cody It's my house. *My* house. 'Kay? He's dead and this is mine. Including this room here, which you know I hate you being in . . .

Woman *Why?*

Cody Because it's a sitting room, okay? 'Sitting.' Supposed to be for sitting and entertaining! You *lounging* in here, middle of the morning, with your feet up and sucking down that damn *Tab* you drink all the time . . . looks lazy. You look like a fuckin' pig, and I hate it!

Woman Wow. Okay, that's . . . well, that's a new one. I mean, you've usually got something *lousy* to say to me, but that is a complete new one. Congratulations, Cody Phipps!

Cody Shut up.

Woman Nice comeback . . .

Cody Fuck that. I don't need a *comeback*. I need a wife who doesn't park it on her fat ass all day, sucking on pop like she was some sixteen-year-old . . .

Woman I wish I was.

Cody What?

Woman That. Sixteen . . .

Cody Yeah, why's that?

Woman . . . Because that was the year *before* I met you. Okay? That's why . . .

She can see Cody react at this but she can't stop now. Not very wise, maybe, but that's how it goes sometimes.

Cody . . . Well, well.

Cody suddenly kicks the back of the couch. The Woman jumps.

Woman Cody . . . God! (*Beat.*) . . . I . . . feel like we're always walking around on pins and, and eggshells here, and I just . . . I cannot take it much longer, okay? I can't! (*Beat.*) I dunno . . . you're just so paranoid, so worried about everybody giving you shit, or disrespecting you or I don't know what – doesn't matter that you do it to me, treat me like the hired help! Snap your fingers or laugh in my face, but life's not about that . . . black or white or any of that crap. It's about being a good guy, Cody. A decent person. And you're not . . . In the end, I'm with somebody who's like all the other guys I grew up around. Not so terrible, but not very good, either. You're just a guy. Just a normal guy . . . which means kind of shitty, actually. Completely average and a little bit shitty.

Cody tenses up, turns to her. He starts to advance slowly, wrapping his shirt around his hand – like a boxer wraps tape around his fist before putting it in the glove. The woman stands, facing him.

Cody 'S that right? Is it? Great. That's really great.

Woman . . . Look . . . Cody . . .

Cody No, that's funny. You're getting real cute with your mouth lately. Must be your little friend over the garage there, making you all clever and smarty-pants like that . . .

Woman He hasn't been . . . no. I was just trying to say that . . .

Cody Make another wish. Like sixteen. Go ahead . . . one more.

Cody continues to move toward her as she backs away. Finally, she comes up against a love seat and is trapped. She looks at him, shit scared. I mean, come on, wouldn't you be? She tries to reach out and touch him. Cody pulls back. The Woman is starting to cry. Shaking her head.

Go on . . . make one. 'I wish . . .'

Woman You wouldn't hurt me . . .

Cody Too late.

Cody smacks her flat in the stomach, doubling her over. She drops to her knees and disappears behind the small couch. He reaches down and hits her again, this time in the face. We can't see exactly what happens, but the sound is sickening.

For a moment, silence. Then the sound of a child waking up on the baby monitor. Cody unwraps his hand and starts off.

Cody exits. The room is empty, the Woman still behind the piece of furniture. After a moment, the Man enters the room. What's he doing here again?

Man Whoah! Geez, that was a bit much! Alright, so maybe it wasn't *exactly* like that. I dunno. Hey, look, I'm a writer – would-be writer, anyway – so, what can I tell ya? It could've happened that way! Easily – I mean, she did get the eye once, this black eye, and so, I'm just guessing. That's all. Actually, I think it's how I *want* it to be, like, so I can jump in there, save her or whatever. That's probably it . . . but no, that was a touch heavy-handed there, so we should go ahead and give it another try . . .

Suddenly, the Woman walks back into the room – how did she get out there? Well, it should seem pretty magical but it'll need to be a theatrical trick. A trap door or something. Anyhow, she walks back in, same as before, except this time holding the Tab can to her eye and carrying the magazine. She sets the baby monitor down and plops on to the couch.

Okay, this is the way *she* described it to me, Belinda did, after it occurred. But, umm, I didn't really believe her. I mean, she swears it was like this but something seems a little off about it, and so that's why I made up the other story. The first one. You guys decide for yourselves. (*Beat.*) Anyway, sorry about that. Told you before that you shouldn't totally trust me on any of this! . . .

The Man smiles and exits. After a moment, the Woman calls out.

Woman Hello. (*Beat.*) I'm in here.

Cody (*offstage*) Why? Why're you in there?

Woman I just . . . because.

Cody walks in, back from his run. Dressed the same as before but wearing the sunglasses up on his head. He moves over toward his wife.

Cody . . . Hey. *Hey.* What happened?

Woman Oh, nothing, no, I just . . . banged it.

Cody Baby, oww. Ouuw! Lemme see . . .

He crouches beside her, lifting the soda can to have a peek at his wife's condition.

Cody Damn . . .

Woman Bad?

Cody Mmm-hmm. Gonna be . . .

Woman Great. (*Touches it.*) Ouuuh . . .

Cody Hey, I'm the one who should be grumpy . . . the person who's gonna suffer is me. The shit I'll get for this'll be unbelievable . . .

Woman S'pose so. (*Beat.*) Good . . .

Cody People'll be saying I smacked you one. They totally will . . .

Woman Right.

Cody (*beat*) 'Cody Phipps, black man, goes on rampage,' shit like that.

Cody laughs at this, as does the Woman. She winces from the pain. He reaches over and kisses her gently. She then allows him to kiss her near the eye as well.

There. Daddy'll make it all better.

Woman Mmm . . .

Cody You should probably use some ice, though. Way more helpful than that soda pop . . . Honey? You should.

Woman I know, but . . .

Cody You want me to get some?

Woman Yeah, but . . . in a minute. 'Kay?

Cody Sure.

He pulls off his sweaty shirt and stretches out – still looks good. Cody plops down on the couch near her, lifting her legs up and then pulling them on to his lap. She smiles.

Woman Thanks . . . (*Beat.*) So, how're your protégés coming?

Cody Hmm? Oh, they're, you know . . . don't know if they'll make regionals, but . . . working hard.

Woman That's good. Nice of you to . . . you know, help out.

Cody Least I can do. I mean, I dump a ton a' cash into the programme, new *uniforms* and shit . . . might as well make sure some of the runners get their shot at a scholarship or, you know. Right?

Woman Sure. That's . . . sure.

Cody Absolutely. (*Beat.*) Baby's okay?

Woman Yeah, he's sleeping . . .

Cody Good. That's cool. I know he's not feeling well. (*He starts to leave.*) So . . .

Woman Where're ya going?

Cody Got a meeting at ten. Should be there a bit before . . .

Woman Why?

Cody You know, check in with everybody, do my emails and shit.

Woman Oh. Okay.

Cody . . . What?

Woman Nothing. I just . . .

Cody *What?*

Woman I was hoping you could take today off, it's Friday and, you know, it'd just be . . . We talked about you taking Fridays off once in a while.

Cody Yeah, but . . .

Woman No, I understand. We were gonna do the picnic thing . . . but, hey.

Cody So tell him we'll get together and do something next week. 'S not a big deal.

Woman Who're you meeting with?

Cody It's some people in from Chicago. The, uhh, you know . . . I told you.

Woman No . . .

Cody Yeah, I did. The one guy's from, I don't know the place – Arlington Heights or whatever – they have the plant out there we want to use for that new line –

Woman Oh.

Cody – the Adirondack line we're gonna add. All the furniture. Remember? (*Beat.*) I told you.

Woman Did you?

Cody Yes.

Woman Huh. Well, I must've forgot . . .

Cody Yeah. You just forgot or something, 'cause I told you.

Woman 'Kay.

Cody kisses her on the bare feet and stands, wiping his neck with the crumpled shirt.

Cody I'm gonna hop in the shower . . . get myself ready. (*Beat.*) Hey, tell our *tenant* to mow that side yard today, would ya? I think he missed it last time . . .

Woman Alright. (*Beat.*) That's a new one . . .

Cody What's that?

Woman Scheduling a meeting on Friday.

Cody What do you mean?

Woman I mean that you don't usually do that . . .

Cody Yeah, I do.

Woman Uh-uh. Not usually. (*Beat.*) Thought you said you like to keep Fridays open during track season . . .

Cody, exasperated, throws his shirt on the end of the couch. Comes over and hovers, leaning in dangerously close to her.

Cody Look, they couldn't . . . Jesus Christ! I'm not gonna *defend* this. What're you doing?

Woman I'm just saying . . . just saying it, that's all.

Cody Well, don't, okay? We do not need all this jealousy crap. 'Kay?

Woman Fine. That's fine, Cody, whatever.

Cody leans down a little closer toward the Woman, letting her get a good whiff.

Cody . . . There, how's that? (*Holds her head.*) No, no, go on, take a good whiff. Nice, huh?

Woman Alright . . .

Cody No, seriously, a little more. Okay? You smell that? I'm nasty right now, got clients coming, so just do not get into your *Desdemona* shit. Have people to meet, that's all . . .

Woman Go then. Should be nice . . . have a great lunch. Make a bundle.

Cody There is just no talking to you . . .

Woman Yeah, well, I sorta like the truth tossed in there every now and then when I'm chatting with a person . . . I'm just funny that way.

Cody Oh shit . . . I'm outta here.

Woman Yep. Go. Maybe we'll have the food without you . . . (*Beat.*) Go on.

> *Cody throws his hands in the air – there really is no talking to her some days. This seems to be one of them.*

Cody Yeah, I will. So I can make us some more money. Money that you have no problem spending . . .

Woman I just spend it to piss you off.

Cody Well, hey, it works!

Woman Good . . .

Cody Yep, great. You have a super day, honey . . .

Woman I will. Thanks. And tell her 'Hi' for me . . . whoever she is.

Cody You are, like, so nuts . . . I mean it. Just completely crazy.

Woman Well, be proud of yourself, 'cause you made me this way . . .

Cody No, uh-uh, that is bullshit . . . total shit and I'm not taking the fall on this one. (*Beat.*) You were pretty fucking *out there* when I first knew you, all the way back at school, but I dealt with it, that's what I did.

Woman That's great . . .

Cody You take the hand you're dealt, 's what my old man always said, and so I did it. And you, sweetness, were just one of the cards God threw my way . . .

Woman I really don't know what the hell you just said, but I'm sure it means something to you . . .

Cody You know exactly what I'm saying . . .

Woman No, Cody, I don't. I really don't.

> *Cody moves closer to the Woman. Towering over her. She tries to hold her own, but hey, let's be honest. This guy can be a bit unnerving.*

Cody I'm saying that, had I been mature enough in high school to see past your *bangs* and your cute little cheerleader skirt, shit like that . . . I probably wouldn't be standing here, having this stupid fucking talk with you right now! Because you would not be in my house . . .

Woman Yeah? Well, I am now . . . but *you* can go. Tell me when and I'll have your shit packed in an hour.

Cody I am not going nowhere.

Woman Well, that's a double negative, but I get your point . . .

Cody I bet you do. I bet you do at that. And I get yours.

Woman . . . And so there we are. Same lousy place we usually find ourselves at.

Cody Yep.

Woman Great. That's really great . . .

Cody starts off, but stops, catching himself. Simmering.

Cody Yeah, super. (*Beat.*) Okay, fine, you wanna know the truth? Huh? Who I'm seeing on the side, 's that it? My *work*, that's who. She's my fucking mistress . . .

Woman Right . . .

Cody It's true. I like it, I'm good at it, and it makes me happy. I *love* making more money than any other guy in this town, 'cause it just pisses 'em off. I dig that. Plus, work doesn't complain, or rag on me about shit, or leave those fucking *tampons* wrapped in toilet paper in the trash for the dog to drag down to the sitting room . . . So, yeah, I love my work. I *love* it, and there is not a damn thing that you can do about it . . .

Cody flicks his shirt at the wall. Exhales loudly.

This sucks. You know that? This whole thing, what we've got here . . . or ended up with. It really sucks. It's shit . . .

Woman No. It's *marriage*.

Cody is about to respond when a child begins to whimper on the baby monitor. The parents look at one another.

. . . So?

Cody Hey, you're always saying 'We both work, you just work here.' So, get to *work* . . .

Cody makes a dismissive gesture with his hand. Does it again.

Don't forget to tell Shakespeare to cut the grass . . .

And with that, Cody is gone. The Woman sits for a moment, taking all this in. A long moment. Then she

*starts to cry. Not a lot – that's hard on an actor, and
we've got a ways to go – but a little. Just enough.*

Woman (*to herself*) It was *Othello* who was jealous! Not
the other way around. Asshole.

*The lights fade on her and up slowly on the Man, who
is now standing in his old spot. He's changed his
clothes – not too much, but khakis and a shirt, tennis
shoes – and seems ready to go somewhere.*

Man . . . See what I mean? I don't really know the whole
story, but those two have got something going on. Some
sort a' trouble. They do . . . (*Beat.*) I mean, it's a *detached*
garage and all, but hey . . . voices carry.

*Lights slowly rise on a new playing space while the Man
is talking. A sort of backyard, with maybe a barbecue
pit or that type of thing. A picnic table. We won't use
it just yet, but I wanted to give you a head's up.*

. . . We're gonna be together again in a minute – the three
of us, I mean – so I just wanted to grab a second here and
sort of set this up, let you know what's going on. By the
way, funny how you never see the kids, isn't it? Yeah.
It's not weird or anything, like in *Virginia Woolf* or like
that . . . it's just my main concern is the two of them. So,
no problem . . . Okay? Good.

*Cody and the Woman enter now, each taking up
positions in the 'backyard' space. Cody is manning
the grill and she is busy setting the table. Plates, forks,
napkins. That sort of deal. The Man looks over at
them and smiles.*

. . . They really are a pretty great-looking couple. I mean,
when you just see them together, from afar. Problem is, I
think it has to be *really* afar, because otherwise you might
hear what they're saying to each other! Still, they are very

attractive people . . . and, in a way, that makes all this somewhat, umm, harder. Not that I . . . well, watch what happens. You'll see what I mean. Sorry! I'm being so *cryptic* and I don't mean to be. Just watch. It's all gonna be okay in the end. It will, I promise . . .

> *He smiles out at us and then moves off, toward Cody and the Woman. They spot him coming – Cody turns back to his grill and the Woman stands to greet him. They hug. Cody catches it.*

Man . . . Hi!

Woman Oh! Hi there . . .

Man Hey. (*Looking around.*) Where's the kids?

Woman Oh, you know, around. Cody Junior's at a play date. Baby's asleep.

Man Great. That's nice . . . (*Another hug.*) Hi.

Cody Shit. (*Beat.*) Don't mind me . . .

> *They laugh at this – not Cody, of course, but the Man and the Woman. They also break their hug and she goes back to setting up drink cups. The Man tries to help out.*

Man Sorry. It's just . . .

Cody What?

Man I dunno. Great to see you guys . . . I mean, *both* of you.

Cody Yeah? Well, then, you better get over here and gimme a big cuddle, too, while you're at it. I don't wanna be left outta the *love fest*.

> *The Man chuckles, then decides to call Cody's bluff. He moves toward the grill, but Cody holds up his chef's tools like a makeshift cross.*

Man . . . I luv you, man.

Cody Get the fuck outta here!

The men pretend to hug, then back away from one another. The Woman smiles at this as she starts on the plastic cutlery.

Cody . . . And you didn't bring your cards, I see.

Man Oh, damn! Sorry. You want me to run back over and . . . ?

Cody Nah, we can do it later. What took you so long? (*Checks his watch.*) It's already ten of . . .

Man Oh, yeah, sorry . . . I was finishing up this movie. On TV. Had to let it wrap up . . . that's the best part. (*Beat.*) See who ends up with whom.

Cody Whatever. (*Beat.*) You want steak or some chicken? I got burgers, too.

Man Ummm . . . maybe a little of each. That alright?

Cody Yep. Same thing I'm doing. High on the protein. No carbs . . .

Man Great.

Cody turns to a covered plate and begins taking off the foil to get at the meat. The Man decides to return and help the Woman. He picks up a pitcher and starts pouring drinks.

. . . Oh, you like *lemonade*? I had no idea.

Woman Very funny. (*Smiles.*) . . . So, what was on? The TV.

Man It was this Hitchcock thing . . .

Woman Nice . . .

Man There's like, some tribute or something. On cable . . .

Woman Oh . . .

Man All weekend. They're playing a *ton* of his films . . . one right after the other. It's pretty great.

Woman I like Hitchcock . . . l think Cody does, too. (*Calls out.*) Don't you, honey?

Cody What's that?

Woman Like Hitchcock movies . . .

Cody Not much. They're alright. *The Birds* was good . . .

Woman Anyway . . .

Man You liked *The Birds*, Cody? Huh. That sounds suspiciously like you having *fun* . . .

Cody Yeah, time a' my life . . .

> *Cody slaps some meat on the grill, seasons it and puts down the lid. Opens the little steam valve.*

Woman And what were you watching? I mean, before you came over . . .

Man Oh, right. Yeah, I was finishing up *Strangers on a Train*. Tonight is *Vertigo* . . . And there's a couple lesser ones later, at midnight.

Woman Really? Which ones? . . . I like him, maybe I'll watch 'em.

Cody You already said that. Said you liked Hitchcock already . . .

Woman I know, I was just –

Cody – just so you do. Know.

Man It's, umm, *I Confess*, I think. And *Marnie*.

Woman Oh. Good.

Cody The one about the liar . . . (*Beat.*) I'm gonna go get the veggies.

Woman Check on the baby, would ya?

Cody nods and heads off toward the kitchen – any of the exits will do. We just need to get him offstage. The Man stops him.

Man . . . You mean 'thief'.

Cody What?

Man She's a thief, in the film. Marnie. Or, Tippi Hedren is, the actress. She's a 'thief' in that one . . .

Cody Same difference.

Man Really? How's that?

Cody She steals shit, right?

Man Yeah . . .

Cody Well, liars just steal the truth . . . 'S the same thing. It's all theft.

And with that, Cody exits. The Man and Woman are left looking at one another – that's okay, they don't mind. An easy smile between them.

Man . . . Man's got a point.

Woman He always does – he's happy to tell you. (*Whispers.*) And it usually has to do with his *mother* . . .

Man Ahhh, right. (*Beat.*) Well, too bad they didn't offer a philosophy course at school . . . he might've aced it.

Woman Probably. He does always get what he wants . . .

Man Yeah?

Woman Oh, yeah. *Always.*

Man Even you? I mean . . .

The Woman looks hard at the Man, unsure how to respond. She looks back toward the house, then moves over toward him.

Woman Sure . . . Actually, the day after my eighteenth birthday my parents were auctioning me off on eBay and Cody jumped in at the last second there!

Man Right! (*Laughs.*) Very funny.

Woman 'S true. (*Smiles.*) . . . But no, seriously, he got me because I wanted him to. That's how.

Man Really?

Woman Yes. From that first time I saw Cody . . . on the bus. The activity bus home one night. Right from then.

Man . . . Wow.

Woman Uh-huh.

Man That's so . . . great. Really.

Woman Why? Why is that great?

Man Oh, you know, because . . . it's true love and all that. Right?

Woman . . . You sure it's not just because I like a nice, thick black cock? Hmm? Maybe that's why . . .

She tries to smile but has to look away, blushing. The Man stops for a moment, as if stunned by this. He then moves down center. Toward us.

Man Okay, obviously she didn't say it like that. I mean, it's *obvious*, right? She'd never say a thing like that . . . God, can you picture her saying that? *Anything* like that? (*He laughs.*) No way. Not at all. *But* . . . it is what I'm thinking, what I've had in my head since the first time I heard about her and Cody. Or any time you see a white girl and a . . . well, you know. I mean, everybody knows those jokes, or stories, or whatever you wanna call 'em. And it's a cliché, I'm aware of that, but . . . a cliché is just some true thing, usually, this truth that gets said, over and over . . . (*Beat*.) Still, she never said that. About Cody's, you know . . . *thing*. That was all me. Not that *I* was thinking about his – you know – just that . . . Okay, let's drop it . . .

> *The Man shrugs and returns to the picnic table, back there next to the Woman, who is turned and lost in thought. Just like we left her. Well, that's convenient.*

Man That's so . . . great. Really.

Woman Why? Why is that great?

Man Oh, you know, because . . . it's true love and all that. Right?

Woman I guess.

Man Well, that's what the ancients used to call it. The *poets*.

Woman God . . . you sound like my dad now! *Droning* on in that English class we had together . . . 'The ancients' view of love was not our own . . .'

Man Right! (*Smiles*.) . . . So, *you* remember that? I mean, that I was . . . ?

Woman Sure. I told you, you used to make me laugh. (*Beat*.) Still do . . .

Man Cool.

Woman Anyway, people don't really use those words any more, do they? 'True love'. I mean, not in a long time . . .

Man No. I s'pose not. But it's a nice thought, all the same . . .

The Woman stands and goes to check the grill. She lifts the lid and turns the pieces of meat, one by one. The Man rises to stand near her.

Woman I wanted to be noticed. That's what it was.

Man Hmm?

Woman The reason I first . . . oh, nothing.

Man No, go ahead. Please.

Woman When I said 'Yes' to Cody, the time he asked me out – to the skating rink – I said 'Okay' because I thought it would make me stand out.

Man Really?

Woman Sure. That's the problem with high school – one of the many problems, anyway. You're so desperate to fit in, and at the same time totally needing to stand out . . .

Man Exactly. Yeah, I mean . . . yes.

Woman You know? And for me, well . . . guess I never really stopped. Doing this, I mean, marrying Cody and staying here – if you could've seen my mom's face! – it's pathetic, really. Not pathetic, I suppose, but . . . sad, almost. That I needed people to be aware of me that badly. Doesn't matter what you look like or how smart you are. No. It's really how you feel about yourself. Who you are. And I was raised with a total sense that I wasn't good enough . . . or that I wouldn't make the right choices. My parents were always nervous that I'd make some mistake along the way. And so, at some point . . . that is what I decided to do. Prove 'em right. I made a 'mistake' they'd never forget . . . (*Beat.*) But I was in love, too. I shouldn't sound so – well, actually I *shouldn't* be saying any of this, but – I loved him . . . Cody. When we got married. I really think I did. He was so . . . different. Rich and black, this big track star . . . you know, *different*. And I like different. Or, at least thought I did . . . the way he used to shine above everybody else at school. I loved that, back whenever. But now . . . (*Beat.*) Some mornings – like really early, before the kids are even up – I'll lay there, up against him and listening to him breathe. Or stare at his face, into those, you know, beautiful *features* of his . . . looking for any trace of what I used to see in him. It's gone, though . . .

The Woman looks over at the Man, to gauge his reaction. He nods and looks back toward the house. They both do – hey, they're not stupid.

Funny thing is . . . I still feel that pull inside *me*. The desire to be different. To be noticed . . . because doing that, marrying him, it made me different, too. And I still get some kind of thrill from it . . . walking into an Arby's or through Wal-Mart, with these two gorgeous brown children in tow. My little *pickaninnies* – that's what my parents call them – with their light-colored eyes. I do. I mean, it might be old hat in a place like New York or wherever, but around here . . . it's still a pretty big deal. (*Beat.*) These faces turning round to get a look at us, the whispering, and me with this fat checkbook and my head all held up high. Defiant. I don't even know why I like it so much. I just do . . .

Man Wow.

Woman Yeah. 'Wow.' Scary . . .

Man No, it's . . . why? Why 'scary'?

Woman . . . Scary that I'm that needy.

She looks at the Man and he trails off. Tries to smile.

Man No, not at all . . . (*Beat.*) Listen, this is going to sound lame, so I'm preparing you now, but . . . see, I always thought you stood out. Completely. I mean, so much . . .

Woman Huh. Well . . .

Man God, that was even worse than I thought! I mean, seriously sad. Forgive me.

Woman No way. I'm keeping that . . . it's all mine.

Man What?

Woman Just that, you know, little tidbit. You put it out there, so I get to have it . . . and thank you.

Man Pleasure – he says, glancing around to see if the husband is about to plunge a steak knife into his back . . .

They both laugh at this – good, that's nice. Just like before.

Woman I think you're in the clear. For a minute, anyway.

Man That's all I need. A minute. I'm much faster than I used to be . . .

Woman Yeah, but he'll kill ya out in the open, that's the problem . . .

Man Damn that 'Flying' Cody Phipps!

She gestures with her hands, making the sound of a jet soaring past.

I gotta get his technique down, that's all . . . the way he used to tear off at the start, remember?

Woman Of course! (*Laughs.*) With his . . .

Man Right! His butt up in the air, and then he'd . . . (*Jumps.*) Whoosh!!

Woman Exactly! With his arms flapping . . . yes, that's it!

The Man does a fair impression of it and they laugh again – but they better be careful. Cody's coming. At the last moment, they both notice.

Woman Hey, sweetie!

Man Cody . . . you need any help?

Cody Nah, I'm good . . . (*Beat.*) Wouldn't wanna break up your *coffee klatch* there.

Woman We were just . . .

Man . . . talking, you know . . .

Cody Yeah, yeah, I know. I do know. Was watching you from the window there, in the kitchen, and . . . boy, you two are like a couple old nannies!

Man That's us!

Woman I was checking the meat for you, and we just got to . . .

Cody Funny, he never talks that much when I'm around. Does he?

Man (*looking around*) Are you . . . I mean, do you mean *me*? 'Cause I'm standing right here.

Cody I know right where you are. Believe me . . .

Woman Honey, please don't . . .

Cody Doesn't bother me. Not at all. You can knock yourselves out . . . I just noticed it. That's all.

Cody takes a quick peek at the grill and then, satisfied, finds himself a nearby chair. He looks at the two of them.

Cody . . . Carry on.

Woman I think most of this is ready. Umm, maybe not the cutlets . . .

Man . . . Yeah, I think chicken's supposed to be . . .

Cody Give it a minute. (*Beat.*) So, what's up? What're you guys blabbing your heads off about? Hmm?

Woman Oh, just, you know . . .

Cody Nope. I don't. I do not.

Man Just, stuff, really. Life stuff . . .

Cody What's that mean?

Man I dunno. We were *chatting*, that's all.

Cody But not about you, I'll bet. (*Beat.*) Am I right?

Man What's that mean?

Woman Cody, honey, let's just . . . would you check these burgers, please?

Cody They're fine. (*to the Man*) I'm saying, I could see you both yakking on out here about shit, but my guess is . . . you didn't say a damn thing about yourself.

Man Why do you say that?

Cody 'Cause I've noticed it. Times we've been together, it's like pulling *molars* outta your skull to get anything at all personal . . .

The Man backs away a little – I never really noticed it, but maybe Cody's right about this. The Man sits at the table.

Man . . . That's true. I'm not the most open guy around. Yeah.

Cody Well, that's big of you . . .

Man Cody, look . . .

Woman Sweetie . . .

Cody No, seriously. I know ya know about us, ya leave your damn *windows* open all day and night – but I don't got hardly two bits of info on you. Was a lawyer. Gonna be a writer. That's it . . .

Woman I'm turning the grill off now . . .

The Woman does so. She starts moving the meat from the metal rack inside the grill to a large serving plate. The Man takes a drink, then smiles over at Cody.

Man . . . because those're the highlights. Honestly, not much to tell.

Cody Bullshit. Everybody's got a story. *Every*body . . .

Man Did I forget to trim your hedges or something? I mean, Cody, what is up with this . . . ?

Woman Guys, can we just . . . ?

Man No, it's okay. He's got something he wants to say, so we should probably just hear it . . .

Cody Yeah?

Man Go for it.

Cody . . . Alright. Fine. (*Beat.*) Why're you really back here? And none of your smart-mouth answers . . . Why did you stop being a lawyer? That's not something people really do. Give up a good job like that. Not usually.

The Man looks long and hard at Cody, then over at the Woman. She's making herself a burger but she's listening. No doubt about that.

Man I just did, that's all. Okay? Just up and quit one day, had my fill of it and walked out. Cleared out my things and that was . . . done.

Cody Huh . . . pretty generic.

Both Cody and the Woman watch the Man, realizing that he doesn't wish to go any further. In a way, though, he needs to. This is the right moment.

Woman . . . Don't feel like you have to . . .

Cody Don't do that. Alright? Don't just always jump in to defend every damn person I have a conversation with. It is pretty fucking annoying . . .

Woman I know that. I know. I only wanted to make this nice, have some food out on the lawn.

Cody The guy can just tell me to shut up, if he wants . . .

Woman Why does somebody have to *tell* you to shut up, why can't you just not say something for once? Why do you always have to have an *opinion* . . . ?

Cody Don't start some shit you can't finish, sweetie, 'cause I'm happy to go at it if you wanna, and I don't give a shit *who's* listening!

The marrieds stare each other down – to her credit, the Woman is holding her own.

Man Alright, alright, *hey* . . . no, Cody's right. That's a total crock – company-line shit. I had to sign a statement, actually, that I would tell that story, or something like it, as what happened, so I got used to it, I guess. Yep. (*Beat.*) But you guys, well . . . you're friends of mine, right? I can tell you the truth. Sure. (*to the Woman*) Do you mind if I have one of the burgers?

The Woman nods, starts fixing him one. The Man watches her as he talks. The Woman brings one to both the Man and to Cody.

I was let go. 'Fired', I guess, is the term they used to use, when our fathers were alive. Well, maybe not your father,

Cody, because he was a self-made guy, but my old man was a mechanic, worked at that Union 76 over on McHenry all his life, and if he screwed up – like, totally ruined somebody's Cadillac or mouthed off to the owner – then he would get fired. He didn't, no . . . But I was. Me. I was fired. For something I did.

Woman . . . I think I'm going to go inside.

Man No, please don't. Okay? I want you to hear this, Belinda. Need you to. Because I haven't really told anyone, so it feels good. Not good, but you know . . . freeing, somehow.

Woman Are you sure you . . . ?

Cody Just let the man talk.

Man Thanks. Yeah. Well, does everybody have what they want, for lunch, I mean? Because after this we may not be . . . just checking. (*Beat.*) I was a good lawyer, fair, anyway. I was very fair with people and decent. And that's not an easy thing, in that job. Not at all, but I was.

Anyhow, I'm on a business trip one time, with some of the people from my office, we were going to, umm, Pittsburgh or some place, I don't remember – it was on United, I recall that, it was with United. And I got there a little late, maybe twenty minutes before closing the flight, but a friend, this dude from down the hall, is up there, getting his boarding pass and he lets me slip in. Into line. Ahead of a few other colleagues . . . and one of them, this lady named Carol, an African-American woman who worked with us, says something out loud. Not a big deal, like, 'Hey, no cuts,' or something, and, you know, the kind of day it was, all rainy and a race through the terminal, I just wasn't in the mood. Not at all. *But*, I let it go. I do. I get my thingie and even use some miles to get bumped up – the last guy to be able to do it, they are totally sold out – and off we go, my buddy and me, down toward security and to the gate. I make eye contact with ol' Carol on the way, toss her a smile, and we're off. Actually, we stop by Mickey D's and grab a McRib each. Those're really good . . .

The Man takes a breather. Cody and the Woman are still there, hanging on his words. Cody heard the 'African-American' thing and his antennae are up.

Cody . . . Where's this going?

Woman Honey, he's trying to . . .

Cody I'm just asking.

Man I'm sorry, I'm rambling. Lemme just get to the . . . we get on the plane. So, we're sitting there, in Business, having our pre-take-off ginger ale or whatever, and people are filing past, bashing into me – I'm on the aisle – with their two bags each and we're talking away and, bam! I get tagged again by some computer case. Right on the elbow. And it hurts, it really does, so I'm about to say something . . . when I glance up, it's Carol. Not even looking. Heading back into Economy – thanks to me, in all probability – and it just makes my associate and I start laughing. I mean, *howling*, really, the two of us, there in the cabin. At some point, I'm not sure when, a bit later – I thought a *lot* later, but – I lean over to him, I lean in a bit and say, really whispering, 'Well, at least they still *sit* in the back of the bus.' Just for fun, right? It's this little joke, we're on an *Airbus*, after all, and, I swear to God, the place goes silent. Like a church for a moment, when the A/C is about to switch over or something . . . I say this thing and a bunch of folks are suddenly looking right down at me. Including *Carol*. See, some old lady back there is messing around with her suitcase, this old Samsonite, and the line hasn't moved at all. Carol is, I mean, she is standing *right* there. Shit . . . I start to sputter, try to stand up, my belt is hooked and it jerks me back into my seat, I spill the drink. A whole parade. I do finally get to my feet and try to explain, say, 'What I meant to say was . . .' and she tears into me, like, well, it was pretty unbelievable. 'S like Angela Davis has suddenly appeared and she's all waving her hands and screaming at me – with the 'mother-fuckin' this and that, like she'd never been to school a day in her life! And I . . . I lost it. I admit it, I just totally lost it there for a bit . . . and I grabbed her by both her shoulders, this Carol woman, not hard or anything, but grabbed her and shook her a second. I shook her and said, 'Hey, Carol stop it! Stop acting like some *blue-gummed chimp*, just fell outta the tree!' (*Beat.*) So . . . just imagine what the next five minutes were like, those last few moments when I'm standing and collecting my stuff . . . it was just so unreal. No, *sur*real. I will never forget that feeling . . . and I didn't apologize, that's the thing. Which is what really does me in, I guess. See, they wanted this formal letter of . . . anyway, I just wouldn't do it. I wasn't gonna back down. I was *defiant*. The firm 'let me go' about three days later. Well, I guess suspended first, but then . . . yeah. My wife left a few weeks after that. Not because it bothered her, I don't think, but because it was the *right* thing to do. Or gave her an excuse, anyway. This was almost a year ago. (*Beat.*) Anyway, Cody, how's that burger?

Cody takes another bite before he does anything. Maybe two.

Woman Maybe we should . . . I don't know. What should we do now? Cody?

Cody wipes his mouth with one hand, then finds his napkin. Uses it. Stands.

Cody Me? I'm gonna go watch the dish . . . maybe that Hitchcock movie you're all so excited about.

Man You did ask . . .

Cody Yeah, I know. Don't mean you always gotta tell the truth.

Woman Cody, honey . . .

Man Maybe I'll head back over to . . .

Cody No, you guys have a nice chat. Go on. Like nothing happened. And it didn't, right? Nothing happened. Other than we found out what a piece of *shit* we got living here with us . . .

> *The Man starts to say something, then stops. The Woman moves to Cody, but he shakes her off. Holds up a finger.*

(*toward the Man*) . . . end of the month. I want you the *fuck* outta my home!

> *Cody wanders off toward the house. Exits. The Man and the Woman sit quietly for a moment. Maybe even longer – no hugs this time. Just silence. Then, out of nowhere, her hand touches the Man's hand. She holds it. So does he. Now, this is interesting.*

Woman . . . Well. I'm sure he's, I mean, he usually doesn't stay mad long . . .

Man Doesn't matter.

Woman No?

Man Uh-uh. Glad I told you. Needed to.

Woman Then good. People should do what they need to do. Mostly. (*Beat.*) . . . Were you . . . I mean, you didn't mean it, though, did you? What you said to her. That woman . . .

Man No . . . not *now*, not when I'm thinking about it. No.

Woman I . . . I'm sure you didn't. Right?

Man Yeah. (*Stands.*) I'm gonna go back upstairs, is that okay?

Woman Oh, please. Sure. Yes. I'll just . . . I'm gonna clean some of this up.

Man Do you want any . . . ?

Woman No, I'm fine. Absolutely.

Man Sorry.

Woman No, don't be, it's . . . it was only *lunch*, right?

Man Sure. I'll see you, then.

Woman I'll . . . uhm, you know . . . call you. Later, maybe.

Man 'Kay.

He moves off, down toward us. She remains and cleans up.

. . . So, that was different, huh? *Very.* Maybe not in the way Belinda was talking about it, but still . . . it was *different.* Yeah. I am *that*, if nothing else . . . (*Beat.*) Speaking of Belinda, and I should've done this earlier, but . . . hey, like Cody always says: whatever. One thing you should know about us. We did kiss once. Yes. I don't mean in the past, not at the drive-in or anything, but recently. Like, within the last couple weeks. Not a big deal, I mean, it was very nice, don't get me wrong . . . but it was just this small little thing. Out on the lawn here one time, when I'm cutting the side yard. I was – ahh, mowing, like I said, or I guess . . . maybe I was raking at that point. Yeah, raking, and . . . (*Beat.*) . . . we kiss.

He takes off his shirt, pitches it out of the way. Finds a rake somewhere onstage – that's the designer's problem. The Man starts working, and, suddenly, the Woman

appears. Glass of water in her hand. Ice cubes. The
Man looks up.

She smiles at him, holding up the drink. He takes
the tumbler and gulps down the cool liquid. She smiles
and, without thinking, reaches over and wipes his
brow. He smiles back. And then they're kissing – kind
of surprising but, believe me, it's happening. This goes
on for a few moments. When they stop, she leans over
and steals a sip from the glass. Moves off.

The Man watches her go. Wistful. Unsure. He shakes
it off and looks back at us. Starts changing his clothing
– he's going to need some jogging stuff. Sweats. Shoes.
Nothing too fancy.

That's pretty much it. Just this nice kiss that comes from
her bringing me a glass of tap water, something to cool
me off. Didn't work! Not after . . . doing that. With her.
I am not cool after that! And it's out of nowhere, that's
the thing that really knocks me out . . . we just kiss. We
kiss like there's a respirator between us, and our lips are
the only thing keeping the other person going. You know
how that is, when you're with someone and you get a bit
close, sort of begin to cross that *no man's land* and there's
no going back . . . (*Beat.*) Amazing.

The Man stretches now, shaking out his limbs. Trying
to loosen up a bit.

. . . You know, while we're gettin' so fancy – like, back
and forth in time and all that – we should probably take
a look at something that happened a while ago, 'cause it's
worth checking out. Yeah, it *definitely* puts a wrinkle in
things . . .

Cody enters, running gear again and sweating through
it. Sits down and starts stretching out.

Can't believe I forgot to mention this! Cody and I met up
one day . . . over at this nature reserve, where they have

these running trails. A mile or so from here. We hooked up there and met. Few weeks after the whole lawn party thing. This is how it goes . . .

> *Cody continues cooling down from his run. Flexing. The Man runs in, a bit out of breath. He stops near Cody and stands there, staring at him. Gradually, Cody glances over at him.*

Man Hey.

Cody What's up?

Man Not much.

> *Cody moves over and the two men look at each other, sizing the other man up.*

Cody I don't like this. I do not like meeting up out here . . . this is gonna be the only time we do it.

Man Hey, you called me.

Cody Yeah, well, no more *calls* then! No emails or drive-bys, any shit like that . . . (*Beat.*) Let's conclude our business and be done with this . . .

Man That's why I'm here. (*Smiles.*) Not because I'm *fond* of you . . .

Cody Whatever, man. So how many times've you talked with her now? I mean, since then. That day.

Man A few. Six, maybe . . .

Cody Six? She's called you *six* times?

Man Something like that . . . and, yes, I make sure she calls from the *house.*

Cody Fine. Okay. And you've met . . . ?

Man . . . a couple.

Cody I don't want to know any more than that.

Man Good.

Cody . . . But you guys aren't . . . I mean, you haven't, umm . . . right? Not yet.

Man That's really . . . not your business. Isn't that what we discussed?

Cody No, yeah, true . . . Whatever. (*Beat.*) How much longer, you figure?

Man What, until you can say something? Or catch us? Hell, I dunno . . . give it a month or so.

Cody A *month* . . . ?!

Man You seem anxious . . .

Cody Of course I am. Come on! What the fuck . . .

Man Of course you are . . . Who is she, by the way?

Cody What?

Man The girl I saw you with . . . out by the reservoir. Last week. She's cute, but really young.

Cody No, that's the . . . I'm training her. She's on the team.

Man *Right.* Look, I know you've told Belinda that you're in love with your work, but please, Cody, do me the favor. I'm a *guy*.

Cody I don't know what you're saying . . .

Man I'm saying, pretty outright, that a person does not do this, this *Mayor of Casterbridge* thing you've got going here, without some reason. A reason like the one I saw you out running with.

Cody No, shit, that has *nothing* to do with this!

Man Oh, yeah?

Cody NO! We ran into each other at the airport there and we were . . .

Man Cody, please. Be honest here. You asked me to take your wife – have her in *trade* –

Cody You wanted to! We got to talking . . . I mean, we were going on about that Jackie Robinson card and, and then *you* brought up Belinda.

Man Cody, I was *there*, remember? Right there next to you and you asked me flat out.

Cody Yeah, but I knew you liked her . . . back in school, I'm saying. I came over to you and . . .

Man No, *I* came up to you . . . saw you and made the connection, and like, *three* beers later . . . you dish up this proposition. A *whopper* of a proposition . . .

Cody I'd just been thinking and you did always like her.

Man So, you were just being nice, then? Gonna let me have her as a *gift*?

Cody No, no, we made a *deal* and now I'm hearing a whole different . . .

Man You gave me your wife. *Asked* me to take her. Now, either you're Henny Youngman or there's something fishy going on! . . . (*Beat.*) I'm only saying this to help remind you – do not forget the truth here. The truth is always of some importance. (*Smiles.*) Just a little tip for you there, buddy . . .

> *Cody stares at him, not sure how he knows all this. Suddenly, the Man seems a lot smarter than he's come off during the rest of the proceedings.*

Cody Hey! Man, we're not friends, okay, this is not you and me talking over old times on some *camping trip*, you got that? Huh?! I'm paying you to do something for me. Do a thing and to place that fucking card back in my hand. That is all . . . you got that?

Man Right. Got it. Yes.

The Man begins to pull something out of his pocket as does Cody. Cody stops and says:

Cody By the way . . . that shit about the woman on the plane was not funny. At all.

The Man stops reaching in his jacket – he smiles at Cody.

Man Hah! Sorry 'bout that . . . spur of the moment thing.

Cody Yeah, well . . .

Man It worked, didn't it?

Cody Yes, it worked. Worked at pissing me off, that's what it did . . . l hate that kind a' thing, just so you know. Any kind of racist shit. Just so you're aware . . .

Man I know. Of course I know. That's *why* I did it . . .

Cody I need her out of my home, but I don't wanna go through all this crap to do it. Otherwise, fuck, I might as well just get a *divorce* . . .

Man Hey, you are going to get divorced! You'll have to . . . you're just going to get everything that you want *in* the divorce. That's why I'm here.

Cody . . . Right . . .

Man Isn't that what we agreed to? Make this as simple as possible. For *every*body . . .

Cody Yeah. It is.

Man Alright, then.

The Man stops talking for a moment, bending over. Stretches. Holding his side in a bit of pain.

Cody You gotta push through the pain . . .

Man You just gotta back off a minute, lemme worry about my own self!

Cody studies him disapprovingly.

Cody Once a fattie, always a fattie.

The Man takes a few steps, flips Cody the 'finger'. Cody fidgets, keeping warm and stretching.

Man . . . Hey, we can't all be Olympians. Or, *almost* Olympians.

Cody Whatever.

Man I mean, you never really made it, right? That's what I heard.

Cody Something like that . . .

Man What happened? I thought you were so good.

Cody Yeah. Well, 'good' don't mean shit. Not out there. Not in sports. Plus, I never even . . . really . . .

Man . . . What? I mean, I knew you went off to school on this big scholarship thing . . . and then you threw a race or something, but that's all I . . .

Cody interrupts at once – intent not to let this notion stand without defending himself. He's obviously done this before.

Cody No, uh-uh, *no*. I didn't 'throw' nothing. If I'd *thrown* it, then I would've lost, and I didn't. No. See, I won . . . *won* it, but I wasn't supposed to.

Man I don't follow.

Cody It was this . . . (*Considers it.*) . . . nothing. Forget it. Where's the card?

Man No, what? Come on . . .

Cody squats down near the Man now, remembering.

Cody . . . They wanted me to be a rabbit for 'em, my Freshman year. And not even my event! I was done for the day with two firsts, but they asked me to go out quick in the five thousand and tire the other teams out, help our guys win – something to do with building my character and shit like that, *unity* – but I was like, 'Fuck this,' and took off running. Never looked back. (*Beat.*) Broke out early. Broke away from the pack – it's a beautiful day, glorious, and I'm feeling good, my dad's there, up in the stands somewhere – so I take off like a shot. Like some *bullet* that got blown outta the starter pistol by accident. And I know I can make it, that's the funny thing. Coach wants me to run my ass off for two, three laps and then drop out, but I take off and just keep it up. I do. You know what I'm like when I get going . . . I mean, bam! I am gone. I practically lap the farthest guy back, I'm that hepped up. Man, I'm flying . . . inches off the ground, the whole race. (*Grins.*) And *that* is how it goes . . . Right up until the moment I break through that tape. Twenty-*six* seconds ahead of the next guy. School record or some shit . . .

Cody stops for a second, thinking back, lost.

I guess I wasn't cut out for 'team' sports . . . which I never knew track was till I got to college; but I beat every one of those motherfuckers that day. And my dad was there to see it . . .

Cody stands and moves off, swinging his arms viciously in the air. The Man slowly stands up.

Man . . . Shit.

Cody Yeah. (*Beat.*) Coach made sure I lost my scholarship 'cause I wouldn't obey or back down. 'Accept responsibility,' I think he called it . . . and, you know, that's what folks wanna talk about, in the end. To dwell on. But my winning, they forgot all about that fact. Anyway, that's as close as I ever got to any gold medal.

Man Wow.

Cody Yeah, 'Wow.'

> *A long silence develops between the two men –*
> *begrudging and respectful. These two just may be*
> *more alike than we first suspected.*
> *After a moment, Cody moves to the Man and*
> *presses a finger into his chest.*

I need to go. Gotta get myself off to work.

Man Cool. I'm meeting Belinda later.

Cody Okay.

> *Cody reaches into a pocket, producing an envelope.*
> *He holds it out for the Man. Cody stops for a moment,*
> *then shakes his head. Laughs.*

Cody Man, it is just too strange! Being in on a thing like this . . . *happy* she's cheating on me.

Man I can stop.

Cody Funny. (*Hands Man the envelope.*) Just do what you need to do. Gimme the card . . .

> *Cody snaps his fingers impatiently, indicating that he*
> *wants something. The Man nods and digs in his zipper*
> *pocket. He produces a single baseball card inside a*
> *thick plastic case.*

The Man doesn't hand it over yet, though. Not quite yet. He glances into the envelope.

Man . . . God, that's a *lot* of cash! You must really hate her, huh?

Cody What?

Man Hate her. You do, right? Which I am just *so-o* fucking curious about . . .

Cody No, I don't . . .

Man Oh, really?!

Cody I'm . . . (*Beat.*) . . . No, I guess I do, actually. Hate her. Never thought of it that way, but, yeah. I do.

Man So . . . ? *Why?*

Cody I dunno. After a while, it's a bit of everything, I s'pose. The way she flosses her teeth, browsing my mail and shit. Her face. All that stuff . . . (*Beat.*) I mean, it's great at first . . . we always looked real nice out there, walking around town hanging off each other's arm. I used to love that – and, yes, she is the mother of my kids and all, stood up to her parents over us – but, hey, after a while, you know how it goes . . . I guess the *novelty* of it just wore off.

Man The 'novelty'? Jesus . . .

Cody Just trying to be honest.

Man So, why didn't you leave her, then? Huh? Why not just, you know . . . ?

Cody Because if I go, I lose. I am the loser and that is bullshit! Bullshit!! No, uh-uh! I will not do that!! I got a place here in this community to think about! A *legacy* and the boys and all kinds a' crap.

I was an *athlete*, I support this town! Cody Phipps is fucking looked up to!! (*Beat.*) 'S the same reason my ol' man stayed – that guy hung in there, built his wife an empire. A goddamn *empire*! That dude weathered fuckin' El Nino over her and you know what? People round here *respected* him. They did. Respected him as he stood there watching her pull away in that motherfuckin El Dorado of hers . . .

Man . . . 'S that right?

Cody Yeah, that's fucking *right* as rain.

Man . . . What *a bitch*.

Cody Don't! Do not say a word, man . . .

Man Oh, come on, that's not exactly 'news', is it?

Cody What?

Man What people thought of her . . .

Cody I don't give two shits what people said about her! *Any*body.

Man Yeah? My ol' man used to laugh his guts out over her . . .

Cody Hey, man, shut up . . .

Man Your 'mommy' running back and forth down Main Street like some goddamn yo-yo . . .

Cody Shut up! Shut up!!

> *In an instant Cody is up in the Man's face, grabbing him by the collar. The Man doesn't fight or cower – just stares into Cody's face.*

Man But Belinda's not at all like your mom, is she?

Cody Hey, what'd I just say?! Huh?

Man She doesn't take off, come running back like your mother used to . . . (*Pokes Cody's chest.*)

Cody (*pushes Man*) SHUT-THE-FUCK-UP!

Man . . . so you can forgive her like your father used to! (*He pushes Cody.*)

Cody You suck my dick . . . piece a' shit like you talking about my *dad*.

> *Cody goes to hit the Man, but he stops – not because he wants to stop but because the Man grabs his wrist. They struggle like Gabriel and the Angel for a moment.*
> *Finally, Cody pulls back and away, pushing the Man to one side.*

Gimme my fucking CARD!!

> *The Man holds it out toward Cody but doesn't move. Silent. It's a stand-off – Cody finally blinks and moves to the Man. Grabs the card from him. Backs away.*

I cannot *wait'll* this thing is over!

Man Me, too.

Cody Good. I'm outta here . . . fuck you.

Man Fuck you, too, bro' . . .

> *Cody gives him the 'finger' and walks off. Angry. The Man turns away and moves back down toward us. Sheepish grin.*

God, sorry for that! Got a touch outta hand, so forgive me. I should explain. You really need to take a good look at the last few moments, decide for yourselves what happened there. I mean, how much is real . . . (*Beat.*) It *happened*, that much I can tell you. We did meet, talked for a bit, he even gave me an envelope. But the rest of it?

Hey, that stuff's for you to decide. (*Beat.*) Can't help you out with everything, wouldn't be any fun!

The Man pulls that thick wad of cash out of his pocket, turns it over in his hands.

. . . This could be my deposit, what I gave them when I moved in. Maybe. Or it's a pay-off for me to take Belinda off of Cody's hands. *Or* for that baseball card, even! Hell, I don't know. I really don't. All I do know is we met in passing at the airport, I moved back to town and *she's* with me now . . . out of their house and living at my place. She sees the children most days, at least for the moment, just until they settle things, and Cody, well, he got exactly what he wanted, too. He did. He finally got – after all those humiliating years of watching his dad take his mother back, time and time again – Cody got a white woman to walk out on him and stay gone. You should see him strutting around town now, telling anybody who'll listen about what Belinda did, and how hurtful it'll be on the kids. How she never would've done this, something so humiliating to him, if he wasn't *black*. Seriously, people have told me he's said that very thing. 'If I wasn't black,' or something like that. Yep. He's gone and pulled the ol' Ace of Spades out, one last time. Wouldn't ya know it? (*Beat.*) Also, I think maybe I came off a little too, I dunno, *something*, in that last bit. Not like myself. (*Laughs.*) But, then, people are so many things, faces, in a given day, maybe that's just some side of me, this other part, that doesn't get out that often but is there. I dunno. But this time – 'cause we're about to finish this off right now – this time out I'll be a bunch more like I was in the beginning. 'The Sensitive Guy.' (*Does 'thumbs-up'.*) This is really about them now, anyhow, settling up and the like . . . I'm just there to be a support to her. To Belinda. Yep. I'm . . . anyway . . .

Lights should probably change here to something more formal – what the hell does that mean? I don't know. But we could use a desk, maybe, and a few chairs. Cody and the Woman should already be seated, waiting. The Man can wander over in his own time. Soon, but you know what I mean.

Man . . . Hello. Sorry that I'm . . .

Woman It's okay. (*Checks Cody.*) I mean, *fine.*

Man Right, right . . . 'Fine but not okay.' I remember.

Woman Yes. That's . . . right.

They sit in silence for a moment – make it a long one. Cody glances around. Checks his watch.

Cody Where *is* this guy? (*to the Man.*) You see anybody out in the hall?

Man Ahh, no, I didn't. I was just . . . no.

Cody Fine.

Man I'm sure he's coming . . .

Cody Yeah? How do you know that?

Man Just hopeful. That's all . . .

Woman Guys, let's not do this. Not right now . . . okay?

Cody grunts and goes back to staring at the wall. The Man reaches over and squeezes the Woman's hand. She smiles.

Cody You two look over everything? The papers I had sent over, and the . . . ?

Woman Yes. (*Looks at the Man.*) You don't have to involve him, this is really just between us.

Cody Hey, he's the one you're screwing now, so he can . . .

Woman I'm really not gonna sit here for that! I won't, Cody, I mean it.

Cody Fine. I'll shut up . . .

Man I doubt that . . .

Cody Fuck off.

Man No, Cody, I don't want to. So I *won't.*

Cody and the Man have one of those adolescent male stare-downs; Cody blinks first. Looks away. Checks his watch again.

Cody Two hundred bucks an hour, ya think he could be on time . . .

Man Right.

Woman Yes. That'd be nice . . .

Cody Man . . . (*Beat.*) You did look at the stuff, though, right? I mean, all the changes from that last draft and the . . .

Woman Yes, Cody, we read it over. *Both* of us.

Cody Good. Alright. And you're sure you want the single payment, instead of the . . . ?

Woman Yes.

Man We do. Yeah. Better to just finish this off, clean, and we can all . . . You agree to the custody schedule and we're fine with the settlement. (*Takes the Woman's hand.*) We don't want your precious house, or your stores, any of that crap. We'll manage . . .

Cody From what, your *book* deals . . . ?

Woman Cody . . .

Cody Just asking.

Man Don't worry about us, okay?

Cody Whatever.

Man Seriously . . .

Woman We're going to be happy. That's what's important. Something *we* never figured out, you and me . . .

Cody That's bullshit, but think what you want.

Woman Oh, I will . . . I'm gonna think and feel and do whatever I want from now on. And you can't do anything about it. You can't yell at me, or, or, or turn Cody Junior against me any more . . .

Cody *Please* . . .

Woman You cannot!! You can't do a damn thing to me . . . none of your silences or mumbling under your breath or, or judgements about my . . . *nothing*. None of the 'Cody Phipps' bullshit that you've gotten away with for so long. (*to him*) You stole my life . . . my adult life . . . but you will never hurt me again! Not *ever*. No, you are not allowed.

Cody . . . You better watch it . . .

Woman No, Cody, I don't have to, I do not have to 'watch' shit any more! (*She laughs.*) When I think about . . . oh my God! The things I gave up, squashed inside of me just to, to . . . what? To keep the peace . . . to go another *minute* or two without you giving me that look of yours! Jesus . . . how could somebody be so stupid, huh?! *How?!* (*Beat.*) I'll tell you how . . . by being scared of your *own* husband. Being so nervous about him looking over your shoulder when you write out a *grocery list* or when he sneers at you reading a book that he thinks has got too much 'talky' shit in it – *Pride and Prejudice* isn't too talky, Cody, it's just a book! I like books!! I never threw

out your *Sporting News*, did I? No, I did not . . . let 'em
pile up next to your chair and didn't make a peep! Not
once. And you know why?! *Because* you wouldn't let me,
that's why . . . because the only sound you ever allowed
in that house was your own voice. (*Beat.*) Well, it's all
yours now, so yell if you wanna . . . there's nobody left to
listen to you.

Cody Shut the hell up . . .

Man *Hey*, Cody! Don't you speak to her like that . . .

Cody I said you watch your mouths, man!! BOTH OF
YOU!! Just watch that kind of fucking shit around me . . .

*Cody stands up and slams his chair against the table,
taking a step toward the Man. The Man remains
seated, not engaging. That's probably best. The
moment deflates and Cody tries to save face – he heads
for the door.*

Cody . . . I'm gonna go look in the hall, check on this
motherfucker.

Woman You do that.

Cody I will.

Man So, go then. Do it.

*Cody starts off, then looks back at the Man. The
Woman, too. A gleam in his eyes.*

Cody . . . But if I ever wanna trade back, you'll let me,
right? Hmm?

*The Man stares at him for a moment, then slowly
nods; Cody smiles and exits. The Woman watches him
go, looking at the door. The Man watches, too, until
the Woman turns to him.*

Woman . . . What's he mean by that?

Man Oh, ya know.

Woman No, I don't. No. What?

Man He's, umm, he's just . . . Cody's just trying to . . .

They look at one another, then the Woman glances over at the door again. After a moment, the Man rises and crosses to us.

Okay, sort of a dilemma here, right? Bit of a pickle . . . do I tell Belinda everything or make a run for it?

The Man glances back at her, then turns pleadingly to us for advice.

I'm serious, gimme some help here. I always imagined a day like this, one where she stumbles onto an airline ticket or a scribbled note on a napkin and asks me about it . . . and I believe that I'd do the righteous thing. Tell her the truth. But the thing of it is, the truth is just so damn . . . elusive, isn't it? In the end. The second you start telling somebody what the truth is – how it goes – it all starts to slip away. Not, like, some lie, exactly, but close. This half-remembered version of one side a' things. And what would the point be? I'll tell you this much – we end up pretty happy. We go and get married not too much later, even have ourselves a couple kids. And we live happily ever after . . . or the equivalent of that, whatever that means today. Yes, we disagree on occasion, I sleep in the guest room every now and then, one of the boys breaks an eardrum swimming, but all in all, we survive. We make it as a couple, and that, my friends, is not easy today. It is work – work that not everybody out there is willing to do. See, people tire of each other, give up on what they've got instead of fixing it, or trying to. It's easier to just . . . start over, go online, bury themselves at the office. *Any*thing, rather than get to the bottom of

223

their own shit. We're weak, that's really what it is. We are
lazy and pushy and we want it all today. Or sooner, even.
Now. And as long as we get it, our fair share – or a pinch
more – well, then, who really gives a fuck what happens
to anybody else? Right? But *I* work at it every day, I do,
because I love her . . . always have. And I can see it on
her face, at night or when we're on the back patio, at that
blue hour when the sun's just dropped down . . . she is
finally at peace. So what the hell am I gonna tell her right
now to ruin it all? Huh? Nothing, that's what . . . I'm
gonna make up some tale about a baseball card I'd given
him from my collection and go with that. Stick with it to
my dying breath . . . (*Beat.*) Quick story. The 'Jackie
Robinson' story. Cody's dad gave him that card – meant
the *world* to him – but Cody offered to trade it to me if
I'd go out with Belinda to the movies that one time.
Time I mentioned way earlier. Remember? See, he was
cheating on her, even back then. He'd met this other girl,
another cheerleader from over at Central, and he wanted
to go out with her. That same night. So, he calls me,
comes over and tells me this whole tale about Belinda
and how I got to help him out. Tells me to go pick her up
at her house, six-thirty, and head out to the drive-in, this
'Showboat' spot, says he'll meet us there, friends are
joining us. The usual line of Cody bullshit. And that's
how I end up seeing a movie with Belinda . . . one that
she doesn't even remember going to but changed my
entire life. See, I would have walked across the Mojave
just to carry her books, but I also knew he was in a pinch,
Cody was. And I hated him, *hated* him, because he picked
on me . . . picked me to help him since I was no threat.
Friendly, fat and always up for whatever. *That's* the kind
of guy Cody Phipps was. (*Beat.*) See, Cody Phipps was
born a nigger. Still is, to this day. And I do know the
difference, believe me, between regular black people and
what Cody is. Oh yeah, absolutely. I never really liked the

guy – yes, back in school I'd hang with him, do some
stuff, but basically just so he wouldn't make fun of me or
knock me around. But Cody was always a nigger, even
back then. A selfish, mean-spirited *coon* who acted like
everybody owed him something. All that sort of post-
Civil War, Malcolm X, heavy-lidded bullshit that guys
like him've been trading on for years. Forty acres and a
mule and always ready to lay down the ol' Ace of Spades.
Well, hey man, forgive us for dragging your sorry asses
over here, 'cause-it-wasn't-fuckin-worth-it! (*Smiles.*)
Now, look . . . I don't really think in that way, use those
kinda terms very often, because the good side of me, the
educated portion, says, 'Hey, no, don't you do that, we're
all God's *chillun*' and so on. But raised like I was, where
I was – by *whom* I was – and that crap is always right up
there, near the surface, waiting to bubble over. Cut me
off in traffic some time, you'll see what I mean! (*Beat.*)
And anyhow . . . it's just a word, right? 'Nigger'. A word
like any other. Only has power if you let it . . .

> *The Man looks back at the Woman – she's still staring
> off. Waiting for her cue. He looks back at us one more
> time.*

I still see him, Cody, some days around town. Running.
Over past the golf course and down there. I don't think
there's too many hard feelings any more. Least I hope
not . . . (*He looks over at the Woman.*) But I'm not gonna
screw this up . . . forget it. I'll make up a lie – I'm a lawyer,
don't forget, ex, so it comes easy to me. Something. I'll
smooth this over and we can get on to all that stuff I just
told you about. That good stuff. I can't wait . . . to be
with her. Finally. After all this time. It's taken a lot to get
here, to this place for Belinda and I to be together. For
her to be happy. 'S worth it, though, right? Sure. I mean,
anything's worth it, as long as you mean well . . .

The Man smiles at us, then returns to his seat next to the Woman. He takes her hand and she turns back to him.

Woman . . . What did he mean, sweetie?

Man Nothing. It's a card, that's all. That stupid Jackie Robinson card he's been talking about . . .

Woman The rare one?

Man Uh-huh.

A quiet falls over them as the Woman studies the Man. She reaches out and touches his face. Softly.

Woman I know what you've done.

Man What? I mean . . .

Woman I do. I'm not stupid, so, I know . . .

Man I never said you were. (*Beat.*) Okay, honey, what? Come on, *what*?

Woman You gave it to him. Didn't you? That card. (*Beat.*) Tell me.

Man I . . . I did it . . . for *you*. I wanted to help.

Woman Oh. (*Beat.*) So, what's he wanna give you for it? I thought you were . . .

Man Just one of his players. His . . .

Woman Yeah?

Man . . . Yes. One of his good ones.

Woman You sure you want to? I thought . . . just don't let him bully you. Okay?

Man I know. I won't.

Woman Because he can do that. Be a bully. And you've got a good heart, so . . . just be careful.

Man It's fine. (*Grins.*) Promise.

Woman Alright, then. (*Smiles.*) You sure?

Man No, yeah. I'm sure. Very sure. Yep. Very . . .

Woman . . . Okay. Then fine.

She smiles at the Man, then looks straight out. He studies her for a moment, unsure what this last word means. Finally he reaches over and kisses her on the cheek. Slowly turns out. They are together now, but lost in their own thoughts. Alone.

Silence. Darkness.

SOME GIRL(S)

Some Girl(s) was first produced at the Gielgud Theatre, London, on 12 May 2005 with the following cast:

Guy David Schwimmer
Sam Catherine Tate
Tyler Sara Powell
Lindsay Lesley Manville
Bobbi Saffron Burrows

Director David Grindley
Designer Jonathan Fensom
Lighting Designer Jason Taylor
Sound Designer Gregory Clarke

The US premiere opened at the Lucile Lortel Theatre, New York, on 9 June 2006 in an MCC Theater production with the following cast:

Guy Eric McCormack
Lindsay Fran Drescher
Tyler Judy Reyes
Sam Brooke Smith
Bobbi Maura Tierney

Director Jo Bonney
Set Designer Neil Patel
Costumes Designer Mimi O'Donnell
Lighting Designer David Weiner
Sound Designer Robert Kaplowitz

Characters

Guy

Sam

Tyler

Lindsay

Bobbi

Reggie

NOTE

The character of Reggie was written in after the original English and American premieres of the play. While she is included in this edition, the play may also be performed as it was first conceived. The previous text was published by Faber & Faber as a single edition.

However, if someone does wish to include the 'Reggie' section in a given production, it seems to rest most comfortably between 'Lindsay' and 'Bobbi' (as published here). Experimentation is welcome, but this order makes the most sense to the author.

Part One

'SAM'

Silence. Darkness.

A standard hotel room. High-end without being too obvious; a resort chain of some kind. Marriott or one of those. A bed, work space, TV, mini-bar. Probably a nice chair.

Guy – thirty-three, fully dressed – sits at the desk and plays with the TV remote just as he is finishing a call on the house phone.

A knock at the door. The man jumps up and crosses to one lamp, carefully arranging its shade. Satisfied, he goes over to the eyehole. Looks out. Takes a breath and opens the latch.

A woman – same age, let's call her Sam – enters with a Starbucks coffee cup in hand. A silent 'hello' from both of them; after a moment, a tentative hug. They venture into the room – the woman chooses the chair, the man moves to the bed. They sit.

Guy . . . Always. You were always the late one.

Sam Sorry! It's bumper to bumper out there . . .

Guy But you made it. Even with the rain. Thanks.

Sam Of course. Sure. (*Beat.*) Used to be a great city, but then, you know. Boom! (*Holds up her coffee cup.*) Thanks to this bunch . . .

Guy Exactly! (*Grabs her umbrella.*) Here, let me take that. Anyway, I'm really happy, because . . . well, you know.

Sam Right.

Guy Because it's so great to see you. It honestly is . . .

Sam Good. I'm glad.

Guy And you look . . . lovely . . .

Sam (*beat*) Pretty nice here. I've never been before.

Guy Oh. Yeah. (*Looking around.*) They're good . . . They've got 'em all over the place now, so . . . a chain, I think.

Sam I mean, why would I, right? Live in town, how often are you gonna stay in a local hotel?

Guy Right . . .

Sam You wouldn't.

Guy No, not usually.

Sam Not for any reason, really. Not even if there was a convention and you were attending or something . . . You'd still just drive home after. (*Beat.*) I mean, unless . . .

Guy What? Unless what . . . ?

Sam You know.

Guy No, I don't . . .

Sam Yes, you do. You know what I'm saying.

Guy I don't, no. Truthfully. *What?*

Sam . . . unless you were seeing someone. Illicitly.

Guy Oh, right. That.

Sam Yes. That. (*Beat.*) So?

The man nods at this and clears his throat. Jumps up and moves toward the mini-bar. Points out various items.

Guy You want anything? I mean, like, a water . . . ?
They've got that Evian . . .

Sam No. (*Points to her coffee.*) Thanks.

Guy Really?

Sam Nope. I'm fine.

Guy I might have some nuts, if that's alright with you.
Cashews.

Sam Go for it.

Guy Even though they're, like, you know, six hundred
dollars . . .

They share a laugh at this, albeit a small one.

Sam Then don't eat them. Right? I mean, that'll teach
'em.

Guy Yeah, I guess. But I'm hungry . . .

Sam Then you decide. Which was never one of your
strong suits . . .

*He nods at this, remembering. On impulse, He snaps
open the canister and begins to eat.*

Guy Geez, no salt. I'm not big on that.

Sam No, you always liked the salt . . . one of your many
vices.

Guy Yep. (*Beat.*) So . . . mmm, they're good, actually.
Not too bad this way. (*He offers again.*) You sure?

Sam Yes. I mean, no. No thanks. (*Beat.*) Oh, I read the
thing you did for that one magazine. Somebody faxed it
to me. It was pretty good . . . clever. Mmm-hmm.

Guy Yeah? Thanks.

The man nods and shrugs. She smiles thinly again and exhales. She sets her latte down on an end table.

Sam . . . Funny how you know so much about women. *Now.* (*Laughs.*) Anyway . . .

Guy Yeah, anyway. So, look, I know this is sort of out-of-the-blue and all, and I appreciate how you might be kinda curious about what's up . . .

Sam Well, I am, that's true. I do want to know that. What is up?

Guy I just . . . look, I needed to see you.

Sam 'Needed'?

Guy Wanted, actually, but there's some need in there, too. Yes. *Need.*

Sam . . . And why is that? (*Beat.*) I only cut to the chase because, you know, my kids are home at three.

Guy Right, sure. (*Checks watch.*) Sorry.

Sam Don't be. It's fine . . . I like when they come home. I just need to be there, that's all . . .

Guy No, I didn't mean that . . . I'm sorry about rambling on about the, like, peanuts and crap. Forgive me.

Sam Cashews.

Guy Right. Those. (*Puts down the nuts.*) I'll get to the point here . . .

A long moment where the man looks at her, trying to decide the best way into this conversation. He eats another nut.

Well – I think I'm gonna have some water, these really do parch your throat after you eat a few.

He jumps up and heads back to the mini-fridge. Grabs a water and breaks open the seal. She steals a look at her watch.

Listen you're probably wondering what I'm even doing here . . . back in the, ahhh, Seattle area.

Sam It did cross my mind, yes.

Guy Right, sure, of course – although I do get back here sometimes. You know, every couple years to see my folks, that kind of thing. But I'm not here for that. To see them.

Sam No?

Guy Nope. I didn't even call them, let 'em know . . . I'm flying out in a few hours.

Sam Oh. Huh. Well . . .

Guy Because I really just came here to . . . you know, I needed to see you. Wanted to, I mean.

Sam . . . Maybe I'll have just a sip.

The man hands over the water, then sits back down. The woman takes a long guzzle, wipes her mouth. Thinks before speaking.

I called your mom once. Just on a whim, like, a year ago. I didn't even remember the number, so I had to look it up in the book . . .

Guy Wow. I never . . . I mean, they didn't tell me.

Sam No, I didn't ask for you. Or leave a message or anything, I just . . . Your mom and I got pretty friendly there for a while, so I was . . . I wanted to hear her voice. (*Beat.*) I thought about calling for you, but in the end I pretended to be somebody else. Selling band candy for my kid's school or something . . . She and I talked for a minute, and that was about it. It was nice.

Guy . . . I never knew that. Huh.

Sam I know. I just said you wouldn't. I didn't tell her it was me, so . . . It doesn't matter . . . it's two-thirty.

Guy Right. Sure, okay, yes. Look . . . I called you, I mean, came into town and contacted you because . . . I just wanted to do something here. Right a wrong or, you know, make things okay.

Sam . . . Huh.

Guy Does that make any sense?

Sam Umm . . . not really.

Guy Well, what I mean is . . . when I think about it, *us*, I'm saying . . . I get a feeling that it didn't end well . . .

Sam Alright.

Guy You know, things end, right? They do, in lots of different ways, for so many reasons . . . and, ahh, we had a really really nice go of it. Back then.

Sam High school.

Guy Yes! Yeah, school. Great times back at Central Valley and a lot of fun, and then, you know . . . we sort of . . .

Sam You ended it.

Guy Uh-huh. Right.

Sam *You* broke up with me.

Guy Yeah, I did. True.

Sam What else did you wanna go over?

The man takes another drink of water and starts to speak. Stops. Grabs more cashews instead. Pops them in.

240

Guy . . . are you mad at me?

She looks at him, then bursts out laughing. A big guffaw that seems surprising for her. The man is a bit perplexed.

Seriously, though. Are you?

Sam I can't believe you'd say that.

Guy Well, you know . . . you carry that stuff around. I think you'd be surprised.

Sam No, I wouldn't. Uh-uh. I would not.

Guy Oh.

Sam Because I do . . . I *do* think about it. What happened. Between us.

Guy Well, good! Let's talk about it . . .

Sam Now?

Guy Yeah . . . I mean, I know you have to go, but we could at least air a bit of laundry, or however that saying goes.

Sam You wanna 'air' this stuff now –

Guy Only if it's okay . . .

Sam – instead of twenty years ago? I mean, you flew all the way here to do this *today*?

Guy It does seem strange, but . . . I just feel that we'd both benefit from . . .

Sam No, great. Fine. (*Leans back.*) Go for it. I can be a little late . . .

The man nods and looks around. He takes off his jacket and folds it neatly. The woman notices.

Sam You're very careful with your things.

Guy Yeah. I picked that up somewhere . . .

Sam You must've, because you sure were never like that when I knew you. Back then . . .

Guy Well, we were just kids, right?

Sam Eighteen. When you dumped me, I mean. That's an adult.

Guy True, but, that's what it seemed like. To me. *Kids*.

Sam Whatever. Whatever you say . . .

Guy You are angry.

Sam Maybe just a touch. Yep.

Guy Huh. Alright . . . Sam, I'm gonna be open with you here. Totally up front. Honest.

Sam That's promising a lot . . .

Guy I know, I know it is, but I'm gonna be, and, well, I just am. (*Beat.*) I think the reason we broke up back then –

Sam Not we. You. *You* ended it.

Guy Yes, but . . .

Sam It wasn't a 'we' thing. 'We' was when we were a couple, *we* decided to start dating, *we* would choose what movie to go to on Friday night, but the finishing it off part? That was you . . .

Guy I know that. I do. I do know it . . . So, yeah, I stopped calling, coming over, but it wasn't any one thing that prompted it, it wasn't . . . And for some reason, I always had the idea that you thought you'd done something . . .

Sam No . . .

Guy Some . . .

Sam I . . . no.

Guy Oh. 'Cause my mom said that, that the two of you had talked, and – not, like, recently, I mean, but back in the day, back whenever – and she . . .

Sam I never said that . . .

Guy No, but implied it, insinuated that I'd led you to believe that you'd done an injury to our relationship and, and –

Sam I don't think that was the case . . .

Guy – and I just wanted you to know, as in better-late-than-never, that it wasn't anything of the sort.

Sam I know. I *know* that . . . I mean, why would I think that? I wouldn't.

Guy Right, so I'm just reiterating for you, then – albeit a bit late in the game – you did nothing wrong.

Sam Thanks.

Guy It was me. All me. I needed to, ahh . . .

Sam What? What did you 'need'?

Guy Or 'wanted' to, I dunno. I felt, like, at the time – I wanted to have my freedom, do the college thing somewhere other than over at, at Community or maybe just pursue my writing stuff. Whatever. And *you* were a girl that I could sort of look at, maybe . . . and see her whole future.

Sam Really?

Guy A bit. Yeah. And that's not bad or anything, it's not, but you're just that type of woman. And I think, if I can say this –

243

Sam Go ahead, you're on a roll . . .

Guy – history has proved me right. It has. You ended up almost exactly like I figured you would.

Sam Oh, have I, now? (*Beat.*) Huh . . .

Guy Well, kinda. (*Beat.*) I mean, still here, with kids and your husband doing what I pretty much would've guessed he'd be doing . . . and back then, when I'm just this scared teenager staring eternity in the face, I could see myself with that produce manager's vest on and I suppose I got nervous and backed out of the situation the best way I knew how . . . (*Beat.*) So.

Sam . . . He's not the produce manager. He runs the store. The whole thing.

Guy Oh. Okay.

Sam He's the *store* manager. There is a difference.

Guy Granted. Sorry . . .

Sam Forget it.

Guy . . . I am sorry. You're not upset, are you?

Sam No, I'm fine.

Guy Because I didn't want to . . .

Sam I said 'I'm fine'. Just believe me, okay? I believe you, so why don't you go ahead and believe me . . .

Guy Alright, I'll . . . yeah. Fine.

Sam . . . And that's really it? That's the *whole* reason why we suddenly just ended like that? Because you had a vision of working at some Safeway for the rest of your life?

Guy Basically, yeah . . . I mean . . .

Sam Not some other girl?

Guy Umm, no, not that I . . . I don't, you know. I don't recall anybody else.

Sam No? You don't?

Guy Uh-uh.

Sam 'Cause I always had this vague, you know . . . this worry about that. Back in 'the day'. Back whenever . . .

Guy No . . . we were going out for, like . . .

Sam Two years. A little over . . . we were 'promised' to each other for two years. (*Beat.*) And you never went to the prom with somebody else? Right?

Guy . . . No. You know that. No, I even . . . I worked that night. *On* prom night. (*Beat.*) It was our senior spring, and after we broke up I was –

Sam *You*, okay? You broke it off. Just say it . . . (*Beat.*) Look, I don't even wanna think about this, not at all, I don't. I'm a mother now, a wife and *mother* and this is like some Ancient Greek history! Why did you have to call me about this? Do this to me . . . ? Huh?

Guy I wanted to . . . I don't know. To just make sure that we were . . . okay.

Sam Yeah, fine, yes . . . we're okay. A-okay. Is that what you needed? Is that gonna be enough to get you back to your something-special-life in . . . where is it, again?

Guy New York. I have a place in Brooklyn now, but I teach up near . . . doesn't matter. It's all New York. City.

Silence for a moment as this all gets processed.

Sam Wow. Jeez, it's amazing how . . . it's all still pretty fresh. You know? I mean, you think it's gone, put in some box under your bed, but God . . . somebody mentions a dance or a boy you knew and it's just, like, *right* there. Instantly it's . . . there.

Guy Yep. That's true . . .

Sam Yeah. (*Beat.*) Guess it's partly due to the whole 'virginity' thing.

Guy . . . Right. I feel the same way.

Sam Well, that's great. *Terrific.* At least we have that . . .

Guy I am sorry about stirring up all the – (*Checks his watch.*) It's almost quarter of.

Sam 'Kay. Thanks . . . (*Beat.*) I know that you're looking at my face. I feel you doing that – it's a skin thing. Sometimes after a baby your pigment can get all . . .

Guy No . . . I wasn't . . . no –

Sam Doesn't matter. Anyway, take care. Good to see you, I guess . . .

Guy Hey, Sam . . . you, too. Seriously. I hope I didn't . . .

She starts off but comes to a dead stop. Turns.

Sam I didn't mean our prom. I was referring to the one over at North Central. That one.

Guy Oh. O-kay . . .

Sam So? Did you go there with someone? To their prom?

Guy . . . Not that I can . . . I mean, this is, you know, fifteen years ago . . .

Sam Please.

Guy I didn't ask anybody to that prom, no. I didn't.

Sam Okay. Not what I heard, but okay . . .

Guy Sam, I would never do that. Something stupid and . . . and . . . hurtful like that. (*Beat.*) I think I . . . There was some girl, a senior friend of – remember that guy I knew from, like, kindergarten? Tim – somebody? Him – and he asked me to just drop in with this . . . really just stop over with this one gal who was his date's friend. A tall girl, played volleyball, I think . . .

Sam Now *this* is what I heard. Go on.

Guy Nothing else. No, we just . . . didn't do the pictures or even, like, a corsage or anything, it was not at all like that . . . I was more like a, what-do-ya-call-it?

Sam I dunno, I'm dying to hear . . .

Guy A, you know . . . a chaperone. More of that, really.

Sam Her 'chaperone'.

Guy Yeah. Basically . . .

Sam And she's a senior. I mean, *you're* a senior, and she's a senior . . .

Guy Right, true, but it felt like . . . you know, like when your brother takes you to something, accompanies you to a . . . (*Beat.*) I left her there, Sam. Didn't even drive her home, or, or . . .

Sam I don't have a brother. Remember?

Guy No, I know, but I'm just saying . . .

Sam I thought maybe it slipped your mind. So much else seems to've.

Guy . . . I thought we even talked about this once!

Sam No.

Guy We didn't? Over the summer there, just before I . . . ?

Sam No, we didn't. Not *ever*. (*Beat.*) We talked about marriage, but not this . . .

Guy Oh. Okay, my mistake.

Sam Yeah, apparently so . . . (*Beat.*) No, I overheard it once, just a mention of it this one time in the store . . . you know, where you almost ended up. In your apocalyptic vision. I was in there, dropping off lunch for my husband and I was looking at something, I don't remember what now, some new thing on an endcap display – cookies or whatever – and I hear a voice, a woman's voice that I recognise, this blast from the past. It's your mother. Your mom, standing in the juice aisle and talking to somebody, a neighbour lady or from the church, and they're going on about the good ol' days, like women do, and somehow they get on the subject of proms. Of big dances. Probably because her daughter – not your mom, obviously, but the other woman – her last kid is getting ready for hers, and off they go . . . chatting about this and that. I don't mean to, but I keep standing there and listening and, boy, do I get an earful! About you, and us, and, well, lots. Lots of stuff. And part of that 'stuff' is how nice you looked – how well you 'cleaned up,' she called it – for your big night. *Prom* night. And imagine me, standing there next to this 'Hearty Fudge Crunch' and I'm thinking, 'What night? I didn't have a big night. We didn't go to any prom.' But of course she wasn't talking about me. Or us. No, this was about you. The night she was referring to was all about *you*. And her . . . some girl. (*Sighs.*) She also said you don't call home enough. Your mom did.

> The man tries to say something but just goes for a quick nod instead. Not much to say, really. He glances at a clock.

Yeah, I know. You don't have to make it so obvious. It's

time for me to . . . need to get going before the, you know. Traffic and all that. So . . .

Guy 'S good to see you. It really, really is.

Sam Yeah, you said that.

Guy Okay, and if you want to . . .

Sam What?

Guy Nothing. I was gonna say, if you'd like an email address or anything –

Sam No, that's alright. No. I'm . . . I should just . . .

Without warning, she reaches over and slaps the man hard on the cheek. His head snaps back as he catches himself.
  The woman exits through the open door, shutting it tightly behind her. The man wanders over to the bed, absently picking up the can of nuts. He eats one or two. Snaps on the TV. Dumps the Starbucks cup in a nearby garbage can.
  He begins to open a drawer in one end-table but is stopped by a light knock. He jumps up and goes to the door, swinging it open.

Guy . . . Hey. (*Points.*) You forgot your umbrella.

Sam Forgive me, that suddenly felt . . . overdue. Just couldn't help myself. So . . .

Guy That's alright. I mean . . . (*Points at TV.*) I'm just checking the news, or, I mean, the weather. I'm flying out, so . . .

Sam Yeah, you mentioned that . . . (*Beat.*) It's so awkward, all this, so I'm sorry for the . . .

They stand there a moment, a curious kind of face-off. The man offers the cashews – she shakes her head 'no'.

Sam . . . I was almost out to the lobby . . . (*Beat.*) This is . . . I don't need her name. I don't. This is so childish! I can't believe that I'm . . . just, look. Tell me what page she's on. Alright?

Guy What do you mean?

Sam In the yearbook. Their yearbook, at North Central.

Guy I don't . . . Why? I mean . . .

Sam Just . . . because, okay? My husband's a Bronco, so I have his . . .

Guy He graduated from there?

Sam *Yes.* (*Beat.*) What page is she?

Guy She was . . . I mean, I'm not . . .

Sam Just tell me. Please.

Guy . . . Near the back, I guess. Last name was 'Walker', maybe? Yeah. Something 'Walker'. She was captain of the voll—

Sam Fine. Thanks. (*Beat.*) It's funny . . . I mean, not 'ho-ho-ho', but still. You want to believe that, at some point in your life, you mattered to someone, that at least when you're young and cute that you . . .

Guy Sam, you did. To me. Absolutely.

Sam Yeah, but I mean, you know. *Really* mattered. Like, Romeo and Juliet type stuff . . . And I always kinda wanted to feel that way about us. (*Beat.*) But I realise now, though, it was just a teenage thing and you moved on almost immediately, so how's that for a wake-up call, huh?

Guy . . . I just gave her a ride.

Sam Sure. (*Picks up umbrella.*) Well, so long . . .

Guy Bye. (*Beat.*) Oh, wait, hey . . . Did I mention I was getting married?

Sam Ahh, no. (*Beat.*) No, you didn't.

Guy Well, I am. Yeah. I'm getting –

Sam – married. Huh. (*Beat.*) Good for you . . .

This time she's gone for sure – the man tries to get in a last hug, misses it. Catches himself without too much dignity lost.

He wanders back to the bed and sits. Starts up again with the cashews. Turns up the volume on the TV. Loud.

Part Two

'TYLER'

The same type of hotel room. Almost exactly. It's designed by the same company, so the details are similar. Twin beds now.

The man is on one bed, directly across from another woman – a bit younger, Tyler is what she answers to – who sits on the other bed. They are in the middle of a discussion.

Tyler . . . Good for you! No, seriously.

Guy Thanks.

Tyler I mean it. That's so awesome.

Guy Yeah.

Tyler Married! Holy shit . . . that's the big one, huh? Totally big step.

Guy Yes, it is . . . it's a, well, yeah. A big ol' step.

Tyler No shit, fuck. *Marriage!* Sweet. (*Beat.*) And *New Yorker* magazine, the same year. Movin' on up, huh?

Guy I guess so . . . yep.

Tyler Gotta say, though, you just never – you know, struck me as the type.

Guy I didn't?

Tyler Nope, not really. Not back then.

Guy Oh . . . well, I always wanted to write but I got a little sidetracked . . .

Tyler I mean about getting married! Not *that* type.

Guy Oh!

Tyler Not during that whole time we were together . . .

Guy Oh. I think I was a bit different when I was here. Unfocused, or . . .

Tyler Yeah?

Guy Uh-huh. Don't really think I was at my best in Chicago. Not completely, but I feel now that I'm . . . you know.

Tyler Then great. That's really nice, I mean . . . marriage is so fucking cool!

Guy Yeah, it should be. (*Smiles.*) So . . . how's all your . . . art stuff going?

Tyler Good, really good. See the earrings I have on? My design.

Guy Wow.

Tyler I'll bet she's hot, if I know you . . .

Guy What?

Tyler Your girlfriend there, or whatever you call it. Fiancée. She's pretty nice-looking, I'm guessing . . .

Guy Umm, yeah, you know . . . yes. A very attractive woman. I mean . . . quite pretty . . . like you, or, umm . . .

Tyler You don't have to flatter me. It's okay. I already know you like me . . .

Guy Yep. Always did . . . always.

Tyler 'Always'. Now there's a word you used to throw around a lot! A – *lot*. 'Always'. (*Laughs.*) She dark or not?

Guy Excuse me?

Tyler Colouring, I mean . . . You seem to go for the brunettes. Mostly. A redhead or two, but mostly dark . . .

Guy Umm, no, actually, she's a blonde. Well, dyes it, I think, the tips . . . what do they call that?

Tyler Highlights?

Guy Yeah, that. She's got highlights. Frosted ends of her hair that're . . .

Tyler . . . blonde. Huh. How 'bout that?

Guy A little change . . .

Tyler An appetite for adventure, I'd say. You always did.

Guy I dunno about that . . .

Tyler No, come on, you totally did! Back then, anyhow. Always had an eye for the toys and whatnot . . . remember? Even wanted me to try one of those, umm, whaddayacallems? Strap-ons . . .

The man shifts on the bed – nervous to get into this subject.

Guy Yeah . . . I s'pose . . . we did a few things sexually that were, ahhh . . .

Tyler What? 'S no big deal, it's just us looking backward.

Guy Right. (*Grins.*) Yes.

Tyler You had your little ways, like me or anybody else. Things you liked, or wanted to try. Experiment.

Guy Sure . . .

Tyler Of course you did. I remember it clearly. Oh, yeah. (*Beat.*) And don't think I didn't notice a couple of our 'greatest hits' in your story there! Which was naughty!

She reaches over and pokes the man good-naturedly in the ribs. He smiles and playfully pushes her back.

Guy Hey, shh . . . don't tell anyone!!

Tyler . . . 'S okay, your secret's safe with me.

A moment grows out of this – they sit staring at one another for a long time. Finally, she leans over and kisses him. He doesn't fight it exactly, but he doesn't really join in.
After a minute, things sort of grind to a halt.

Tyler Look, I don't wanna force you . . .

Guy I just, well, you know.

Tyler No, what?

Guy I'm . . . I mean, I told you. I'm gonna be married, that's all.

Tyler Exactly. 'That's all'. (*Beat.*) I'm saying I don't care. Get married.

Guy Yeah, but . . .

Tyler You're not having the wedding here, are you? Not *today*, right?

Guy No, it's in a few months, but . . .

Tyler So okay. I'm fine with that. More than fine . . . I'm happy for you.

Guy Thanks. It's a very big –

Tyler What? . . .

Guy – step, I guess. And . . .

Tyler Is that what's stopping you?

Guy You mean from . . . you?

Tyler Uh-huh.

Guy Of course! I mean, you know . . . I'm supposed to be, what's the word?

Tyler I dunno. I don't know what you're supposed to be. Tell me.

Guy . . . honest. That's what. I need to display some fidelity here.

Tyler Oh.

Guy That's the general idea, anyway.

Tyler . . . You sound like you're really thrilled about it.

Guy Shut up! (*Laughs.*) I am . . .

Tyler Yeah, I can tell.

Guy Seriously, don't, come on . . . This is very hard.

Tyler What is? (*Touches him.*) This?

Guy Hey, Tyler, honestly . . . don't. You shouldn't do that.

Tyler I know I 'shouldn't'. I completely understand that . . .

Guy Okay . . .

Tyler But I hardly ever do what I'm supposed to – that's why my friends have a bunch of kids and I have *fun*! Don't you like fun? You used to . . .

Guy Of course, sure, I do. Yes.

Tyler Then let's have some. Old-time's-sake fun, and then you can go do whatever sort of little wedding crap you feel the need to . . .

She tries to kiss him again – bingo. He allows it a bit more this time. After a moment, though, he pulls away.

Tyler You know, after the thirty or fortieth time you do that, I will start to get offended . . .

Guy I need to stop.

Tyler . . . Oh. Alright. Whatever.

She sits back a bit – close enough for him to start again if he chooses, but far enough to maintain dignity if not.

Guy Believe me, I'd love to just, you know, dive right back in there.

Tyler Where? (*Casually spreads her legs.*) Here?

Guy Come on . . . really! I would. But I've kind of taken this vow-thing here, and I need to stick to it . . .

Tyler I see. Okay.

Guy Thank you.

Tyler Then you're doing it for her.

Guy Right.

Tyler As a kind of, what? A sort of gift for her . . .

Guy In a way, yes.

Tyler Got it. (*Beat.*) But if that wasn't the case, you'd jump my bones?

Guy . . . Pretty much, yeah.

Tyler You still find me attractive?

Guy Very.

Tyler . . . But it's a moral thing. Or some kind of deal like that.

Guy Umm, yes, 'moral,' I suppose. Yeah. Or 'ethical', maybe. I get those confused.

Tyler Doesn't matter. What you're saying is . . . you want to but you'll stop it for her. This woman.

Guy Right. I don't wanna let her down.

Tyler Even if it just happens here, with nobody the wiser . . .?

Guy I think so. Yes. I mean . . . *I'd* know.

Tyler Well, I hope so!

They share an easy laugh at this one. Her hand on his knee.

Guy I would, yes. Like . . . feel . . .

Tyler No, I get it. Cool. You've made a little change in your character. That's good.

Guy Thank you. For understanding, I mean . . .

Tyler Of course. Sure.

Guy Thanks.

The woman smiles and looks around. Scans the room.

Tyler . . . Can I smoke in here?

Guy Umm, yeah, I think. It's a smoking room, but I don't see an ashtray . . .

Tyler That's alright. I'll use a glass.

She jumps up and goes to a tray containing an ice bucket and two glasses. She quickly unwraps one and moves to the chair. Sits as she's lighting up. The man watches.

You're not a smoker.

Guy Nope.

Tyler So why'd you get a 'smoking' room?

Guy . . . I actually got a room like this because . . . for you, I guess. So you could smoke.

She sits back for a moment and takes a long, deep drag. Blows the smoke in the man's face.

Tyler Look at you, Mr Confident! (*Smiles.*) . . . I remember that *you* didn't mind smoke so much.

Guy (*smiles*) It's true, I sort of like it . . .

Tyler Huh. (*Drags.*) Here, want some blow-back?

She indicates for him to come close – he leans in and she puts her mouth next to his. They are almost touching. She blows a fine line of hazy smoke into his mouth.

Guy Mmmm . . . (*Breathes.*) Good stuff.

Tyler If this was a joint, we'd be flying soon. 'Member?

Guy Sure.

Tyler The good ol' days . . . (*Beat.*) Should I roll us one?

Guy No, that's okay. If you don't mind.

Tyler Wow. Swore off that, too, I'll bet.

Guy A little. Yeah.

Tyler Huh. (*Grins.*) Guess I'm still a bit too wild for ya, huh? Same ol' me.

A smile from the woman. She darts forward and kisses him, holds it a second, then moves back. He can't help himself – the man reaches over and pulls her close.

Tyler . . . Don't forget about your 'vow' thingie.

Guy Right.

The man nods and sits back a touch. He reaches over and puts his hand on her face – she allows it, looking right at him.

. . . I still want you, though. Like, in that way. I think you're really really sexy.

Tyler Nice. Good . . .

Guy Yep. Always did . . . Always.

Tyler That's very cool to hear. Since we haven't seen each other in a few years . . .

Guy Uh-huh, yeah. It's been a while.

Tyler . . . It's easy to fall out of favour, or just off somebody's radar, you know? I've known a few men that way – I'm mad about 'em for a couple months, then, bam! Totally gone, just these tiny green blips on my screen . . . Guys are like that sometimes. And women, too, actually.

Guy No doubt.

Tyler . . . It's simple to forget guys. But I never forgot you. Isn't that funny?

Guy Yeah.

Tyler It is to me. I mean, no offence, but you weren't like some amazing person or anything, you were just this dude, we spent however long together, and yet . . . I do think about you. 'S crazy.

Guy I know. I mean, you're the same way for me. Just always kind of buzzing around up there in my skull . . . (*He makes a 'bee' sound.*) Bzzzz . . .

Tyler Mmm. Romantic . . .

Guy You know what I'm saying!

Tyler I do, I know, I'm kidding . . .

Guy 'Kay. See, and that was part of the deal here. Why I got a hold of you.

Tyler Really?

Guy Yep. It's . . . well, I just wanted to see if we could talk.

Tyler Absolutely.

Guy Great. Okay . . . So.

Tyler This oughta be good.

Guy Yeah, let's hope. Right? (*Beat.*) What I've done is start to travel around a bit, here and there, and stop in on a few old girlfriends. Say 'hi', that kind of thing. Before I get hitched . . .

Tyler Say 'hi'. Huh.

Guy Yeah. Well, that and other stuff . . .

Tyler O – kay . . .

Guy Do a check-in, you know? Get caught up to date with 'em, make sure that we are, you know: no harm, no foul. That sort of thing.

She finishes the smoke and drops it in the glass. Studies it for a moment.

Tyler . . . How many?

Guy What?

Tyler I'm saying, how many little stops are you making?

Beat.

Guy Oh.

Tyler You can round it off if you want to . . .

Guy Ahh, let's see . . .

Tyler I'm not jealous, so don't worry.

Guy Four for right now . . . maybe five. It's expensive, so I'm just doing the . . . Plus, working out everybody's schedule and all that, so . . .

Tyler Huh. Interesting.

Guy Just figured it'd be a good way to start my new life. This whole thing I'm about to embark on . . .

Tyler It's not a cruise . . .

Guy True! 'Embarks' probably not the exact word I'm looking for . . .

Tyler What are you looking for?

Guy . . . I dunno. Some other word.

Tyler No, I mean by doing this. What are you trying to do here?

Guy Hell, I don't know! (*Grins.*) Right some wrongs or whatever. Little bit of windmill tilting, that kind of thing . . .

Tyler This was one of our downfalls, I think . . .

Guy What?

Tyler . . . I never knew what the fuck you were talking about!

Guy That is a problem.

Tyler 'Windmill'?

Guy It's from *Don Quixote*.

Tyler Oh.

Guy No big deal.

Tyler Right, the old dude on the pony shit, sure. You lost me there.

Guy Sorry. Look, the thing I'm doing here, going around and meeting up with girls like you . . . is probably kind of fanciful, or you know . . . quixotic. But it's really an emotional thing, too, it is . . . and so I'm doing it.

The woman nods, taking it in. She gets up and takes the glass to a little sink around the corner, fills it with water.

Tyler I understand. (*Beat.*) So am I on a list or something?

Guy List?

Tyler Is this, a, you know . . . this stop. To see me. Is it on a . . . ?

Guy No! No, nothing like that. Not a big formal thing like a list. I'm not, you know, Bluebeard . . . checking the wives off as I go!

Tyler Who?

Guy Sorry! Literary figure, it doesn't matter. What I'm saying is, no, I wanted to see you because I had the need. It felt as if our situation ended in some bad way – or less than perfect – and so I wanted to track you down and ask if there was anything that we needed to . . .

Tyler Is that what you're doing? Going around to all your fuck-ups and trying to make 'em better?

The man looks at her. Starts to say something but just nods.

Guy . . . Sorta.

Tyler Wow. Shit . . . that's funny.

Guy I know, it's crazy, right?

Tyler No, not at all. Totally sounds like something I would do!

Guy Really?

Tyler Sure. I mean, I'd never do it – I'd blow the money on clothes or pot or some shit – but the idea, I'm saying the notion of it . . . that's pure me.

Guy Good. I mean, glad you understand.

Tyler Oh, yeah. I completely get it. It's messed up, don't get me wrong . . . but I get it.

They look at each other. The woman laughs a bit. Shakes her head.

Tyler Damn . . . I'm glad we didn't ever end up together! Married, or whatever.

Guy Probably for the best . . . (*Phone rings.*) Sorry.

Tyler Yep . . . (*Beat.*) Why me, though? . . . In what way did you feel you fucked me over?

Guy Hmm?

Tyler Just asking. See, I always sort of felt I broke up with you . . . that you finished your Master's and, I dunno, felt the need to go off and become some big citizen or what-have-you, a member of society. And I recall this one fight, screaming and shit on the stairway, but I can't really remember you being the cause of anything.

Guy You can't?

Tyler Nope. Not anything serious, at least.

Guy Well . . . I mean, we had a nice time together, *very*, but I was just coming off a relationship, and I'm, I don't think that I ever really gave us a, you know, a real chance. So, I just don't wanna feel that you might be harbouring, like, some sort of . . . ill . . . toward me.

Tyler 'Ill'?

Guy You know . . .

Tyler Did you become Amish or something?

Guy Come on! You know what I mean . . .

Tyler I *sorta* know what you mean . . . when you're not talking like you're in that one Harrison Ford movie.

Guy Okay, really cute . . .

Tyler But, no . . . I do not think 'ill' of you. (*Smiles.*) Now Godspeed . . .

Guy Very funny! Don't . . .

Tyler Then don't act like some fucking doofus! (*Laughs.*) I like you. I've always liked you . . .

Guy Me, too. I mean, you . . .

Tyler I told you, I'd start up with you again right now, if you wanted to.

Guy I know, and I appreciate that. I mean, appreciate *knowing* it . . .

Tyler Okay, then. (*Grins.*) So, you're off the hook . . . with me, at least.

Guy Good! Thank you. (*Beat.*) It's strange, you know, being here again with you because . . . I'm not sure. It's so all mixed together, these feelings. Of lust and, like, fear and, well, a lot of things. (*Beat.*) It's just, I dunno, some general sense of this that keeps gnawing at me . . . a kind of faint memory of hurting. Of me hurting or being hurt or . . . I dunno.

Tyler Huh. No, I don't . . . Nope . . .

Guy Well, good. That's good because I do feel it. This burst of hurt that I've always wanted to get to the bottom of . . . (*Beat.*) That's the deal when you're a writer, I guess. Doesn't matter how much it stings or how painful it is for you or the other people in your life . . . you just can't let shit go! You gotta turn it over and study it and poke it and –

Tyler – sell it?

Guy No. (*Beat.*) Well, yeah, at times some scrap of life will find its way into a story and that may get sold, but . . . hey . . .

The woman studies him and the man stares back at her.

Tyler Anyway, no. There was nothing like that . . . I mean, I was pretty fucked up most times back then, but . . . no. (*Beat.*) I mean, unless you did something to me in my sleep or whatever!

Guy . . . What's that mean? I'm . . .

The man studies her, waiting to see if she continues.

Tyler Nothing. It's just . . . (*Waiting.*) I'm only joking around. Jeez!

Guy Oh, okay. God! (*Beat.*) Must be nerves!

Tyler No prob'. (*Laughs.*) Shit, hope she's worth it . . . this fiancée person.

Guy I think so. Yes.

Tyler Hmm. You think . . . or you *know*?

He thinks about this and shrugs. She smiles at him.

Guy That's just it . . . I don't know. I haven't really known anything, not ever. (*Beat.*) I'm out here, running around the country, but for what? I dunno. I just, with you it feels . . .

Tyler Go ahead.

Guy I'm not sure my being here is so much about us or anything, the relationship I had with you, or if the 'hurt' thing I was talking about, that I mentioned a minute ago . . . (*Realising.*) Ohhhh . . . God. It's about her.

Tyler Who?

Guy I think that I came here feeling like I did something to you, all this 'hurt' stuff . . . but it's really her I'm thinking about.

Tyler 'Her' who?

Guy Just some girl. This . . . person in LA that I . . . the girl that I left for *you*. I maybe felt so shitty about what I did to her by leaving that I just . . . plunged in with you, did whatever. All the, you know . . .

Tyler Naughty bits.

Guy Right. Those. (*Beat.*) Gave myself to you physically, but all that time I was really feeling . . . I don't know. Something. Bad, I guess. About her. (*He tries to smile.*) Wow. I suck . . .

The woman wipes at one eye quickly – was it a tear? It's gone too fast to tell. She turns away when he tries to check.

Tyler Well, at least you know it – some folks, they never figure that shit out about themselves . . . they'll go around sucking for years without ever noticing.

Guy Hey, I'm a quick study! Sixty times or so and it's locked in there . . .

He raps the side of his head – she smiles at this and turns back to him now. They sit for a moment in silence. Waiting.

267

Tyler So, that answers that.

Guy What?

Tyler (*Grins.*) I wasn't always stoned . . . there was a lot of phone calls you made in those first few months. I mean, *lots*. To California. I used to look at 'em on our phone bill when it'd come, that same number, over and over . . . and each call was, like, ten seconds! Just a hang-up, really, but they charged you a full minute for it. The fuckers! Anyway, yeah . . . I'd catch you doing it sometimes, right after you hung up and you'd make up some elaborate lie about it, but I knew what you were doing. I mean, after a while. (*Beat.*) Look . . . it is never cool to be second, you know? In a relationship. It's not. And I was a distant second there for a bit! But then you started coming around and so, what the fuck, you just go on and let things happen. That's fine. So, yeah . . . I think you're right. I was not always your big number-one top priority during our time together. Not by a long shot . . . and I'd tell myself, 'Hey no problem, we are not that kind of couple.' I mean, you can talk yourself into *anything* if you say it enough. But it's not really true. That shit hurts . . . (*Elbows him.*) You prick. I should've been harder on you back then!

Guy Maybe so . . .

Tyler Oh well . . . (*Beat.*) Whatever.

Guy Yeah.

Tyler . . . You bad boy, you.

> *The woman smiles; reaches over and squeezes the man's face.*
> *The woman digs in her purse and pulls out a cigarette. She lights it, blows some smoke in the man's face. He grins.*

Guy Mmmm . . .

Tyler Man, I do not get you. You are something else, you know that?

Guy That's what they tell me . . .

Tyler And I don't just mean about the smoke.

Guy I know.

She slides a bit closer. The man doesn't move away.

Tyler . . . Want a little more? Just some blowback . . . (*Indicates.*) They're French, so it's kinda nice . . .

Guy No tongue. (*Smiles.*) Promise?

Tyler Okay. Promise. Scout's honour.

Guy Just a little smoke and then we should . . . We should probably . . .

Tyler Yeah. Here we go . . .

The woman leans in, their lips nearly touching. The smoke curls out of her mouth and drifts over to the man.

Part Three

'LINDSAY'

Another version of the same room. New pictures and lamps. The man is seated in the chair. Bottle of water in one hand.

Another woman – Lindsay is her name – is standing up. She is older than the man, nicely dressed. Just removing her coat.

Guy . . . Here we go. Okay.

Lindsay Look at you . . . The Prodigal Son returns . . . This is the part where you say something charming in return. That's how it works. That's why they call it banter . . . Am I speaking too quickly for you?

Guy No, sorry, not at all.

Lindsay Because I don't really need to have this conversation. I don't. It is not necessary to my life . . .

Guy I know that.

Lindsay You asked for it, not me.

Guy That's true, and I appreciate it, that you drove over here. For me.

Lindsay I didn't do that. Not for you.

Guy Oh.

Lindsay Don't get that idea, no. Do not get that into your head . . .

Guy Okay . . .

Lindsay I'm here for me. That is all . . . I'm here for one person only, and that is me. Me, myself and *I*.

Guy Okay, Mrs Bergstram, I get it.

Lindsay . . . Fine. Then fine. (*Beat.*) And call me
'Lindsay', for God's sake. After all this time, you can at
least do that . . .

Guy Sorry. 'Lindsay'. I don't know why . . .

Lindsay Good, then let's leave it.

*The woman crosses to the bed and perches on the end
of it.*

Guy . . . 'S fun to be back here.

Lindsay Is it?

Guy I mean, yeah, kind of. In our old room. 127.

Lindsay Uh-huh. That's true. (*Looks around.*) Although
you'd hardly recognise it with the, umm, you know . . .
changes.

Guy Yep. All new stuff. (*Takes it in.*) Lots of memories,
though. *Lots.*

Lindsay Well, you're right about that. I do have a
number of memories about the room, this place . . . I do.
And *some* of them didn't even end up in your article.
(*Beat.*) It's astonishing to me how vampiric you people
are! How cannibalistic. Writers. God, it's amazing that
you can even . . .

Guy I just . . . It's mostly all made up, Lindsay . . . what
I do.

Lindsay Well . . . whatever lets you sleep at night. (*Sighs.*)
It's . . . what was the name of it again?

Guy Oh, umm, 'The Calculus of Desire'.

Lindsay Right! Nice. Lyrical. (*Beat.*) And is there anything new out there that I should be . . . aware of?

Guy Ahhh, no, but I'm . . . you know. Just sold off the movie rights, so . . .

Lindsay Oh goody. (*Pointing.*) I do remember this fondly, though . . .

Guy Yeah, me too. (*Beat.*) I never even liked Boston until I met you . . .

Lindsay Really? Well, that's a shame. It's a lovely city . . .

Guy No, it is, I know that, but at the time . . . I mean, me just outta school and at my first big teaching gig, I was pretty . . .

Lindsay Lost. That's what you used to say to me. 'I feel lost.'

Guy Well, I was. I mean, felt that way . . . for a while, really. After grad school. (*Beat.*) Anyway, it was a tough first year.

Lindsay Only year.

Guy Yeah. I think I was just too young. That was part of it, anyhow . . . way too young to be teaching some grad lit course.

Lindsay I was a year younger than you when I started here. Dissertation to finish, but still . . . Can you imagine?

Guy That's wild . . .

Lindsay Well, it was a different time.

Guy That's true.

Lindsay Yes. A different era, at least. We all cared a bit more then, were all more committed or something . . .

Guy That's what they say. I mean, you know, on CNN and stuff. The seventies . . .

The woman looks over at him and stops. Studies him closely.

Lindsay I started in the eighties. Late eighties.

Guy . . . Oh. Sorry.

Lindsay Eighty-*nine*. (*Beat.*) It doesn't matter. Has nothing to do with this, actually. I'm just going on here because . . .

Guy Right. I just meant your field, like, in Women's Studies.

Lindsay We call it 'Gender Studies' now. Some of us are actually trying to keep up with the times . . . (*Shifts about.*) Why're we here? Hmm?

Guy Umm, well . . . I guess I wanted to see you again, basically.

Lindsay Because of this wedding?

Guy Yeah, and just – I wanted to. That's why I've been travelling around to . . . anyhow, I just felt the need.

Lindsay Well, that's nice, I suppose, it's lovely to know that our time with one another meant something more than just a paycheque from a publisher, it is, but . . .

Guy Listen, I know that you've got no reason to trust me here and it's certainly been a while, but . . .

Lindsay Yes, that's part of it. Part of the confusing side. I mean, your call came at work, at my work, so it was . . . I'm glad I got the message rather than my teaching assistant.

Guy Me, too.

Lindsay My point is . . . you didn't need to do that. You're getting married – I'm *still* married.

Guy I know. Believe me, I know . . .

Lindsay Then why do it? After what we went through, all that happened . . . why do that to me? Hmm? Risk that?

Guy I dunno. I'm sorry, I thought that . . . I didn't wanna just show up there on campus, you know? I mean, he's still on faculty, right? Teaching?

Lindsay Of course. He's the Dean, now.

Guy Oh, really? Well, that's . . .

Lindsay It's nothing. Doesn't matter.

Guy Right, but . . . you know, I thought I might run into him or whatever. See him in the hallway and that sort of thing, make a scene, and I didn't want that. (*Beat.*) For you . . .

> *She waits for a moment, looking at the man to see if he's being serious; he seems to be. She nods. Silence.*

Lindsay You left at the end of that second semester, so . . . you probably have no idea, I mean, no real sense of how hard things were for me. There for a while . . . after we were spotted.

Guy No . . . I mean, not really . . .

Lindsay Well, how could you?

Guy Right.

Lindsay You never called me to check. Not once, not even a single time.

Guy No, that's . . . true enough.

Lindsay We got caught and you . . . well, you took the first train out, as they say. Figuratively speaking.

Guy Yeah, I'm . . . Yes. I did a bad thing there. Skipping town.

Lindsay Yes, I'd say that. Quite a bad thing.

Guy Uh-huh. I was scared . . . let myself get all spooked by, like, the *spectre* of an angry husband, I suppose, and just ran. Ran off.

Lindsay Leaving me behind.

Guy I did do that, Lindsay . . . and I am very sorry. It's bothered me ever since then. Honestly.

Lindsay I see.

Guy It really, really did. *Does.* And that is kinda why I'm here . . . back in the area. Before I go off and get all married myself.

Lindsay . . . Before you get the chance.

Guy Hmm? What do you mean?

Lindsay The chance to become the jealous husband. The cuckold.

Guy Well, I hope not, but . . . yeah. Yes. (*Smiles.*) I deserved that.

Lindsay Yes.

Guy Anyway, this is a sort of *Pilgrim's Progress* for me.

Lindsay Don't you mean 'Rake's'?

Guy Touché. (*Beat.*) Geez, I'm an idiot for not offering you something . . . here. Water?

Lindsay That's fine.

Guy It's the French kind. 'S that okay?

Lindsay Yes. I have nothing against France. I mean, specifically . . .

The man jumps up and crosses to a small fridge. Pops it open and pulls out a bottle of water. Takes it to the woman. The woman opens the bottle and takes a long drink. He waits.

Guy Anyway, it's good to see you.

Lindsay Well, I'm here. Take a look.

Guy I'm glad you came.

Lindsay Me too. It's important.

Guy Yep. I agree.

Lindsay No, I don't mean . . . not for us. No. I mean for him. (*Beat.*) I fibbed a bit saying it was just for me. All this. I also did it for him . . .

Guy Who?

Lindsay For my husband. It's an awfully big step, letting me come here.

Guy I don't follow . . .

Lindsay He urged me to see you. Today. (*Beat.*) He's waiting downstairs for me . . .

Guy Huh?

Lindsay Sitting out front in our Subaru.

Guy Oh. Shit . . .

Lindsay Yes, he really wanted me to do this. Felt that I needed to.

Guy So, you told him . . . what?

Lindsay Everything. That you contacted me. About your wanting me to come here . . . about 127. All of it.

Guy You did.

Lindsay Yes . . . (*Beat.*) I mean, he already knew about before, all the details from the first . . . So yes, he knows. Now.

Guy And, wow . . . may I ask 'why?'

Lindsay Not really. I mean, not if you're asking if you have the right to ask me, then I'd say, 'no', No, you do not. You lost most of your rights with me when you took off . . . back whenever. (*Beat.*) You lost the *rest* when you wrote about it . . .

Guy Okay. I just meant . . .

Lindsay Whereas he stuck with me. Stayed in a relationship that I had totally and completely betrayed with a man that he hired. Had given a job to.

Guy I know that.

Lindsay That's what he did, and that's why he is sitting out there right now. Drove me over here so I could find out just what on earth you might be calling me for . . . at this late date.

Guy . . . Just so . . . so that I could . . .

Lindsay That's why he is in the parking lot, pretending to read the *USA Today*. Because he cares for me. About me.

Guy I understand.

Lindsay And so, the big question now is . . . why are *you* here? Back here after all this time . . .

Guy So . . . I can say that I'm, you know, to let you know that I'm sorry.

Lindsay Oh. Well, maybe you should run out to the car and let him know, too.

Guy I don't . . . I'm probably not prepared to do that. At this time . . .

Lindsay No, I didn't imagine you would be. (*Beat.*) That's not why he came, by the way. For an apology.

Guy No?

Lindsay Not at all. He came to support me. As *my* support. Isn't that just amazing . . . a person who'd do that? (*Beat.*) I think older men are very giving in that way.

Guy Yes, that's – he's quite special. (*He cringes.*) God . . . that sounds really bad, doesn't it? Coming out of my mouth.

Lindsay Pretty much, yes.

Guy I could tell, as I was saying it . . .

Lindsay Well, good, at least you felt it.

Guy Yeah.

Lindsay That's something . . . (*Beat.*) And what exactly, if you don't mind, what're you 'sorry' for? Hmm?

Guy You know . . .

Lindsay No. I don't, actually . . . uh-uh. You tell me. There's *so* much . . .

Guy For all the . . . what you said. When I ran off – I did get another job, so it was not technically 'running', but – took off when things came out.

Lindsay I see. So . . . not for doing it. Not that?

Guy . . . Umm . . . no. I mean, yes, that was probably wrong, too, but –

Lindsay – but mostly you're sorry for us being found out. Getting caught.

Guy Basically.

Lindsay And that's what you wanted to tell me?

Guy Overall. Mostly that . . . and for the leaving-you-hanging part, too. It's a sorta bad habit with me. Since I was a kid, actually . . . as someone recently pointed out.

Lindsay I see.

Guy I didn't want anyone to get hurt by our . . . That was never my intention.

Lindsay I wouldn't think so. Very rarely is that the reason behind an affair –

Guy True.

Lindsay – but that is almost always the *result*. Hurt.

Guy Yeah. I know.

Lindsay Someone being hurt.

Guy I think . . . I've done a lot of that, in this particular instance.

Lindsay Oh, I doubt that.

Guy What?

Lindsay That this was very 'particular'. Not judging from what I've read.

Guy . . . I'm sorry, but . . . what're you . . . ?

Lindsay I think you're the kind of person who leaves a *bunch* of hurt in your boyish wake . . . all the time. I'll bet 'hurt' is your number-one by-product.

Guy Well, I mean . . . if you're referring to the story, it's fiction, but . . .

Lindsay Ohh, don't sell yourself short . . . you can hurt people with your eyes closed. I could tell the first moment I saw you, and yet I plunged in.

Guy This isn't . . . Listen, I didn't come out here for this . . .

Lindsay I know that, I know, but it's all I'm prepared to give you. The truth.

Guy Look, maybe we should just . . .

Lindsay You probably need to get going, right? I mean, that's your MO. When the going gets tough . . .

Guy I know, I know, 'the tough get going'. Right?

Lindsay I was gonna say 'run away and hide like a fucking child', but . . .

Guy Lindsay, listen . . . you have every reason to resent me. Resent how I left things, but I came here to make amends. Some sort of, ahh, complete reparation for all my . . . behaviours.

Lindsay Oh. Oh. (*Beat.*) Alright . . . Fine. And how might you go about that? I'm very curious, how?

Guy Well, I . . . I . . .

The woman studies him for a moment, then abruptly stands up and crosses to a window. Opens the curtains and looks out. After a moment, she waves. She returns to the bed.

Lindsay . . . I told him I'd do that. Just so he knows everything's okay. (*Beat.*) But let's get back to this making-it-all-better notion. That deal.

Guy Alright . . .

Lindsay What do you propose?

Guy I'm . . . I hadn't really given it too much . . . like, the specifics, I mean.

Lindsay No, I didn't imagine that you had.

Guy I do want to, though . . .

Lindsay 'You want to' or you're going to?

Guy I . . . will. Yes.

Lindsay Because I don't want you to try, it only works if you do it. No matter what.

Guy No, you're right. Okay. I'm *going* to.

Lindsay Good. That's very good.

The woman takes another hit off the water bottle. Drains it.

And, so, then, how do you help me, you know . . . get back some of the dignity I lost? A small bit of that back . . . ?

Guy Well . . . I could . . . I mean, I suppose I could go out there, you know, to the car, and talk to him. If that's what you really *really* want . . .

Lindsay Hmm . . .

Guy Something like that. I don't see what we gain by it, but . . .

Lindsay No, you're right. It doesn't really even out . . . not after all the time that's passed. Uh-uh.

Guy Or I could . . . ahhh . . .

Lindsay You wanna know what he thinks? My husband, I mean . . . what he thinks you should do?

Guy Ummm . . . no, what?

Lindsay This woman you're marrying . . . you haven't said much about her . . .

Guy Not that much to tell, really . . .

Lindsay She'd probably be surprised to hear that.

Guy I mean, not so much. Studying to be a nurse, and, ahhh . . . you know. Some girl is all. This girl that I'm . . .

Lindsay Yes?

Guy I mean, she's *terrific*, of course, she's definitely that. But –

Lindsay – what? She's what?

Guy Nothing. I just . . . I'm not really so keen to drag her into this.

Lindsay I see. Fine. (*Smile.*) She's younger than me, right?

Guy Hmmm?

Lindsay 'Younger' than me.

Guy Ahh, yeah. Yes. She's twenty-three. Well, in August.

Lindsay Nice. How nice. Youth. (*Beat.*) Back then, when it was over, I was sure that was one of the reasons, the *main* reason, that you didn't stay. That you left me. My age.

Guy . . . No, not just that . . . I mean, no.

Lindsay Well, that's what I imagined. Told myself, anyway. That it wasn't for a real reason, not some reason that would actually matter . . . but because I was older than you.

Guy I liked your age. I did . . .

Lindsay And the fact that your bride-to-be is so young sort of nails it for me.

Guy Lindsay, no, it really wasn't . . .

Lindsay So tell me something – what's the, tell me what you think would be the most hurtful thing you could do to her?

Guy Listen . . .

Lindsay This fiancée of yours . . .

Guy I don't even want to . . .

Lindsay It's speculation. That's all. We are just imagining. So . . . what would it be?

Guy I dunno.

Lindsay Well, what if . . . you cheated on her? Even though you're not married yet.

Guy . . . She'd hate it. I mean, what do you think?

Lindsay I believe she would, because she trusts you. She's put her trust *into* you.

Guy Yes.

Lindsay See, that's what my husband thinks, too. He said that very thing. That the worst thing wouldn't be what we could do to you . . . but to her. For you to hurt her in some way –

Guy Oh.

Lindsay – and I agree. I agree with that. Because it's the other person who feels the pain.

Guy Right. Maybe we should, umm . . .

Lindsay So, I mean, since you've *promised* to make things all better . . . that's what we'd like you to do.

Guy I'm not following you . . .

Lindsay We would like you to sleep with me. Again. *Now.*

Guy What? . . . Why?

Lindsay Because you don't want to. And she wouldn't want you to, either.

Guy But, I don't see where that . . .

Lindsay It's not really for you to see. It really is for somebody else. These someone *elses* that you hurt a while ago and didn't have the guts to say 'I'm sorry' to. (*Beat.*) Do you want the drapes open or closed?

Guy Wait, no . . . Look, I realise that you are mad, Lindsay, I get that now.

Lindsay Good, I'm glad that's coming across for you . . .

Guy I do understand that. Totally. But I cannot . . . no. I can't.

Lindsay Yes, you can.

Guy No . . .

Lindsay Yes . . .

Guy Noooo . . .

Lindsay I said 'yes'.

Guy Ahh, and I said 'no', okay? I mean, I can do this all day long, if you'd like, but . . . (*Beat*) I *want* to do something here, I do, but I can't do . . . that.

Lindsay You said you *would*. You said you would make it up to me.

Guy I know, I know that, but . . . I can't.

Lindsay Can and will. You *will* do this! Do it while my husband sits down there in our Outback and waits for me . . .

284

The man takes this in. The woman takes another sip of water.

Guy Why would I do that? I mean . . . and you, why would *you* want to? It's . . .

Lindsay Does she know?

Guy What? Does who know . . . ?

Lindsay About your little trip here.

Guy You mean . . . ?

Lindsay You know *exactly* what I mean. Does your girlfriend know about this?

Guy . . . No. God, no.

The woman moves to her coat, takes a piece of paper out.

Lindsay Shall we call her now? It's Alex, right? My husband tracked her down.

The woman moves to the phone, starts to dial.

Guy What're you – Wait! Lindsay, don't! Stop!

Lindsay Then I'd get my pants off if I were you. I'd like to get this over with . . .

Guy But I can't do this! I really . . .

Lindsay Yes, you can! Yes, you are quite capable of fucking me. You are. And I bet you'll enjoy it too . . .

Guy Shit, Lindsay . . . this is . . .

Lindsay You used to do it all the time, all the . . . every minute that I'd let you in the beginning. Back then.

She begins to undress – taking all her clothing slowly and methodically off. Placing each item on the desk.

Lindsay Always here. This was our little place . . . any time that we could escape. Remember? (*Beat.*) The love was nice . . . we were nice as a couple, I think, but it wasn't that that kept me coming back – it was your promise of a future. This big, bold future that you would whisper to me about. That's what I was in love with. Tomorrow. The tomorrows that you kept offering me.

Guy . . . I remember that . . .

Lindsay I'm sure you do. It was easy enough to say, apparently . . . all of that's simple when you have no want or hope of ever seeing it through. Then it is simply fiction and as whimsical as a fairytale – and you were good at it, I'll give you that. An expert at making an honest, practical woman like me fall for it. Gobble it up! (*Beat.*) And then a call, one single call from a colleague could make it all go away . . . that courage of yours. Your bravado. That's why you teach it, I suppose, and write it, too. *Fiction.* Because it's what you deal in as a person.

> *The woman is undressed now – she sits on the bed and waits. After a moment, the man begins to undress. Removes his shirt carefully. Over his shoulder:*

Guy . . . He's not going to come up here, right? For Polaroids, or anything?

Lindsay No.

Guy Not come bursting in, the middle of all this?

Lindsay I promise you.

Guy Because that would suck . . .

Lindsay This is just between us. (*Beat.*) And her, of course . . .

Guy Who? (*Thinks about it.*) Oh . . .

Lindsay Will you tell her?

Guy Are you . . . No, of course not!

Lindsay Good. Then you'll have to live with it. Carry it around . . . like I did. I mean, until I came clean . . .

The man is down to his boxer shorts. He sits on the bed.

Guy I can't believe this . . .

Lindsay Just pretend we're between classes –

Guy Okay. So . . . The deal is, if I do this . . .

Lindsay Shhh. We can talk later. Later when we're done. After . . . when I'm lying there, in your arms . . . you can tell me all about it.

Guy About what?

Lindsay . . . The future. The future I'm about to miss . . . Just lie back. Lie your head back and . . . go on. You can relax, I know you can . . . close your eyes and let yourself go. I want some music.

The man lies back and does what she asks. Closes his eyes. She turns on a radio in the room.

. . . Tell me something. Something you remember about us. Here. Keep your eyes closed and tell me . . .

Guy Okay, umm, I can . . . I can see us, I mean, recall us . . . on Thursdays. On each Thursday of that first, that semester before Christmas . . .

The woman quietly goes to her coat and slips it on. Puts on her shoes and gathers up her clothes.

I was going off to Seattle at the holidays and it was killing us, for me to do that, but I'd promised my folks that I would and the two of you – you and your husband – he

287

was on sabbatical in the Fall and you had agreed to meet him. Over in England. He'd taken a group of grad students on a theatre trip, do you remember?

Lindsay Of course I do. Of course . . . Go on. Keep your eyes shut and go on. Further.

Guy . . . But . . . right before I left, like the hour before we both had to fly out, we met here.

The woman opens the door and slips out, leaving it ajar.

. . . Rolling around in the sheets, I mean, no idea if we could make it to Logan or not . . . not even caring about it. We weren't worried about . . . tomorrow. No, we . . . God, it was so . . . it was just so . . . nice. Very nice.

After a moment, the man looks around. He sits up and doesn't get it for a minute – then he realises. All of it.

He will not be having sex with Lindsay tonight. She just wanted to shame him; to prove to him that he would still be willing to do it.

He stands up and crosses to the window. Looks out. He quietly lifts his hand and waves. Returns slowly to the bed and sits. Alone.

Part Four

'REGGIE'

That hotel room again, refigured by somebody to have a more open, airy feel. Bigger windows. A softer colour palette.

The man is standing at the door, just letting someone in. A girl of twenty-five or so – this one goes by 'Reggie' – enters into the room and stops, looking around at the pleasant surroundings.

She fiddles with a large Starbucks cup in one hand.

Reggie . . . Nice. Very nice. (*Toward a painting.*) I like the *flamingos* . . .

Guy Thanks.

Reggie No, seriously, this is really nice. Big.

Guy Yeah, no, you're right – it's definitely big. Probably more than I needed, but . . .

Reggie Hey, why not? Live a little . . .

Guy Exactly! (*Smiles.*) That's what I thought. I asked 'em for an upgrade this time, at the front desk.

Reggie Yeah?

Guy Uh-huh. I figured 'what the hell', right? I've got one of those cards, those . . . you know, where you get points and all that crap; they accumulate each time you sleep over at one of their other resorts but, I mean, hey . . . when am I ever gonna visit Bali or some place like that? Take a free weekend in Tonga . . . (*Smiles.*) I've been

travelling so much throughout the States, though – lately,
anyway – it's better if I at least enjoy the nights I do
spend away from home . . . like this.

Reggie Makes sense. (*Beat.*) Oh . . . but I thought you
said you were getting married. On the phone you did.

Guy That's true, I did, yes . . .

Reggie So, I mean . . . wouldn't it be good for that? A
bridal suite or that sort of thing, down the road?

Guy No. (*Beat.*) See, no, because . . . we got the whole
thing – the honeymoon package, I'm saying – from my
in-laws. To be. My in-laws-to-be arranged this trip to
Mexico, some hotel that they recommend and so, yes.
That's what we're doing.

Reggie Got it. (*Smiles.*) Then, yeah . . . an upgrade's
perfect.

Guy I thought so. (*Beat.*) Corner room makes all the
difference sometimes. A little balcony or whatever . . .
terrace.

Reggie I bet it does . . .

Guy Seriously.

Reggie Well, however you did it . . . it's pretty nice.

Guy Yep, I agree. Glad you like it. (*Beat.*) You're not . . .
I mean, are you married or anything? I don't really . . .

Reggie Uh-uh. I'm not anything . . . not yet.

*They smile at each other and then drift into a kind of
silence.*

I gotta say . . . I never expected to hear from you.

Guy No?

Reggie Nope. Not really . . .

Guy Well, I'm . . . I was your brother's best friend. Kelly and I were always very close. In school, I'm saying.

Reggie Not lately, though.

Guy No, that's true, not so much in the past . . .

Reggie Fifteen years . . .

Guy Right! Not for a while, not for . . . yeah. A decade or so, but . . .

Reggie I told him I was coming to see you and he was knocked out by that. The idea that we were meeting, the two of us . . .

Guy Really? It's not so crazy, I mean, me being in the same town and everything . . . I don't get down to Dallas very often, if ever, so it'd be hard to, you know. Keep in touch.

Reggie Yeah, but this is . . . it's not by happenstance or however they call it. Right? (*Beat.*) Is that a word, 'happenstance'?

Guy I think so . . . or something like it. Very close to that.

Reggie I believe that's right. 'Happenstance'.

Guy It could be . . .

Reggie Well, you're the big-time writer . . .

Guy Ha! Teacher, really. I just . . . well, both. Now. I'm both.

Reggie Even worse. You should know better.

Guy I know, I know! I think that is it – 'happenstance'. Yeah.

Reggie Anyhow, you're not here by that. Chance or anything – you're here in Seattle to see me, aren't you? Isn't that what you said?

Guy That's true . . . I did say that.

Reggie Anyway, I didn't tell him the whole . . . I fibbed a little.

Guy How's that?

Reggie I told Kelly that you called me out of the blue –

Guy – which is true . . .

Reggie Yes, but – anyway, I said you called me up, that you were in town for just the day and thought we should say 'hello', catch up on old times, grab a bite, etc. All that kinda stuff . . .

Guy Oh, I see. Got it.

Reggie Which, of course, just made him ask more questions like how'd you get my number, how come you hadn't called him in so long, etc. You know, 'brother' crap.

Guy Sure, that's natural . . .

Reggie Yeah. (*Beat.*) He said he'd wanted to talk to you ever since you did that story of yours, the magazine one that he read – he sent me a copy on my work fax which got me totally busted! – and I guess he even wrote you or something, to your agent, maybe, but never heard anything back . . . which bummed him out. A lot. (*Beat.*) He asked me to give you this, by the way. Here. (*She holds out a piece of folded paper.*) It's his work number and stuff . . .

Guy Thanks. I don't think . . . No, I would've seen it if he ever . . .

Reggie Doesn't matter. He was just surprised, is all.

Guy I'll check with my . . . Maybe it got mixed in with a bunch of other . . . (*Beat.*) I haven't been so great about keeping up with everybody from school.

Reggie No biggie. It's hard . . . I'm only twenty-six and it's already hard. Email helps, but still . . .

Guy Yeah, email's great for that. Quick note here and there. (*Beat.*) 'S that what you are now? Twenty-six? Wow, time just . . . you know.

Reggie Yep. Flies . . .

Guy That's the one! (*Makes a jet noise.*) Whoosh!

A short laugh between them. Reggie takes a sip of her coffee.

Guy So . . . it's . . .

Reggie You look a lot older.

Guy Yeah?

Reggie Uh-huh.

Guy I suppose I do, sure. That long ago, I must . . . I mean, you do, too, although not . . .

Reggie Well, of course I do. Of course I would.

Guy Right . . .

Reggie I was a kid. A child, really, but you were . . . I can remember exactly what you looked like back then, exactly, and I've always had that image in my head . . . of you, I mean.

Guy I get it. Sure.

Reggie And so for the last few days – and all the way over here – I've been imagining you, but this younger guy that I knew back then. The guy that was always hanging out at our house and sleeping over and all that stuff, etc.

293

Guy Uh-huh. (*Beat.*) I don't think you can use that right there . . .

Reggie What's that?

Guy Nothing . . .

Reggie No, what? What can't I use?

Guy 'Etcetera'. I mean you can, of course – you can do whatever you want, I guess, that's the beauty of English! – but it's not proper.

Reggie Why, what'd I say?

Guy Oh, I don't remember exactly, but when you were listing all that stuff – 'sleeping over' and those other – you kept saying 'and' between each thing, which is basically the same as using 'etcetera' at the end. I mean, basically.

Reggie Huh. (*Beat.*) You really are a teacher, aren't you?

Guy It's true . . . (*Smiles.*) Listen, you can say whatever you want, I'm sorry for even . . . it just gets to be habit.

Reggie No problem. I get it. I do. (*Beat.*) Etcetera.

They share a smile this time. The man glances at his watch and Reggie catches him.

I'm not keeping you from anything, am I?

Guy No, God, no . . .

Reggie Good. That's good . . .

Guy I just . . . forgot the date, that's all. I've got a . . . whole . . .

Reggie Oh. (*Beat.*) You're not really good at making stuff up, are you?

Guy Not really.

Reggie Not for some man who makes his living doing it.

Guy Exactly! (*Grins.*) Yeah, that's something I should work on . . . my lying skills.

Reggie They do come in handy!

Guy I know, I know! Okay, I'll put that on the list – although there's a few people out there who'd disagree with you! They'd say I'm a plenty good liar as it is . . .

Reggie I bet . . . (*Beat.*) What 'list'? You have a list?

Guy Sure. My 'to-do' list. Self-improvement, that type of thing. Work out, read more, be a better friend . . .

Reggie Etcetera. (*Smiles.*) See? I know how it works . . .

Guy Right! (*Grins.*) I had no doubt, Reggie. None at all.

Reggie Good.

Guy Funny that, how we all ended up calling you 'Reggie' . . .

Reggie Not that funny . . . I mean, when your idiot parents go and name you 'Regina', what choice do you have? 'Regena, Regina!'

Guy Ha! (*Laughs.*) It was a family name, wasn't it?

Reggie Who cares?! It's just a nasty thing to do to your kids . . . shit like that. Imagine the variations.

Guy Oh, I think I've heard a few of 'em . . .

Reggie I'm sure! Even made up a few, if I recall . . .

Guy I stand before you an accused man . . .

Reggie Not yet.

Guy What?

Reggie Nothing. I'm kidding. (*Smiles.*) It's funny, though, that you mention a 'list', or putting that on your list –

Guy Yeah, why's that?

Reggie – and then you call me like you did, just like that. (*Snaps her fingers.*) It's weird.

Guy Why? You've lost me here . . .

Reggie I'm just . . . I was gonna call you, I guess. Or had thoughts about it at least, a few times over the years.

Guy . . . Really?

Reggie Sure – it was on my list, anyway . . . (*Smiles.*) To do.

Guy Huh. How come?

Reggie You know. (*Beat.*) Same reason you called me, probably.

Guy I'm . . .

Reggie Because of that one time.

Guy Oh. Are you . . . ? (*Beat.*) I mean, if you feel like we should . . .

Reggie We never spoke about it and I didn't tell anybody and so I've just always wanted to, you know, clear the slate on that one . . . see if we could, I dunno, sort it out somehow.

Guy I understand. I do. I really do understand . . .

Reggie Don't say that – don't go on about 'understanding' me about it, okay, because . . . that makes it seem like I just brought it up and you're surprised by the whole thing. Taken aback. Etcetera. (*Beat.*) It is why you contacted me, right? Yes?

Guy . . . Yeah. It's something that . . . Yes, Reggie.

Reggie Okay, then.

The man moves over to the mini-fridge and looks inside. gets a bottle of water out for himself.

Guy Anything?

Reggie I'd take a beer if they have it . . .

Guy Umm, sure. It's . . . Coors Lite or Bud. It's a pretty generic selection, I'm afraid, for such a swanky . . .

Reggie Bud.

The man nods, snags a bottle and brings it to Reggie. Opens it on the way over. She smiles and takes it as she sets her Starbucks cup down. Gulps down some hops and grains.

Reggie Wow. Super cold.

Guy Hope that's okay . . .

Reggie Hey, I'm not English. I've turned out to be a pretty complicated girl, but at least I don't drink warm beer . . .

Guy Right! No wonder they colonised the world . . . 'Some ice, some ice, my kingdom for some ice!' (*Beat.*) Sorry, that was dumb . . .

Reggie No, I just don't get it . . . What's it from?

Guy Oh, ahh . . . *Richard III*. Shakespeare.

Reggie I got that part. I'm not retarded . . .

Guy Of course not! I didn't mean . . .

Reggie I'm kidding. I'm pretty retarded in terms of crap like that. 'Trivial Pursuit' and that sorta junk . . . (*Beat.*) It's a quote, right?

Guy Yeah . . . 'A horse, a horse, my kingdom for a horse!'

Reggie Right, right, yeah, I've heard that one. It's Shakespeare.

Guy Exactly . . .

Reggie Huh. So, why's he want one so badly? A horse, I mean?

Guy Oh, he's, umm . . . you know. He's about to get killed because, for all the bad stuff he's done. So he's trying to escape . . .

Reggie Ha! How appropriate! (*Laughs.*) That's a good one . . .

Guy I'm lost. What're you . . . ?

Reggie If you don't get it, then don't worry about it. (*Beat.*) You guys used to play that all the time, remember? 'Trivial Pursuit'. You and Kelly would sit down in the basement for hours doing that thing, with all those little coloured chips . . . (*Laughs.*) My dad used to call it 'Frivolous Pursuit'.

Guy Right! (*Grins.*) Pie pieces. That's what they're actually known as. The little wedges of, ahhh . . .

Reggie Whatever. You two would do that downstairs and my mother'd scream her head off every Friday when she was vacuuming down there and she'd get five or six of 'em jammed into her Hoover . . . She hardly ever used to yell or anything – my mom, I mean – but for some reason that really bugged the shit outta her. Those little bits of plastic getting swallowed up in her hose . . .

Guy I remember that. Sure.

Reggie Yep. And you'd go running back home to your place, any time she'd start up at Kelly . . . he always had to just stay there and take it but I noticed that you would disappear . . . I was only, like, little at the time but I noticed that.

Guy I probably did, you're right . . . I never liked to get in the middle of family stuff like that. Even at my house, I'd take off outside or go down to the school. (*Beat.*) Conflict's not, like, my favourite thing.

Reggie Yeah, I can see that. I mean, it's there in your writing, too . . .

Guy Oh. I mean, huh. So, you've read the . . .?

Reggie The fax, remember? Kelly got me in trouble, I had to at least read the damn thing!

Guy Right!

Reggie Your character in that . . . all those run-ins with women and his big defence is to slip away. Get out through the window, etc. Whatever it takes to save his own skin . . .

Guy Right, but . . . mostly it's for comic effect. Irony and all that. The, ahh, repetition of a motif – the hasty exit – is a classic sort of . . . umm . . .

Reggie Still . . . I don't figure you made it all up.

Guy Mostly I did. It's . . . satire. A send-up of sexual politics and based on *Candide*, as well . . . It's, ahhh . . . Anyhow, doesn't matter.

Reggie No? So, then, it's all just this big . . . fantasy?

Guy Well, I mean, certain episodes – an incident or a phrase, that kind of thing – can't help but seep in, but . . . yes, it's from the imagination. Mostly.

Reggie Got it. (*Smiles.*) Whatever you say, Shakespeare.

Guy "Shakespeare'. Ha! That's a good one . . .

Reggie Well, you always did want to be a writer.

Guy I think so . . . in some way, yes I did. Yeah. (*Beat.*) You can't possibly remember that, though. No way!

Reggie You'd be surprised. I remember a lot of stuff . . .

Guy Sure, but . . .

Reggie I used to watch you – you were my favourite of Kelly's friends and so, yeah, I used to follow you guys around, spy on you and all that crap. I overheard a bunch, things you wouldn't even remember now . . .

Guy Oh yeah?

Reggie Sure . . . I was stealthy. A regular little Mata Hari.

Guy Well, don't forget what happened to her . . .

Reggie Why, you gonna shoot me?

Guy Oh, I don't know – is that how she died? I have no idea, I was just saying that . . .

Reggie Really?

Guy I mean, yes, I think I do recall that she was killed or something, executed for being a, you know . . . yeah. Spy.

Reggie Uh-huh. But a sexy one . . .

Guy True.

Reggie Like me. (*Grins.*) I turned out kinda sexy, don't you think? I mean, objectively speaking and all . . .

Guy Umm . . .

Reggie Damn, come on! Give a girl some credit here . . .

Guy Of course you are, Reggie. Of course. It's just . . .

Reggie What?

Guy You're my friend's little sister . . . Kelly's sis. So . . .

Reggie Never stopped you before.

Guy Look . . .

Reggie I'm just saying . . .

Guy I know, but . . . (*Beat.*) Anyway, yes, you've turned out to be a very beautiful woman, but you're not just some gal here. You and I are . . . we're . . .

Reggie Connected?

Guy No, I was gonna say . . . I mean, yes, we are. Grew up together, same neighbourhood and all, but . . .

Reggie Anyhow, the point was that I liked you best of Kelly's pals and I really did overhear a bunch of crap that you guys said to each other . . . no joke.

Guy Like what?

Reggie Ummm . . . stuff about classes, giving each other the answers for tests and jokes that you heard from people – I heard you tell him that there was a girl, some girl at school that you had the hots for – that one redhead that you dated for a long time – shit like that.

Guy Oh. Huh. (*Beat.*) That's . . .

Reggie Am I even close?

Guy Yeah, not too bad . . . you little snoop!

Reggie Ha! (*Grins.*) What else're you gonna do when you're that age?

Guy Watch cartoons or something! (*Laughs.*) So, you said that you were thinking about getting a hold of me . . .

Reggie Yep. That's right . . .

Guy How come? Seriously . . .

Reggie You know . . . right? I mean . . .

Guy I guess, but, it's . . . Why now? So much later in life?

Reggie Just 'cause. (*Beat.*) Actually, I wrote it in my journal – I never spoke to anybody about it, no one – and I promised that I'd give it fifteen years for you to ask me to marry you, but if you hadn't done it in that amount of time, then I was gonna tell on you . . . say something to somebody. My mom, at least.

Guy Really?

Reggie Something like that! I don't remember how I worded it exactly, but some sort of crazy statement along those lines. Yep. (*Beat.*) Hey, I was a kid, what can I say?

Guy Wow . . . that's, you know . . . (*Beat.*) I never knew that you kept a journal. At eleven?

Reggie Uh-huh. I wanted to be a writer, too . . . because of you.

Guy . . . No . . .

Reggie It's true.

Guy And you . . . I mean, isn't that what you do now? Or . . .

Reggie Sort of. Journalist, anyway, but mostly freelance.

Guy Still, that's . . .

Reggie It's whatever. Pays the bills. I do human interest stories and that kind of thing. Stories like ours . . .

Guy What do you mean?

Reggie Nothing. I mean, I'd never do it, but this'd make a hell of an article, us meeting again, after all this time . . . what you ended up doing, and me, how things affected me, who I turned out to be. That sort of deal. (*Beat.*) Like you did with that story of yours, but without all the – what'd you call 'em? – motifs.

Guy Reggie, listen, I never . . . I think maybe we should talk.

Reggie We are. We're doing that right now. Talking.

Guy I know, but . . .

Reggie Just like I promised we would, in my journal . . .

Guy Uh-huh, right, but . . .

Reggie I gotta tell you, you just made it under the wire! (*Laughs.*) Almost to the day . . .

Guy How's that?

Reggie The date on that entry, I remember it because it was my birthday – You might not know that, but it happened the night you slept over, on my twelfth birthday because mom wanted Kelly to have you stay with us so he wouldn't bug us girls during my party . . . That's the night it happened. Us.

Guy All that we . . . I mean, it was just a kiss. That's all.

Reggie That's all?

Guy Yes . . .

Reggie . . . I was twelve. Not even, 'cause it was before midnight.

Guy I know, but . . .

Reggie I can't help it. I'm a journalist, so I stick pretty close to the facts . . .

Guy No, I get it, I do, I'm just saying . . .

Reggie What? What'd you wanna add to that?

Guy Just that I didn't . . . you know, I never . . .

Reggie No, what?

Guy I didn't mean anything by it.

Reggie Oh.

Guy I mean, not that it wasn't good, or . . .

Reggie You enjoyed it?

Guy No, but . . .

Reggie You didn't? Oh. (*Beat.*) I did.

Guy I mean, no, I didn't enjoy it, like, in some sexual way or whatnot, but of course it was nice, of course it was . . .

Reggie It was nice, huh?

Guy Yes. Nice, and tender and, ummm . . . sweet . . .

Reggie Etcetera.

Guy Yeah, right. Etcetera.

Reggie Did I use it okay that time?

Guy . . . I'm trying to be serious here.

Reggie Me, too. I'm being totally serious right now. (*Beat.*) And that's how you remember it? Just like that? 'Sweet' . . .

Guy Mostly. It was . . . I mean, it only lasted a few . . .

Reggie It was a kiss. A full kiss on my mouth. My twelve-year-old mouth . . . eleven, technically. I was technically still eleven.

Guy I know that.

Reggie Good. I'm glad . . . (*Beat.*) And what else?

Guy 'Else'?

Reggie I mean 'what else happened?' I want to see if our stories jib so that I can then close the book on this and move on with my life . . . Not that it's this major episode, but still . . .

Guy Reggie . . . I'm very . . .

Reggie What– else – do – you – remember? (*Beat.*) You made it in on the time-limit thing, but I'm still mulling over the story deal or talking to somebody else – my mom, or Kelly – so it's up to you . . .

Guy Please don't do that.

Reggie I need some closure.

Guy Fine. Then let's . . . fine. I'll . . . Just don't do that.

Reggie Tell me then . . .

Guy We . . . God, it's been so long that I . . . I guess that we . . .

Reggie Why're you here? Tell me that. Why did you call me up and come to Seattle? I don't get it . . .

Guy I was . . . I dunno, I felt like I wanted to . . . I wanted . . .

Reggie What? What did you want?

Guy Or needed to, maybe . . . I needed to get this off of my chest with you. Before I get married and everything, I wanted to talk about things and just, you know . . . say, 'Hey, I know this happened and all and I still think about it, play around with it in my head so she must, too, so we oughta . . .' That's about as far as it ever goes, but I do weigh it out every so often. I do, Reggie . . .

Reggie Good. Well, that's good to hear . . .

Guy And I was – this is the truth – I was in town recently, a few days ago, seeing my, umm . . . this conference thingie I attended . . . and I happened to see you. Just crossing the street in front of me, like something out of a movie, or . . . (*Beat.*) Remember the way that Janet Leigh's boss in *Psycho* strolls right in front of her car after she stole all that money from the bank and he looks at her – there's a whole weird moment there – but he just keeps on walking . . . we had one of those. I mean, I don't know if you saw me – or that film, even! – but it was just like that on my side. I'm in this little rented Ford Focus and suddenly there you are in front of me in the crosswalk, carrying a Starbucks cup and talking on your cell. Fifteen years later and I had no doubt, none, that it was you . . . (*Beat.*) I flew outta town the next afternoon but it kept gnawing at me – that image of you in the middle of the street there – so I tracked you down in the white pages, found you and called. I left that message on your machine . . .

Reggie That's funny. I didn't even notice you . . .

Guy It didn't seem like you did, but I couldn't stop thinking about it.

Reggie . . . And so you called. You rang me up.

Guy Yeah. Called and flew back here so that we could . . . whatever. So that we might have a moment like this one. Or . . .

Reggie I get it. (*Beat.*) Do you remember touching my ass?

Guy . . . No. I don't, Reggie. Honestly. No.

Reggie Because you did . . . (*Laughs.*) I didn't even know I had one of those back then – it was just my little ol' behind, something that my daddy would pinch and my

mother would pat and . . . whatever. Etcetera. But that
night, when everybody else was asleep – my friends,
anyhow, I think Kelly had snuck off to try and get you
guys some beer from our neighbour's garage, they had a
fridge that they kept out there – you and I were . . . we
were both in the kitchen and we were laughing about,
I don't know what – -you were probably making fun of
me, like usual! – and somehow, I mean, you were
suddenly just right there, in my face, and I was scared
but I didn't leave, I didn't pull away or anything; it was
like a truth-or-dare or something, like in spin-the-bottle.
No big deal. But then . . .

Guy . . . I kissed you.

Reggie Yes. We kissed. We kissed and I . . . grew up,
right there. Instantly. I became this, like . . . suddenly I
was aware of things. Of me. And I kissed you back, only
for a few moments, but we were doing it like some
couple. We were kissing and you whispered, 'I'm gonna
marry you some day.' You did. You said that to me and
then . . . then I felt your hand on me, down on my . . .
in my . . .

Guy . . . I didn't mean to, Reggie, I really didn't . . .

Reggie You hand was there, slipping into my panties and
I was . . . you made me all . . . (*Starts to tear up.*) That
was too much. You did that and I looked at you – I can
remember looking right into those beautiful eyes of yours
– and I . . . I . . . anyway, afterwards, I went back up to
my friends, all my sleeping friends who were still just
girls, some girls that I was never gonna be like again.
Not ever. (*Beat.*) The next morning, down at breakfast –
remember how my mom always used to line up all the
cereal boxes on the picnic table we had on the screened-in
porch out back? – I was looking for you, just to see what
you were thinking, smile at you, something . . . but you'd

already gone home. Snuck back down the street in the early morning to your place. You ran away . . .

Guy I'm . . . Jesus, Reggie, I am so, so sorry if you . . . you feel like I'm responsible for . . .

Reggie What? 'Responsible' for what?

Guy I dunno. I didn't really get to the end of that thought . . . I figured I should just get it out there while the going's good. (*Grimaces.*) I'm trying hard to be honest here . . . I really, really am.

Reggie At least you're funny . . . sort of. You were always funny.

Guy Thanks . . . that's a very . . . thank you.

Reggie nods and turns away, wiping at her eyes. The man sits on the bed and waits. It's definitely her move.

We were just . . . it's okay, I think. I mean, yes, we probably shouldn't've done it, let it happen, but we're, you know . . . we were just kids.

Reggie No, don't say that! Do not say it that way.

Guy What do you mean?

Reggie I was a kid. Me, I was . . . a little girl, but you weren't. You were not a child at all. Uh-uh. You were sixteen . . .

Guy No, I was . . . this was . . .

Reggie October. Twenty-third of October, remember? My birthday . . . three days from now . . .

Guy Right . . . (*Checks his watch again.*) Of course.

Reggie Your birthday's in August. I looked it up because I couldn't recall it and it's August. Seventh. You were already sixteen.

Guy Okay, fine, yes . . . that's true, but . . .

Reggie But what? (*Beat.*) You were a man, doesn't matter how you wanna spin it – maybe you couldn't vote or go to war, but you had a car and all – you knew what was happening. You had no business doing that with me. Not that night or ever.

Guy Reggie, you're . . . No, you're right. I didn't realise that you . . .

Reggie I'm not gonna lay the whole 'you ruined my life' dish on you because I'm not even sure that's true . . . I am who I am, who I turned out to be or whatever, but you had some part in it, I guess that's all I wanted you to know . . . your doing that – to me, on that night – had something to do with this . . . what you see before you. (*Beat.*) Cute, smart, hard-working, kinda fucked-up, sexually inappropriate at a pretty early age, just making it some days and other times, off the charts and laser sharp . . . etc. Etcetera. (*Smiles.*) Just thought you should know, that's all.

Guy I'm . . . God, I'm so . . .

Reggie I don't really still expect you to marry me, by the way. That part was kinda silly . . . even back then.

Guy . . . Reggie . . .

Reggie I should get going . . . There's always traffic around here these days. (*Picks up her coffee cup.*) But that's life in a city for you . . .

Guy Right . . . (*Grins.*) I suppose so.

Reggie Most of us are really – people, I mean – we're basically to blame for our own shit, I absolutely believe that. It happens and it can be awful or amazing, whatever . . . but's it how we deal with it. That's the trick – what we do after, that makes all the difference. (*Beat.*) I guess I just needed to tell somebody about it. You and me. Share it with another person for a second . . . what happened there. How it, you know, affected me. (*Beat.*) It was just too much for a kid to handle all on their own – I mean, it's a kiss, right? Just a kiss. Get over it! – but it's hard . . . it's just so damn hard to . . . I dunno. Let it go, I s'pose. To let you go . . .

Guy I get it, I do, and I'm glad you did this. Told me that. Truthfully.

Reggie Yeah?

Guy Yes.

Reggie And, so, that's it? I mean . . . we just walk away now?

Guy No, I . . . look, I don't care what you do. To me, I'm saying . . . If you call someone, your brother or the . . . God, the police, even, then so be it. It doesn't matter. I guess what I wanted to say, to acknowledge when I saw you in the street there, was that for a long time I've known I did something wrong – and believe me, the bullshit since then hasn't been minor, either, but – this was a bad one. That time with you, in the kitchen where I touched you, it was bad and I'm . . . I really just . . . I swear at the time I didn't realise it, in the moment; then it was just, you know, late, and we're laughing and it's your birthday so I decided to give you a kiss, this innocent little kiss but it got, it sorta spun out of control. It did. It just . . . got away from me for a . . . Yes, I should've known better, or stopped myself because I was the older one, the teenager, you're right, but I was . . . I never meant to hurt you! Not ever. I, I always liked you, Reggie, I did, and I just let things get all . . . (*Beat.*) I'm really tired, exhausted by all my running from stuff. From me.

SOME GIRL(S)

Away from who I am. All I can say is I'm sorry for it and if I can do anything to . . . you know what I mean. So, forgive me. Please. That's what I'd like . . . is for you to find some way to forgive me, Reggie. Because I'm . . . just . . . I can't . . .

Reggie Okay then . . . (*Makes a gesture.*) It's off the list. You're free to go.

They smile at each other briefly, then return to silence. Reggie stands up and moves toward the door. The man follows her.
Without warning, Reggie grabs him and pushes him up against a door, looking deeply into his eyes. Dead quiet.
She kisses him. Long and hard. He responds.

Reggie There. That's what a *woman* kisses like . . . See the difference?

Guy Yes. I do, yeah.

Reggie . . . Then good.

Without another word, Reggie goes to the door and opens it up. Disappears down the hallway. The man watches her go, slowly closing the door after a long while. He crosses to the bed and sits. Breathing heavily in and out.

311

Part Five

'BOBBI'

The room again, in a slightly refigured state. A different bedspread this time, or something like that. New curtains.

Another woman – this one goes by Bobbi – is standing over by the window, looking out. After a moment, a flush. Sound of water running. She can't help but look around the room a bit. Tentatively.

Bobbi . . . Then good . . . because I was so unsure.

The man's voice from offstage – in the bathroom. Nearby.

Guy (*offstage*) Huh?

Bobbi It wasn't tomorrow, was it?

Guy (*offstage*) What?

Bobbi I said 'tomorrow'. I almost turned around and came back tomorrow . . .

Guy (*offstage*) Really?

Bobbi Yep. In the elevator . . . I was riding up and, I dunno, I suddenly thought to myself, 'God, I can't remember now, which day did he say?!' I almost went back to the house . . . I left the paper there with the details on the counter. (*Beat.*) And then when you answered the door with your hair all wet, you know . . .

Guy (*offstage*) Sorry, no, you were just a bit on the early side, that's all . . .

The man comes out of the bathroom and crosses to her. Stops and adjusts a lampshade.

Guy . . . Anyway, hello.

*The Man smiles and saunters toward her, then
hesitates. She looks at him, then turns a cheek and
allows him to kiss her.*

Bobbi Hi. There.

Guy You look great.

Bobbi You too. You're . . .

*The man smiles as he looks at the woman, waiting for
the rest of that sentence. Laughs. Goes to her and
gives her a hug.*

Guy Thanks. Hey. God, it's . . . hello!

Bobbi Hello, stranger.

Guy Yeah. 'Stranger.' (*Chuckles.*) That's a good one. And
no, it was today.

Bobbi Good!

Guy This is it. Yes.

Bobbi Right. (*Beat.*) So, this is . . .

*The man doesn't respond immediately; he steps back
and takes a long look at the woman. She really is
something special.*

Guy Geez, you look, well, you know . . . fantastic!

Bobbi Thanks.

Guy Really. So . . .

Bobbi That's . . .

Guy You really do. Your hair, it's . . .

Bobbi Same as always. Highlights.

Guy Longer, though? (*Beat.*) My, ahh – whatever-you-call-it, my fiancée – she's got those.

Bobbi Oh, really?

Guy I mean, not exactly like that, but she just . . . has some right here. She calls it 'framing her face'.

Bobbi That's . . . huh. Nice.

Guy Not as stylish as yours, though. (*He points.*) Uh-uh. Your boyfriend must love your – I mean, if you're with somebody now – he must really . . .

Bobbi I'm not. (*Beat.*) You know, on the way over here, I had a crazy idea that she'd be here, with you. The two of you, and I'd have to . . . you know, be on display or something.

Guy No, God, that's . . .

Bobbi Well, I didn't know what to think! I mean, calling my parents, and then that email from you with all those details . . . I dunno . . .

Guy I know, I'm sorry . . . but I'd never do that. Make you feel all uncomfortable . . .

She looks over at him, sizing up this last comment. Waits.

Bobbi . . . So I was one of 'em, huh? The lucky ones . . .

Guy I don't know about 'lucky' . . . but, yes, Bobbi . . . I really wanted to see you.

Bobbi And you came all the way down here to LA because you dreamed about it one time? That's why?

Guy Not just that, just dreamed . . . I'm saying that I, you know, I really considered it there for a moment.

Bobbi My sister?

Guy Yes. (*Beat.*) Pursuing that. See, this is all part of the 'honesty' thing I'm working on, so . . .

Bobbi But we're . . . I mean, we're the same.

Guy Well, not exactly, no.

Bobbi We're twins. Identical twins.

Guy I know, that's true . . .

The man doesn't finish this thought. The woman studies him.

Bobbi So, it'd be like, the *same* thing. (*Beat.*) I mean, it's not like you could've talked us into doing it together or anything . . . no way!

Guy I understand, but . . .

Bobbi Then what's the point?

Guy The point?

Bobbi We went out for three years . . . I even thought we had a shot at getting engaged there for a bit – I mean, we sure talked about it enough! – but then . . .

Guy Absolutely we did. *Yes.* And that's part of why I came.

Bobbi . . . And yet you were wanting to be with Billi?

Guy Not always, no. God, I'm not saying that . . . (*Beat.*) I'm trying to help you understand that, at some point – for a minute there – I thought about being with her, too. What it would be like to sleep with her instead of . . .

Bobbi It'd be the same.

Guy It couldn't be. I mean, not exactly the same . . .

Bobbi No, but, like . . . almost identical. We're *twins*.

315

Guy I know that! I get that part.

Bobbi That's weird . . .

Guy I just . . . It's hard to explain.

Bobbi Yeah, because it's weird. That's why. Guys are weird!

Guy Sometimes we are.

Bobbi *Most* times. (*Beat.*) And that's how I ended up a stop on your little journey? By you just dreaming about it?

Guy It just felt wrong – when I started to think it through, I mean – so I decided to come down and let you know that.

Bobbi Well, I appreciate that part. It's been a while . . .

Guy Yes. I'm not great with letters and stuff . . .

Bobbi No, not for a writer.

Guy Right.

Bobbi I heard that you had a story in something pretty recently –

Guy Yes.

Bobbi – but I never saw it.

Guy Oh. You . . . you didn't? It was very well received. Went over well . . . (*Beat.*) I'm sure I've got a copy in my satchel if you want me to . . .

Bobbi No, I don't read all that much. Not any more. (*Beat.*) Except X-rays . . .

Guy Right. (*Grins.*) Anyway, so yes, you start to make plans, like, all the wedding plans, and your life – this part of your life, anyway – begins to come back up for you.

Bobbi . . . Like vomit . . .

Guy No! (*Laughs.*) But . . . it kind of eats away at you as you're picking out a tux and your Cancun tickets, so I figured that I would just jump in there and try to right some wrongs. Be pro-active about it . . .

Bobbi Very cool. I respect that. (*Beat.*) And, so . . . how many people are you gonna see?

Guy Umm . . . you're the fifth that I've actually seen.

Bobbi Huh.

Guy Yes. There were supposed to be six or seven, but . . .

Bobbi Too much flying around?

Guy No, not that, no . . . four I saw. Met with and, ah, that was interesting.

Bobbi I'm sure it was.

Guy Yeah. Another one set it up at the airport and didn't show – that was outside of Austin, in Texas – and one, this one girl . . . we only stopped dating a few years ago . . . I went over to her place, some new apartment that she's got, and knocked at the door. She was in, caught her at home, but she looked at me, stared at me like I was a vacuum salesman and then, in a split second, wham! The door's slammed in my face. I'm not kidding you . . . I'm standing there, moving my mouth in, in, like . . . utter surprise. It was completely *mutual*, our split . . . and that's what I get when I go to see her.

Bobbi I guess maybe it wasn't as 'mutual' as you remembered . . .

Guy Yeah! (*Laughs.*) Maybe not . . .

Bobbi What was her problem?

Guy I dunno! I mean . . . we really did do it together. Breaking up, I mean.

Bobbi No, I'm sorry . . . I meant wrong with her. Why'd you stop liking her?

Guy Oh. Umm, you know . . . (*Flustered.*) We were just . . . Stuff.

Bobbi . . . Like?

Guy She was clingy, kind of, and a bit too . . . She gained a lot of weight from a knee injury she got skiing. It made her a very unhappy person.

Bobbi Huh. Well, that's interesting.

Guy It's whatever. History now.

Bobbi . . . And, I'm sorry, but I guess I'm a little slow – I'm here because of?

Guy Because you're important to me. (*He smiles.*) See, I started this whole business by – You sure you wanna hear this?

Bobbi Oh, yeah.

Guy I started by making a chart, but I realised pretty quickly that, well, basically I had a fair number of women to choose from . . . a group of *many*. So I wrote down names of the ones that I felt remotely responsible for, our problems, I mean . . . and after a bunch of revisions, I narrowed it down to, like, the finals. Top five or so. The ones that I felt were, ahh –

Bobbi – Yeah?

Guy Truly instrumental. Pivotal.

Bobbi Huh.

Guy I mean to me and where I'm at now. As a person . . .

Bobbi I see . . . (*Beat.*) Well, I'm glad I made the cut.

Guy What're you . . .? Of course you did! Bobbi, you were, I mean . . . you were easily up there at the front. You *were* the front. I saved the best for last . . . (*Clearing his throat.*) I'm a little . . . you want anything?

> *The man grabs a water from the mini-bar. The woman stares at him for a moment, really giving him the once-over. The man becomes a little uncomfortable.*

Bobbi . . . So you never heard about her?

Guy Who?

Bobbi My sister.

Guy No . . . I know she was going to go do that internship over in Europe . . .

Bobbi She did.

Guy Well, that's great!

Bobbi Went for a couple months.

Guy Nice.

Bobbi . . . And then she came back here, to Stanford, actually.

Guy 'S a good school . . .

Bobbi Yes. Got a scholarship there, and was doing her sports and stuff . . . and then got . . . she got cancer.

Guy . . . Shit, what?

Bobbi Yes.

Guy R-really?!

Bobbi Uh-huh. Leukemia and died. (*Beat.*) I think that's what helped drive me toward medicine.

Guy Oh, Jesus . . . Bobbi, I'm . . . I'm sorry.

The man stops cold – this really rocks him. He sits back a little, trying to take it all in.

Bobbi She came back from Brussels and she went to school for a bit but at the end there, when she was really bad, she had to be . . .

Guy But . . . I mean, was she . . . ?

Bobbi Funny thing was, of all the, you know, people she knew – she was such a popular girl – those last few days, when she was rolling in and out of consciousness . . . Billi was asking for you.

Guy *What?*

Bobbi She was.

Guy I don't . . . Why would she . . . ?

Bobbi I don't know! I mean, that's what I could never figure out . . . and, so, when you wrote and said . . .

Guy Bobbi, nothing . . . I'm telling you the truth here . . . *nothing* happened. Between us. I never . . .

Bobbi You sure?

Guy No, I . . . I mean, yes. Of course! I'm absolutely sure. (*Beat.*) This is a horrible shock . . . Oh my God.

The man slowly puts his head down – not crying, but trying to cope with it. The woman reaches out and touches his shoulder.

Bobbi . . . Don't take it too hard. I'm just fucking with you. (*Beat.*) She lives up near Santa Barbara.

The man looks up – the woman is grinning. She starts to laugh. Moves over toward the desk.

Guy What, what're . . . ?

Bobbi Look, I'm sorry, but . . . I couldn't help it.

Guy Why the . . . I mean, why in hell would you do that?!

Bobbi I mean, please, come on! *Listen* to yourself here . . . this whole, me even being here is absurd! 'Right some wrongs'?

Guy I am!

Bobbi You're . . .

Guy I mean, I'm trying to . . .

Bobbi You are looking up old girlfriends! That's all you're doing.

Guy No, I'm not, I'm –

Bobbi Don't. Seriously, we're grown-ups now. I mean . . . for the most part. *I* am, anyway . . .

Guy But, Jesus, that's not a nice thing to . . . don't do . . . Even if I deserve it, don't do that! God! (*Beat.*) Look, I think we got off on the wrong foot here . . . with this whole sister thing, which was – okay, maybe I was using that to get you here, because . . . I didn't know if you'd come just to see me. You want me to be honest? . . . I had this, this moment, a thing in Chicago, where I realised I had to see you, to –

Bobbi So *see* me then, talk to me . . . ask for my sister's number, shit, I do not care! But don't pretend that you're just dying inside to make it all good between us . . .

Guy I'm not! I mean, I am, but . . .

Bobbi Don't do that.

Guy I really *do* want to . . . (*Softer.*) I do, Bobbi . . . I've always wanted to . . . I know it's taken some time, but I've . . .

They stand for a moment, facing each other. The woman relaxes against the desk as the man stares at her. A slight movement.

Bobbi This is *not* one of those moments where I'm really hoping that you'll kiss me, okay?

Guy I know.

The man backs up a bit, just to give her a little space. He starts in again, using a new approach this time.

Guy What I was trying to do in this case was to let you know that I never did that, went after your sister, or anybody else for that matter . . . because I liked you so much. Respected you.

Bobbi I see. And . . . did you lose respect for me when you got out there to Chicago or something? All that respect you had for me?

Guy . . . No, not at all!

Bobbi Then how come I didn't hear from you or anything? That part I never could quite . . . You just took off . . .

Guy I . . . because I was . . . (*Beat.*) I met someone.

Bobbi Oh.

Guy Yes. I met this other, sorta hooked up with another girl out there and, well, you know how serious I am about the whole monogamy thing, so . . .

Bobbi But . . . you were supposed to be being monogamous with *me*. Then.

Guy Right.

Bobbi So who was she? Who was she that you'd start a . . . ?

Guy Just a girl. Some girl, that's all.

Bobbi 'Some girl' that you . . .

Guy Yes. That I did that to you with. It was a mistake. A huge mistake . . .

Bobbi Okay. See . . . now I get it. After all this time. I *now* get what one phone call would've taken care of . . .

Guy I should've called you or . . . called. I started to, dozens of times, but I –

Bobbi That would've helped . . .

Guy – I kept hanging up. I'd phone you but then I'd chicken out. (*Beat.*) I didn't want you to not like me.

Bobbi But you didn't really want me to like you, though, either. True?

Guy Sorta. It was complicated . . .

Bobbi So you sorta just disappeared on me there. I mean . . .

Guy . . . I went with the 'clean break'. I didn't want to muddy it up with a bunch of talk.

Bobbi I see. Okay . . . (*Beat.*) Well, we're probably done here, aren't we?

Guy What? No . . . we're just getting started. Bobbi, you can't leave without us first . . .

Beat.

Bobbi Yes?

Guy . . . I dunno! Without giving us a chance to . . . to . . .

The woman suddenly stops and digs in her purse. She pulls out an envelope and holds it out toward the man.

Bobbi Here. It's a gift certificate. For Williams-Sonoma.

Guy Huh? . . .

Bobbi You said you're registered there . . .

Guy No, I can't accept a . . .

Bobbi Look, don't be an asshole about this, *too*, okay? Just take it.

> *The woman moves straight toward him; he backs up. She takes the envelope and shoves it into his shirt pocket..*
> *The man reaches for her arm and holds it, trying hard to pull her close and explain.*
> *The woman remains where she is. Stares hard at him.*

Guy Bobbi, please don't let a misunderstanding from the past – this sort of rotten behaviour on my side – ruin our reunion here! (*Beat.*) I do feel bad about what I did to you . . . my part in all that, but –

Bobbi Which *part*? The fantasies about my sister or the dumping me for some-other-girl-at-random stuff? Huh?!

Guy Prob'ly all of it. You're right. I mean, if I really . . .

Bobbi What?

Guy If I was to really examine it, to really really get down to the –

Bobbi But you never *really* do, do you? The work, I mean. Not ever.

Guy Well, yeah, I . . .

Bobbi No, you don't. Not now. Not then.

Guy What's this if it's not me trying to . . .?

Bobbi This isn't work. Oh, no. Not what you're doing here . . .

324

Guy Don't say that. I'm trying to –

Bobbi You're making sure you haven't missed out on something! That is *exactly* what you're doing!!

Guy No, I – I'm . . .

Bobbi Yes, you wanna know that this nurse of yours – isn't that what you've said she studies? – that she's the best deal you can get. The nicest, the sweetest, the prettiest of the –

Guy No, that's not true, I'm –

Bobbi Bullshit. Bull-shit!! I *know* you. Man, I'd love to just . . .

Guy What? . . .

Bobbi I would love to know how many you actually had there, on your 'chart' thingie. Seriously. How many girls? How *many*? I'll bet the sum total is pretty staggering . . .

Guy You think whatever you want . . .

Bobbi Oh, I will.

Guy Go ahead, do.

Bobbi I *do* and I'm going to!

Guy Fine! (*Beat.*) God . . . we can at least be civilised about this, can't we? I mean, Jesus, even if we just end up as, you know . . . as –

Bobbi – 'friends?' You were not just about to say that, were you? Huh?

Guy . . . No . . .

Bobbi Geez, I hope not . . .

Guy I just –

Bobbi I mean . . . why would I want to be pals with you, huh? 'Buddies'? Especially *now*. I mean, I barely wanted to see you! (*Beat.*) God, you always were this grandiose guy, but I had no idea . . . really, not until *this* moment, that it might actually be pathological.

Guy SHIT! Bobbi, I always meant well.

Bobbi Fuck you. (*Beat.*) That is pathetic. Oppenheimer meant well. Pol Pot *meant* well. It's not about the meaning, it's about the 'doing'. Guys always mean well – right before they fuck somebody over . . .

Guy Oh, come *on* . . .

Bobbi What?

Guy I mean, please, that is not . . .

Bobbi "Not' what? You think it's okay as long as it's just one person rather than a dozen? Or a million? When is *hurting* okay? When you say so, or is it just open season, all of us going at it in any way we see fit?

Guy Look, I'm not saying it's alright to –

Bobbi Seriously, if you have the answer, tell me . . .

Guy – but you can't, you *cannot* equate like, some war with me not calling you!

Bobbi Why not? Who says I can't? Because when you do what you do, what it sounds like you've done – a *lot* – people get hurt. Injured. A bit of them, some piece . . . it dies. They lose something that will never come back. Not *ever*. This part that you decide you can just take from them and damage . . . piss on.

Guy I, I didn't 'take' anything from . . .

Bobbi You did! From me you *did* and you didn't care. You did not even look back, and *that* – that one little

brutal gesture – makes you more than just an ex-boyfriend.
You are like a killer. An assassin. Some emotional
terrorist who's just out there . . . (*Beat.*) No . . . you
know what the truth is? This – all this stuff that you do –
makes you a not-very-nice person. And that is as bad as it
gets, far as I'm concerned –

*The woman moves toward the door. The man follows
closely.*

Guy Bobbi, this is not what I wanted, I mean, hoped to
happen here . . .

Bobbi Well, then. Surprise . . .

*The woman starts to walk out. The man hurries ahead
of her and blocks the way.*

Guy Wai, wai, wait – just wait a second! Please don't
leave! Listen, I ran away and all that shit, yes, I know
that, but I *did* look back! I . . . I think I've been searching
for a way back ever since. I'm . . . I mean, it's *so* obvious
now! Look! Here.

*The man pulls out his wallet. Holds up a photo toward
her. She takes the wallet and studies the photo.*

Bobbi . . . She's pretty.

Guy No – thanks, but, no – what I mean is, a little
similar, huh? Yeah. She's even in medicine . . . I've been
deluding myself all this time. What we had – have – what
there is between us, it's *undeniable*.

Bobbi . . . You're sure you don't mean my sister?

Guy Come on! Please . . . Bobbi . . .

*The woman reaches over and hands back his wallet.
Waits.*

Bobbi Why didn't you come back then? I mean, before
this? *Why?*

NEIL LABUTE

Guy Okay, yes, that's an excellent question. Right! Or, Jesus . . . here's one for you: why'd I ever leave in the first place? Huh? I even applied to UCLA for grad school *and* I got in – didn't know that, did you? – no, you didn't because I lied to you about it . . . Tore up the letter and said I 'had' to go to Chicago, Northwestern was the only place for me . . . Why?! Why do we do such blatant, foolish shit that destroys our lives? I don't know, that's the answer. I do not. I can only speak for me, and the truth of it is . . . I just wasn't ready. This incredible girl comes over to me in the student union one day and sits down across from me with her lunch . . . I'm *nineteen* years old! It's my only defence. I was a kid and I . . . Bobbi, I fucked up. I . . .

Bobbi God . . . that's, I can't . . . no, I can't accept that.

Guy What? I'm –

Bobbi I'm sorry, but . . .

Guy It's the *truth*!

Bobbi I don't care! It's too . . . No. *No.*

The woman tries to push past him but the man grabs on, holds her tight. She struggles and they go down to the floor. Hard. She tries to crawl away but he holds on.

Bobbi Don't! Stop it! Don't do some last-ditch, shitty thing that we'll both be sorry for . . .

Guy No, *please*! Just hold up! Listen to me for a moment. Really, don't do that, walk out and . . .

The woman tears at him as she gets to her feet. He holds on to her and they bump into the nearest nightstand, knocking the shade on the lamp. A microphone on a cord drops down, dangling there. Silence.

Bobbi What is that? What is that?

Guy It's a . . . this is just . . . a mike.

Bobbi 'Mike'? Like a microphone?! Why is there a . . .? Why?!

Guy . . . It's . . . because I'm . . .

Bobbi Are you taping this? What we're saying to each other?! Huh?!

Guy Yes! Yes, I am taping our . . . but it is not a . . . Bobbi, I'm . . .

Bobbi Why? *Why* would you do that? Why the fuck would – (*Pulls away.*) STOP!

Guy I can explain!

Bobbi Go ahead . . . try.

The man stands slowly, gathering himself. Tries to tuck his shirt back into his pants. He opens a drawer and displays a micro-recorder. He sets it down on the night stand.

Guy Could we not . . . Listen . . . I had this thought . . . just a sort of crazy notion about my . . . You said you never read my story, that was in the . . . For years I've tried to write, you know, while I'm off teaching . . . and then suddenly I found my voice. I did. In my own romantic foibles! (*Tries to laugh.*) See, and now, all the sudden, I'm an author and respected and, you know, I got this taste of, this minor taste of some celebrity. Okay? So I was, I just thought, you know, what the hell, I'd keep doing it. I was approached by *Vanity Fair* so I started taping all these different conversations, and . . . and . . .

Bobbi And obviously didn't give a shit that somebody might get hurt.

Guy Okay, see . . . but, no . . . I really do believe this stuff is mine, though, once it happens – it's out there in the atmosphere and if I wanna use it or alter it a bit to expose a greater truth . . . who's to say that's wrong? Hmm? Who?

The man looks over to see Bobbi holding her hand in the air – he nods at this.

I acknowledge that you may disagree with that, may feel that what I do is pornography almost . . . but either way, whether I'm a shit or a fearless cartographer of the soul – I mean, I had a review that said that very thing. I did – no one is in any way exempt from screwing up once in a while, I don't care who you are! (*Beat.*) But . . . I don't want to keep getting sidetracked, here.

The man stops, tries to figure out exactly where he's going with this – he's doing well now, but he needs an ending.

Point is, what I said about seeing you again is true, all my feelings for you.

Bobbi Really?

Guy Completely! I really did have this desire to see you again.

Bobbi Yeah, and maybe even make a buck or two off of it!

Guy (*beat*) Fine, yes, I sometimes use the people around me to further my career . . . well, Bobbi, that makes me an 'American', frankly, and that is about it. Look, I'm not even one of these authors who're out there right now pretending like all their shit is real or, or . . . hiding behind the persona of some twelve-year-old boy – I don't do any of that! I am just me and I write amusing stories while changing the names of everybody involved and I don't see who's getting hurt by it. I really don't. (*Beat.*) I'm not, like, you know . . . doing this all haphazardly or anything. It's,

330

it's . . . for *Vanity Fair*! Now, just because I'm an author doesn't mean I'm not able to have human . . . stuff. I can't help it if I'm complex. (*Beat.*) Does that make me some big, despicable creature just because I continue to search? To reach out for my happiness on a profoundly human level? I don't think so. And I'm not trying to take anything away from what I've done to you, now or then, I'm not – I did such a . . . stupid, stupid thing back so many years ago, and I'm *sorry*. *This* was my fault, all of it. I was just young and dumb and, I dunno, goofy, and, you know – those were my good qualities! – I'm a guy, Bobbi, I'm bad at this; I found this . . . amazing woman . . . and she liked me. Me! And that just didn't compute, it did not make sense, no matter what she said to me . . . so I made myself believe it wasn't true and I ran off. Like . . . like a fucking idiot. (*Beat.*) But I've grown up since then, I have – all this being with other women and writing about it and telling myself that I should go visit my past before I marry . . . I realise now, it's all about *you*! I don't care if you buy that or hate me or laugh in my face . . . (*Tears up a bit.*) I need you and I'm . . . ohh, boy. No way I'm gonna top that, so I'll just leave off right there. It's you, Bobbi. Not your sister, not anybody else I've ever known, not even this girl I'm supposed to marry . . . no one. Just you.

The man stops now and waits – the woman doesn't even blink.

. . . I wish you'd say something.

Bobbi It's late.

Guy O-kay . . . is that metaphoric, or . . . ?

Bobbi I think sort of all-encompassing. (*Glances at her watch.*) It's very late.

Guy Yeah, but we could . . . what're you saying here? I'm . . .

Bobbi Nothing. I have to go. (*Wavers.*) I just . . .

Guy What?

Bobbi I don't know. It's such a shame, that's all.

Guy What is?

Bobbi Everything. You. Me. *Us.* (*Beat.*) What a waste . . .

Guy Bobbi . . .

Bobbi It's for a hundred dollars. The gift.

The woman steps around the man and goes to the door. Exits. The man stands for a long while. Frozen in place.
Finally he moves over to the tape player. The man presses 'Play' and listens to a snippet of conversation with Bobbi. He presses 'Stop' and takes the tape out of the machine. The man begins to pull the tape from the cassette casing. A long spool of brown spills out of it.
After a moment, the phone rings, and he answers it.

Guy Hey, hi . . . Good . . . No, I'm fine . . . Oh, nothing, I'm just . . . I think I'm tired. I'm really tired and . . . Interview just ran long, that's all. How was your class? . . . (*Laughs.*) I miss you . . . Listen, you know what? I think I'll catch a red-eye back after my next . . . No, tonight. Why? Because I wanna see you. That's why . . . And I love you, too . . . I do, honey, very, very much . . . and always will . . . Yes. I promise . . .

As he speaks into the receiver, he begins the slow process of winding the tape back into the case. Carefully, inch by inch.

Will always and always and . . . yes . . . always . . .

Silence. Darkness.

HELTER SKELTER

Helter Skelter was first presented at Theater Bonn in Bonn on 7 February 2007, performed by Birte Schrein and Yorck Dippe, and directed by Jennifer Whigham.

The play was revived under the title *Things We Said Today* as part of the short play festival 'Marathon A' at Ensemble Studio Theater in New York City on 31 May 2007, performed by Dana Delany and Victor Slezak, and directed by Andrew McCarthy.

Characters

Woman
Man

Silence. Darkness.

    Man sitting at a table in some chic restaurant, sipping a drink. After a bit, he checks his watch. Muzak playing.

    A Woman arrives, carrying a shitload of packages. The Man stands and helps her with the stack – we see now that she is pregnant. Very.

    A kiss happens. Nothing amazing, just a peck. She sits.

Woman . . . 'S crazy out there.

Man I know.

Woman I mean, seriously. It's, like, *seriously* crazy on the street today.

Man I agree.

Woman People shopping.

Man Right.

Woman They'll kill you. They would actually be happy to *kill* you if it'll help them . . .

Man I'm sure.

Woman With a spot in line or something. To grab the last . . . whatever-it-is that they want.

Man Or *think* they want . . .

Woman Exactly! It's amazing.

Man Uh-huh.

Woman And a little frightening. Christmas.

Man Every year . . .

Woman God! It's . . . (*Beat.*) I love it.

> *They look at each other and burst out laughing. Ho-ho-ho.*

Man I picked up a few items – that video game they want. (*Beat.*) And you? Anything good?

Woman Oh, you know, a couple things . . . little stuff, for the kids. My sister. Nothing that's gonna matter two months from now, but it's a start. (*Beat.*) Imagine if we'd waited until after the holiday – if we'd come down here the weekend after Thanksgiving? It'd be, well . . . absolute chaos.

Man Oh yeah.

Woman You know? Unreal . . . Already it's, like, so unpleasant, so out of the realm of how it should be, the delicious fun that you can remember from your childhood . . .

Man Whole thing's been commercialised.

Woman That's right.

Man Turned into an advertising circus . . .

Woman Yes. It's . . .

Man . . . a shame, really . . .

Woman It absolutely is – and a *sham*! It's both.

Man . . . Oh well. (*Laughs.*) What're ya gonna do?

Woman I don't know. Complain?

Man I suppose . . .

Woman That's about it. Max out those cards and complain to someone you love . . .

Man So true.

Woman Cosy up with a loved one in a chic little eatery and bitch about the state of things. It's the way of the world . . .

Man I agree. And we can do just that – either here or once we get back to the hotel . . .

Woman Perfect. (*Beat.*) 'S what we do every year, isn't it?

Man Mmm-hmmm.

Woman How many times have we done this? I mean, these little shopping getaways?

Man Ohhhh, God . . . at least since we moved. If not that first Christmas than at least by the . . . yes, second one for sure.

Woman That's what I was thinking. At least that long.

Man Yep. (*Beat.*) They're fun, right?

Man takes a gulp of his drink, finishes it. He glances at the Woman and smiles. She returns it.

You want anything? I could easily do with another one . . .

Woman Sure. Yes. Bloody Mary, maybe? (*Grins.*) I'm kidding . . .

Man 'Course. (*Grins back.*) So?

Woman . . . Surprise me.

He stands up to go off and get the order filled. She puts up a hand, stopping him.

Do you have your phone?

Man Hmm?

Woman Your cell . . . do you have it on you?

Man I'm . . . sure, yes. It's right . . .

He starts to feel his jacket, patting the pockets, and to search. She watches him while removing her own phone from a purse.

Woman I ran mine out of battery. (*Smiles.*) You can take satellite photos with it but it can't hold a charge for more than, like, twenty minutes!

Man . . . That's so true . . .

Woman Did you find it?

Man Yeah, it's . . . one of these pockets . . .

Woman I just want to call the sitter. See how the kids're doing . . .

Man Lemme see . . . it's . . . I called them earlier, anyway, said 'hi'. They were fine.

Woman . . . Good. (*Waits.*) You don't have it?

Man Maybe I . . . did I leave it in the room?

Woman No . . .

Man I didn't?

Woman Uh-uh. Impossible . . . I called you before lunch, remember? *And* you rang the kids.

Man Oh, right . . . so . . .

Woman Did you try the inside one? I've seen you put it in there before . . .

Man reaches inside his jacket. Feels around. Nothing.

Man Nope.

Woman Huh.

Man Can you believe that? Maybe I've . . . Did I leave it somewhere? In the sporting goods store, or that . . . ? God, I hate this!

Woman It's not in that pocket, right there?

Man Hmmm?

Woman There . . . where the bulge is. That one.

Man No, it's . . . I checked that one already.

Woman You did?

Man Yes, when I first . . .

Woman Just try it again. Please. (*Beat.*) For me.

Man Fine, but I . . . (*Feels inside.*) Nothing.

Woman Really?

Man No . . . (*He pulls out his wallet.*) See?

Woman Oh, it's your . . . sorry, I thought that shape was your . . .

The Man is close enough to her – she suddenly reaches over and feels the pocket for herself.

Man What're you doing?

Woman There . . . isn't that it? Right there?

Man That's . . .

Woman I can feel it. In the corner.

The Man reaches in and digs around – makes it look a bit elaborate. He finally retrieves it.

Man Ah, there it is! Got stuck in the fabric.

Woman Was that it?

Man Yes. Tucked up in that, you know . . . bit of cloth where the pocket attaches to the . . .

Woman I see. (*Puts her hand out.*) May I?

Man Ummm, yeah, lemme just . . . I'm . . .

Woman I can dial it.

Man Fine, go ahead, I just wanna . . .

Woman I'll do it.

Man Wait, I'd like to make sure . . .

She gets a hand on the thing as the Man is pulling away – the phone crashes to the ground. Shatters.

Woman . . . oh.

Man Now look what you've done! God . . . (*Picks up the pieces.*) I don't think I can even get this to . . . Why did you have to . . . ?

He struggles with the battery, trying to replace it. She watches him carefully.

Woman Do you want me to . . . ?

Man I've got it. *Wait.* (*Fighting it.*) Damn!

Woman What?

Man I think the case is . . . I can hear a piece of it rattling around in there. Listen.

He shakes the thing and it does indeed rattle. She frowns at this.

Woman Well, it's . . . or maybe you can . . .

Man Maybe it's broken, OK? *Maybe* that's the story . . . my phone got broke.

Woman Sorry.

Man It's . . . doesn't matter.

Woman I am sorry. (*Beat.*) Do they have a . . . ?

Man No, I'm not going to go wandering around the city, looking for a place where they can fix the thing, I'm not doing that . . .

Woman . . . I wasn't . . .

Man Let's just get our stuff together and go back to the hotel. You can call from in there . . .

Woman Fine. (*Beat.*) Are you sure you didn't just turn the battery over by mistake? I know that in the past I've . . .

Man Will you *stop*? Please? I'm sorry, but I do not want this becoming some . . . big . . . thing here, OK? One of those Greek dramas . . .

Woman It won't, I'm just trying to . . . although I don't know what you've got against a 'big thing' happening . . . if it's worth it.

Man We'll be back in fifteen minutes. Can the kids wait for a few seconds or do ya have to get on a line *this* instant? Huh?

Woman . . . I can wait.

Man Good.

Woman Yes.

Man Thank you.

Woman I'll be happy to wait until we get back. (*Beat.*) If . . .

Man What?

Woman I said: if. *If* you do something for me . . .

Man Now what?

Woman Give me the phone. Hand it to me, just as it is – in pieces – and let me have it.

Man What're you . . . I don't get your . . . ?

Woman I want to fix it, when we're back – I want to put it all back together and plug it in and then I want to turn it on. Do you hear me? I want to turn on your phone and watch it light up and then I want to check the last few numbers you've dialled. Today . . . (*Beat.*) I'll wait to call if you'll let me do that – without you touching it.

The Man stares at her. Speechless. He slowly sits down in his chair.

Would you help me with this coat? Seems very hot in here suddenly . . .

Man Of course.

He hops back to his feet and moves to the Woman – leaves the phone on the table.
She removes each arm from the jacket and then stands to smooth out her dress – it is long and icy white. She is wearing pearls with it.
As he goes to sit she snatches the cellphone from the table and pops it into her handbag.

Don't do that . . . what're you doing?

Woman What I said I'd do – but without your permission.

Man Why?

Woman Because . . . I promised myself, just now, that if you handed it over – your cell – without some . . . *elaborate* game, then fine. I'd let it go at that . . . but you didn't. You did not, so . . . (*Beat.*) That's why.

Man . . . That doesn't really help me. (*Beat.*) And why're you wearing that *dress*? It seems a little . . . something for shopping . . .

Woman It probably is. (*Beat.*) A little what?

Man Ummm . . . 'summery', maybe? Or . . . I dunno. Youthful?

Woman Hmm. Well . . . (*Beat.*) It felt right this morning, when we were getting ready.

Man Oh.

Woman You didn't notice it then . . . when you were getting on your slacks and your shirt, it didn't seem 'a little much' then?

Man I guess I . . . I didn't realise. No.

Woman You were going in and out of the room . . .

Man Yes, I know . . .

Woman . . . back and forth into the other part of the suite, doing things. *Texting.* (*Beat.*) It never struck you as too much then?

Man I didn't . . . Sorry, no. Just now is all.

Woman I see. (*Studies him.*) You can sit again if you'd like . . .

Man I'm not sure yet.

Woman Really?

Man No, I . . . I dunno. You're acting . . . all . . .

The Man looks around, realises that this is pretty silly, then sits back down. Checks his watch.

Woman So?

Man What?

Woman Do we have a deal?

Man Listen . . . honey . . . we can . . . I can probably get the thing to work, if you just give me a minute with it. I'm . . .

Woman I know you can. Of course you can.

Man So, then, lemme . . . you know. Let me do it back at the hotel, when we're alone . . .

Woman No, I'd rather do it myself, actually.

Man Come on, let's not . . .

Woman That's what I want to do. OK?

Man No, it's not, *actually*. It's not OK. I'm actually kind of sick of this behaviour . . . (*Beat.*) I mean, what're you doing with all this, huh? Some kind of . . . I dunno . . .

Woman Who do you think it's going to be?

Man What? (*Waits.*) Excuse me?

Woman The first number I find there – which'll be the last one, really, right? The one that comes up first'll be the one that you called most recently . . .

Man . . . Yes, but . . .

Woman I'm curious . . . who?

Man It's . . . ummm, lemme think.

Woman Any idea?

Man Probably . . . no, not you . . . I was . . .

Woman Got it?

Man No, but . . . Oh, I know who it's gonna be – and this should be nice and embarrassing for you – it's your sister! That's who.

Woman Really?

Man Yes.

Woman And why's that?

Man Because . . . sweetie, look around you. OK? It's the holidays. You're not exactly the easiest person to shop for . . .

Woman Ahhh.

Man Yeah, 'Ahhh.' (*Beat.*) I called her to get some gift ideas and, and . . . you know, we talked for a bit, I asked her how things were going at school, that sort of deal. Had a nice little chat.

Woman I'll bet.

Man Now what's that supposed to mean?

Woman Just that. I'll bet you had a nice chat.

Man We did.

Woman I'll bet . . .

Man Look, I'm . . .

Woman I'll just bet you did.

Man Alright, this is getting kind of . . .

Woman What? Tell me.

Man I don't know! Silly, I guess.

Woman You think I'm being silly now? Is that what you think? That I'm . . .

Man Yes, I do. A bit.

Woman I'm sorry . . .

Man It's fine, it's probably just the . . . you know, being pregnant and the walking all over the . . . shopping, right?

Woman Yes, that's true. I walked all over.

349

Man Really?

Woman Yes – much further than I thought I would. Further than I told you I would.

Man You did?

Woman Much. Much, *much* further. (*She starts to tear up.*) Oh yes . . .

> *He starts to move, to stand and go to her, but she stops him with a word.*

Stay! Sit down and stay right there . . . No. Don't.

Man But I'm . . . Honey, you're . . .

Woman How long?

Man What?

Woman I'm asking 'how long?' If I hadn't walked past her street, down past the park and all the way over by the water – I was thinking about that little cheese shop at the end of her block, the one that you've always *loved* – if I hadn't done that and seen you, watched the two of you out there on her steps . . . the steps *out*side, that lead up into her house, how long would you say that this has been going on? Hmmm?

Man I'm . . . it's . . . I can't really . . .

Woman Yes, you can! You can find within yourself the very last decent thing that might happen in these circumstances, and you can say to me how long this has been happening.

Man . . . No.

Woman Yes, you can.

Man But . . . we're . . .

Woman It'll hurt less if you just do it – like when they shoot an animal. Quickly helps. (*Beat.*) Go on. *Please.*

Man Fine – six years.

Woman . . . years?

Man Yes.

Woman Years? Did I hear you correctly? Did you say '*years*'?

Man I did, yes. Six.

Woman So . . . since before her divorce? And . . .

Man Uh-huh.

Woman Before she left her husband . . . before that time, you two were . . . on her steps there? So to speak . . .

Man I s'pose. (*Beat.*) It's been a while now . . .

Woman I see.

Man Right before we moved to the new house. Off to the suburbs, I mean . . .

Woman Really?

Man Around there. I didn't write it down or anything, so I'm . . . It's a guess.

Woman Got it.

Man I'm not proud of it.

Woman Well, that's something.

Man I'm not . . . Listen, I want you to hear me on this, one thing about this before . . .

Woman Yes?

Man I dunno, before you go and get all . . . you know, worked up about it. Or however you do. (*Thinks.*) This is only one little part of me, the man that I am. *Me*. I'm an OK guy, basically, and I think you know that fact. You do. I've always been – this all sounds ridiculous now, but – I'm a person who loves you, and the kids, too, which I know that you rationally believe to be a truth as well. It is, it's true. (*Beat*.) I didn't want this to happen but it started out as a comforting thing and it just . . . well, it just grew. The way things do. It took on a life of its own and I can't say it's wrong or immoral or whatnot because that would be hurtful to the little good that's come from it – and some has, if you believe it or not. There have been times when a few moments of . . . you know . . . kept me feeling sane. Or normal. Something. So it's not my place to badmouth it so that I can try and save face here, with you. I'm sure you feel differently and that's OK, that's expected, but I just want to say that we're not all one thing, right? Good or bad or like that. We're just . . . people, folks who make mistakes, who do good or bad *things* but they aren't really what defines us. (*Beat*.) I see you glaring at me and that look in your eyes and I'm not defending myself, I'm not, I'm really just saying, 'Hey, honey, it's still me. I'm still the guy you married.' I'm very sorry to have hurt you and I don't feel proud of – No, I'm just gonna leave it at that. I'm sorry.

The Woman has listened to all of this quietly. Taking it in. She waits another beat.

Woman . . . and is she? Do you have any idea?

Man What?

Woman If she's proud of what's happened? My *sister*.

Man No, I don't – I mean, we don't really talk about it much, so . . .

Woman No?

Man Well . . . yes, obviously we speak, I'm not saying that, but . . . it's mostly, you know. What you saw. There. (*Beat.*) 'S physical.

Woman Right.

Man Anyway . . .

Woman Is it at all hard saying something like that, or do you find that it just spills out of you . . . ? Hmm?

Man Look . . . I'm trying to be adult about this.

Woman Why? (*Beat.*) Why now?

Man Honey . . .

Woman I don't get that part. When people have done the most outrageous . . . shit, right? When you go and do this completely bad and adolescent thing that will hurt so many people and is just, like, off the charts, out-of-this-world insane – sure to cause the downfall of an entire . . . *family* for years to come, how come the urge immediately afterwards is always to get sensible? Huh?

Man I don't know.

Woman Why?

Man I'm . . . maybe because it's . . .

Woman Why would that be? (*Beat.*) How come it's never *before* – just before you lean over and kiss the woman who is married to a friend of yours and is related by blood to the woman you're sleeping with . . . the lady that you've filled up with the seed of your loins . . . (*Pointing at her belly.*) Do you even see this? What's going on, right here?

Man Of course I do . . .

Woman Well, that's good. That's the best news I've had all day . . . (*Smiles.*) And you two never thought about just saying something to me, or, like, running off to some . . . you know, *tropical* isle or like that?

Man No.

Woman Why not? Why not go for broke with this, since it's already taken on all these . . . biblical proportions. Why didn't you go ahead and 'take the cake' with it? Hmmm?!

Man I'm not sure . . . (*Beat.*) I did want to, if you must know. A few years ago.

Woman Really?

Man Yes. I even . . . I dunno, drew up the plans for it all – the itineraries or whatever.

Woman Ahhh. (*Beat.*) Maps?

Man Excuse me?

Woman You know . . . the little guidebooks, with the maps tucked inside. (*Beat.*) I seem to remember some of those showing up around the house. 'A few years ago.' Was that a coincidence, or . . . ?

Man . . . Yes. I mean, no. (*Beat.*) I bought them.

Woman Perfect.

Man But she didn't want to . . . your sister did not want to go through with it, so I put the tickets back on the charge card and I didn't worry about it again . . .

Woman 'Tickets.' *Wow.* (*Dazed.*) And why not?

Man What do you mean?

Woman My sister. Why didn't she want to leave with you to points unknown? Why ever not?

Man I think she . . . No, I know this, actually. For a fact. She didn't want to hurt you.

*The Woman turns and looks at him – they remain in
silence for a moment. Suddenly, she bursts out
laughing. Really laughing, hysterics.*
     *The Man watches for a moment, then looks around.
Finally he tries to calm her.*

. . . Honey. Stop. Come on, stop it. Will you please . . .
sweetie, stop this. Stop. Stop it! STOP!!

*And, as suddenly as she began, the Woman does stop.
It is deathly quiet again.*

You're making a scene . . .

*A last little burst slips out of her mouth – she throws
a hand over her lips and stops. Wild-eyed.*

Woman I'm sorry – don't know what came over me.

Man It's OK, I understand, but . . . you know.

Woman No, what? What should I know?

Man We're . . . this is in public. So . . .

Woman I see. (*Beat.*) Like when I saw you kissing my
sister on her porch? Like that kind of 'in public'?

Man . . . I guess. Yes.

Woman I see. Just wanted to be clear.

Man Fine.

Woman Make sure we're talking the same language here
and all that . . .

Man 'Kay.

Woman . . . because I certainly wouldn't want to cause a
misunderstanding between us. To be the one who creates
a *rift* in our . . . little lives. God forbid I do that.

Man Honey, can we just, please . . . ?

Woman What?

Man I dunno. I was just throwing it out there to, you know . . . maybe get things started. To *jump*start this. Get us out of here . . .

Woman Oh. I see. (*Beat.*) Then, no . . .

Man 'No' what? (*Beat.*) Alright, this is going nowhere, so . . . look, I think I should . . .

> *He clears his throat and leans in closer to his wife. Just so that he can speak a bit more quietly.*

Let's clear the air here, alright? I do not want you to . . . to take this on your shoulders, to carry the burden of this. I don't. (*Tries to smile.*) It's a mess, I'm aware of that, I know it, but it's not what I . . . what I'd wanted for us. *Any* of us. This is one of those things . . . you know when you hear someone say, 'It just happened,' well, that's exactly the case here! Yes, it happened and it's wrong and all that, I realise that part of it. I do. But what're you gonna do, right? I mean, we've very logically and naturally come to this juncture and the more we . . . I don't know what I'm trying to say, but the harder that we work to place blame on somebody's back, the worse off we're all going to be in the end . . . I can feel it. (*Beat.*) We can be civil about this, seems to me, civil and, and understanding and work toward clarity . . . work together for a better tomorrow. I'm just babbling on here, but I think there's some truth in what I'm saying – Tomorrow is another day and you and I are going to learn from all this, to grow and become richer, better people because of it, we really are, and I'm including your sister here . . . adding her into the mix because, believe me, I have spoken about all this with her – at least over the course of these six years that we've – it doesn't matter. No, what's important right now is healing. A

356

sense of love and forgiveness that the children can feel,
no matter how much we tell them about this . . . and I
vote for very little, actually, I think complete knowledge
now would do nothing but breed heartache and
resentment and, and, like . . . *fury* for no good reason.
(*Beat.*) Honey – bear with me on this, OK, because I'm
just thinking out loud here, but I feel pretty – listen, we
can get through this. We can. I don't know how exactly
or in what configuration yet, but we'll get through it.
Through it and, you know what? Maybe even on to some
better thing . . . That probably sounds . . . but maybe so.
We might. We could still break through to some richer
and more beautiful place because of what we've done
here . . . your sister and me. (*Beat.*) So, ummm . . . can
we go now? Honey?

Woman No, no . . . this is perfect. Right here. In this
restaurant.

Man I don't get why . . . are you hungry?

Woman No, I'm not . . . no. I just don't want to be alone
with you. I don't want that, ever again – after that . . .
what you just spewed – so I'm very happy to stay right
here . . .

Man Well, yeah, but . . . I mean, you can't stay here the
rest of your life. Right? OK, yes, we have some things to
work out . . . to talk about, but . . . we can't . . .

Woman How do you know that? Hmmm?

Man I don't know what you're . . . I'm lost.

Woman Why can't I be here for the rest of my life? How
can you be so sure this isn't the last place I'll ever visit?

Man Because that's . . . it's not . . . you know.

Woman No, I don't. I've realised today that I do not
know anything – *every*thing that I thought I knew or

357

believed has flown out the window and I'm starting from scratch. I mean, yes, normally I would meet you in here and have a drink or dinner and we'd leave at the end, life goes on . . . but now, after what has happened to me . . . how do I know this isn't the last place on earth for me? Or you? How would I really *know*?

Man This is . . . Listen, let me get you back to the room and I'll . . . I'll go home, head up on the train so you can . . . please . . .

Woman Because you don't want to create a scene, right? That's it, isn't it?

Man No, I just . . .

Woman Tell me the truth. For once – apparently – just say what's true. (*Beat.*) That's what it is for most people, so . . .

Man No . . . I mean, yes, that's true, the idea of us having some knock-down, drag-out in the middle of this place isn't my idea of a great day, *obviously*, but no . . . this is me thinking about you now. And the baby.

Woman Ohhh, right. Yes. Of course. The baby. Our baby. That I'm carrying . . .

Man Yes.

Woman Which, if I'm not mistaken, I had inside me a few hours ago, back when I was down the street from you and watching you put your tongue into my sister's mouth, your hands going up and down her body, across her soft skin – you mean that baby, right? The one right . . . (*Points.*) . . . *here*.

Man That one. Yes, I do mean that one. (*Beat.*) So, can we go?

Woman No, I told you already . . . I don't want to be

alone with you ever again. That rules out the hotel, even
with you leaving for home . . . because I can't fathom
standing up and you helping me with my coat and us
walking out together – you carrying these packages
because you think that somehow that'll *mean* something
– and helping get me back to the hotel, upstairs with all
the other guests in the elevator, having to feel you pressed
up against me since it's crowded and one of those smiles
that you do when we're . . . No. That can't be.

*They sit for a moment, waiting for something else to
be said – for now there is only silence.*

Man . . . I could put you in a cab. What about that? I'll
just run out and . . .

Woman No. (*Beat.*) You're thinking logically now and
you need to quit that . . .

Man Honey . . .

Woman Stop saying that! 'Honey.' (*Beat.*) Now, you've
got to stop being so practical . . .

Man . . . why don't you let me just . . . ?

Woman No, I said. *No.* (*Beat.*) No . . . cabs or train fares
or calling our lawyers after making it through the holiday
for the kids' sake and all the rest of it. NO!

*She slams the table top with the palms of her hands for
a bit of emphasis. The china rattles. The Man looks
around.*

Man Well, what then? I mean, I'm trying to . . .

Woman What? Finish that sentence, please.

Man . . . hoping to . . . forget it. Go ahead.

Another little burst of laughter; she can't control it.

Woman Sorry.

Man It's not funny . . .

Woman No, I agree with you. I so, so agree with you on that. It's not. At all. Funny.

Another burst overtakes her; she fights to overcome it.

Forgive me . . .

Man Whatever.

Woman Yes. Whatever. Like the kids say . . . now I understand what they're getting at.

Man Hmm?

Woman What-*ever* . . . (*Beat.*) You know how I think this should end? Us?

Man . . . how?

Woman Spectacularly. Vividly. *Operatically.*

Man What does that mean? (*Changing tone.*) I'm, listen, I feel terrible about this, that you'd find out the way you did . . . Can't I just try and make it up to you? I know it might take a, a, a long . . . but can't I?

Woman Oh no. No, nothing like that. Don't think so plainly now . . . you've plotted and planned like a military general for years – *years* – at least help me finish it off with some of the glory and astonishment that this union of ours deserves . . . *Please* do that.

Man . . . but . . .

Woman We don't think outside the box any more, do you realise that? Not just you and me, but everybody, that's what I'm saying . . . The world has come to a stop. We're off our rockers, completely mad, but we just keep limping along, acting like it's all OK and nothing out of the ordinary could be happening . . . happening right under our very noses! And all we want to do is get on with it, to, to keep going to work and down to the grocery store and off on vacation in the summer and that's it, that's enough for most of us. Each morning we pick up the paper over our cereal and we see . . .

She stops for a moment, marvelling at this thought. Grins.

. . . my God, the things that we're witness to! Tsunamis and hatred and atrocities of such magnitude that it takes your breath away . . . really, sucks it right out of your lungs and whisks it away; but you know what fools us, tricks us into thinking that it isn't really happening down the block and in our state and across the ocean? We get used to it always being somebody else. It is *always* some other person who has their legs blown off in the marketplace . . . never you that gets into the automobile accident that sends you smashing through the windshield and having to have your face rebuilt, no, it never is . . . Why is that? I don't know. (*Beat.*) So we go along believing that our children will grow up strong and true and that are husbands will be faithful and we plan on dying peacefully in our sleep and that is how we kid ourselves into taking the next step and the next one and each one after that . . . (*Turns to the Man.*) But I don't believe that any more. Those kinds of lies. I believe we're *extraordinary* . . . each one of us, capable of such amazing things and phenomenal heights. I really do. But do we do it? Do we go off and do those things – nail our demands up on the door of a church, making ourselves heard *each* and every day? NO, is the answer . . . no, we don't. Not most of us. The things we say today are forgotten at the second, the very *second* that they slip from our mouths . . . (*Thinking.*) You'd like nothing more than for me to go quietly right now, leave this place and accept a quick divorce and maybe no one at your work would even realise that some change had occurred in your life! I do believe that's what you wish could happen, there in your heart of hearts – and I'm giving you the benefit of the doubt on ownership of that particular organ – but that isn't what's going to happen here. It's not, my dear, no, it's not . . . so get that idea right out of your head. You and I are going to finish off in the most awe-inspiring way and you'll see it on the news tonight and hardly be able to believe that you, yes *you*, were a part of it . . . now, how many people can say that?

> *She sits, waiting for an answer – the Man shrugs. Quiet. She is about to say something but she catches herself. A tiny smile.*

As children we do nothing but read all these stories . . . tales of wonder and of myth. *Legends.* And we never question if they're real or imagined – we just simply believe. Medea and Joan of Arc and, and the girls who followed Charles Manson up a hill one fateful night . . . they were all just people at one time . . . like you and me and anyone else. (*Beat.*) And then a thing happens, some *thing* happens inside them or to them . . . they wake up or get pushed off a ledge, a light turns off or on and snap! They are never the same again – and off they go on their merry way. Maybe to wander about the city first . . . block after block after block, trying to imagine that what they saw wasn't really true but they know it is, they *know* it, and that's when they stop and buy a dress, a dress that is perhaps too young for them, yes, far too '*youth*ful', but it reminds them of a time when they were lovely and carefree and of an age before they'd ever-even-heard-your-name – you were right about what I wore out of the hotel this morning, good for you! – and then they make their way over to a restaurant where they know their husband will be waiting for them . . . but that's how it happens to people. People just like me – real and normal and not at all fantastic or anything special . . . this is the *only* way that many of us will ever have the world turn its weary head toward us one time in our entire lives. This is how we become . . . *remembered.*

Man What're you talking about? Honey . . . sorry, sweetie . . . I don't get what you're saying.

Woman You don't? Really?

Man No . . . I mean, I follow you, some of your ideas there, but you're not making . . .

Woman Here's what I'm saying – that *this* is how it all begins. With a single step. (*Beat.*) This . . . is . . . what . . . we . . . become . . .

> *Without warning, the Woman picks up a steak knife off the table and plunges it into her protruding belly. It sticks there, wedged deep inside her flesh. Her eyes grow wider but she remains lucid, even as she screams out.*

AAAAAAAAWWWWWWWWWWW!!!!!

> *Somehow she pulls the blade out, then slams it back in. Deeper.*
>   *The Man is frozen for a moment. When he finally reacts, it is too late – he reaches for the Woman but she is too quick for him. She has pulled the knife out again and holds it in her hands.*

Man Oh my God . . . oh my God . . . OH MY GOD!!

Woman Now . . . what . . . do . . . you . . . do? Now . . . what?

> *The crimson stain is growing on her dress. The Man can't seem to decide what to do. He shuffles back and forth.*

363

Man OH MY GOD . . . SOMEBODY HELP US . . . HELP US!!

Woman Now what?

Man HELP US, PLEASE! SOMEBODY HELP! SOMEBODY!

Woman Now . . .

Man HELP! HELP ME!! PLEASE HELP!! PLEASE!!!

Woman . . . what?

The Woman continues to hold the knife, pointed toward the Man; he finally bolts and runs off. Desperate.

The Woman slowly turns out toward us – carefully puts the knife down on the table. Sits back. Hands on her belly. The stain continues to spread.

Sound of muzak growing to a roar. Overtaking everything.

Silence. Darkness.

A SECOND OF PLEASURE

A Second of Pleasure was first produced at 59E59 Theaters, New York, on 24 July 2009. The cast was as follows:

Kurt Victor Slezak
Jess Margaret Colin

Director Andrew McCarthy
Scenic and Lighting Designer Maruti Evans

Characters

Kurt
Jess

Silence. Darkness.

   Two people standing in Penn Station. Near a departure gate.

   Each of them carries a travel bag. After a moment, the woman (Jess) looks over at the man (Kurt). She speaks.

Jess . . . alright, here's the thing.

Kurt What?

Jess The thing of it is, I don't really want to go. I don't. I guess that would be the actual 'thing' of it.

Kurt Oh.

Jess Yeah.

Kurt I see.

Jess I know I'm standing here and I've got my bag in my hand and all that, but if you were to ask me right now, 'Hey, you sure you wanna do this, sneak off to the Cape this weekend?" I'd say, 'No, not really.' I would, I'd say that. 'No thank you, I don't.'

Kurt But . . . you already said 'yes' before.

Jess I know I did.

Kurt I mean before now. Today. This minute. You said 'yes' earlier this week.

Jess You're right. I did do that.

Kurt And that was, like, Tuesday or something.

Jess Late Tuesday, I think, but yeah. Yes, it was.

Kurt So, I mean . . . you had all week to say something. (*Beat.*) Train boards in, like, ten minutes . . .

Jess I realize this is sudden. Unexpected.

Kurt Very. It's very much that . . .

Jess I know. I didn't want to do this. I mean, I did, I did want to tell you earlier . . . call you or something, an email – but then today I had this . . . a thing happen. Something happened and it gave me this idea that I should say something.

Kurt So . . . you gave it a lot of thought, then?

Jess Huh?

Kurt I mean, it didn't just pop into your head this minute, when we were buying tickets or whatever. You mulled it over.

Jess Well, I didn't . . . you know, I wasn't up at night because of it, but yeah. I tried to find the right approach to . . . but then I'm suddenly standing there buying snacks and thinking to myself, 'Gosh, I really need to say something! I do, and right now.'

Kurt Oh.

Jess That's what I was doing when you touched my shoulder and said, 'You okay? That's what I was doing at that very moment.

Kurt I see.

Jess I was coming to a decision about it.

Kurt Without me.

Jess No! I mean, yes, alright – it's not like I was purposefully trying to leave you out, it's just that, you know, it's sort of a one-sided deal, that's all. Right?

Kurt I wouldn't know.

Jess Come on . . .

Kurt Seriously. I'm big on sharing. On being open about stuff, whether it's painful stuff or not.

Jess Oh, please.

Kurt I am. I'm completely that way.

Jess Fine, I understand.

Kurt No, I don't think you do or you wouldn't approach my feelings in so *cavalier* a manner. My feelings.

Jess I'm not being . . .

Kurt You're riding all over them, absolutely you are. This minute. Like one of the Seventh Cavalry or something. It couldn't be worse if I was some Sioux squaw, running along the riverbank with a baby in my arms, trying not to get shot in the back. I mean it . . .

Jess That's a little dramatic, isn't it?

Kurt I think it's a pretty suitable metaphor.

Jess Well, it's a bit much, I think. Plus, you couldn't really . . . I mean, you're a man. It doesn't even work, your analogy.

Kurt I know that, I know, but you get my point.

Jess I do, yes, but it's . . . it just seems kind of *grand*, that's all.

Kurt You think?

Jess Sort of. I mean, '*squaw*?' Really?"

Kurt I'm hurt, so I lashed out. Sorry.

Jess I understand, I'm just saying, isn't it better that I bring this up now than in the middle of dinner tonight or tomorrow during a walk along the beach? I'm trying to be fair to both of us . . .

Kurt I see. This is you being 'fair.'

Jess Well, in a way, yes. Trying to be.

Kurt Great.

Jess I really am . . .

Kurt Terrific.

Jess See, now you're just angry. Getting all huffy and everything . . .

Kurt No, I'm not. I'm really not.

Jess Sounds like it to me.

Kurt I'm not. I'm just taking it all in. Dealing with it as our train's leaving.

Jess It's not going yet, we've still got a few minutes.

Kurt Whatever. Doesn't really matter now, does it? It's moot.

Jess Is it?

Kurt I think so. I think it was invented for a moment like this, that word. 'Moot.' Just like this moment right here.

Jess I don't know. What I'm saying is there's still time, whether we both go or just you, there's still time to get on board.

Kurt That's comforting . . .

Jess Oh God . . . (*Beat.*) Lemme walk you down. Okay?

Kurt This is unbelievable.

Jess . . . I can't help it. I needed to say what I was feeling.

Kurt And you did.

Jess Yes I did, I did do that and I'm glad. I'm sorry if it feels . . . but I am glad. So. (*Beat.*) The rest is up to you . . .

Kurt Wow, you've got an answer for everything today! That's great . . .

Jess I'm just being practical. No reason that you shouldn't enjoy this, I'm just letting you know up front that I can't do it this time.

Kurt Well, not exactly 'up front.' No, that would've been Tuesday night, up front. Wednesday morning at the latest.

Jess Right, yes, that's true . . .

Kurt No, I think you'd have to go ahead and call this 'last-minute,' what you're doing here – besides thoughtless and shitty and maybe even mean-spirited. I think this would go down as 'last-minute.'

Jess I deserve that, so go ahead . . .

Kurt I don't know if you deserve it or not. It's just how it makes me feel. (*Beat*) You haven't said 'why' you're . . . you know . . . nothing about that. Yet.

Jess Because. I feel bad for him.

Kurt Oh.

Jess That's why. Okay?

Kurt Bad?

Jess Yes.

Kurt You feel 'bad.'

Jess Yes, I do.

Kurt For him? You mean 'him' him?

Jess Yes. My husband.

Kurt Got it.

Jess I was packing when it started. Going up and down stairs and throwing a suitcase together, having already laid the groundwork – heading off to Boston with some friends, getaway with the girls, blah-blah-blah – and I see him, sitting in the kitchen in his suit, still in his suit jacket and having cereal for dinner . . . (*Beat.*) It was a kid's cereal and I was watching him, leaning forward with his tie hanging in the bowl, almost touching the milk, and it hit me. It did. Right then it kind of hit me like a shock or something, a little bolt of lightening. I sat down on the stairs and, and I . . . I couldn't breathe for a minute, watching him. (*Beat.*) And I realized that I was feeling something that I hadn't felt in a long time. For him. My husband . . .

Kurt My. My oh my.

Jess Yeah, I know . . .

Kurt This is a surprise . . .

Jess Believe me, for me, too.

Kurt I'm sure.

Jess I mean, we've done this before. You know? Done it and I didn't think twice about it or what it meant or how he might feel. No, I just did it. But not today.

Kurt . . . so you can't go. That's what you're saying. Don't want to now.

Jess No, I can't. Not this week, anyway.

Kurt Not *ever*, maybe, from what I'm hearing.

Jess I'm not sure. Honestly, I don't really . . . I'm confused by it myself.

Kurt Right.

Jess I am – I hope you believe me but this is the best I can do. Try and identify my feelings . . . put my finger on it.

Kurt And I appreciate that. Would've been nice if you could've put your finger on it, like, say, Thursday or something, but . . . (*Beat.*) Hotel's booked now and everything.

Jess I know! I can pay you half of it, if that helps at all, or . . .

Kurt No, come on, you know it's not just about that. The cost. Please.

Jess I know. (*Beat.*) It was just that image of him, sitting there in the breakfast nook with that carton of Count Chocula. I saw him with a puddle of brown milk in his . . . there in his bowl and it all made sense to me, what I'd been doing to him. The hurt that was piling up because of this. Us.

Kurt 'Us.' You mean 'us' us?

Jess Yes. You and me. (*Beat.*) But as I sat and watched him eat, trying to scoop up those little marshmallow pieces with his spoon, I felt a kind of pleasure. Only a second, really, but it was so deep and so honest that I remembered everything about why we had come together and married and had our children and lasted this long.

Kurt Jesus, that's . . .

Jess Through sickness and money troubles and recessions and a war and even you and me. We had weathered all of that and we were still together – that man in there and me. Because of a kind of pleasure we brought to each

377

other, something that – if I'm at all honest about it – we'll probably never have a chance of finding. Us two. (*Beat.*) Just being honest.

Kurt Yes. Brutally honest.

Jess I'm sorry.

Kurt You could've . . . I mean, you could just say 'I can't make it this time.' Don't have to be all Bram Stoker about it: drive a stake through my heart.

Jess I don't know. Maybe I do.

Kurt God, that's . . . shit. Wow. (*Beat.*) Look, if that's the case, then okay. I understand. Hell, I feel the same way. Every time I look at one of my kids and I say how bad I feel about missing a soccer game, that kind of thing – I don't, can't stand that crap. I hate soccer, actually – but I detest lying to them.

Jess No, I agree. I've always hated that part of this . . .

Kurt Not so much with my wife because, well, I dunno, I'm not sure. She's an adult and can fend for herself, I suppose, or maybe I'm just so used to it, after doing it so often over so many years that it's really become not just natural but kind of, umm, comforting . . . in a way. It warms me a bit, to look into her eyes and deceive her.

Jess Oh. Well, I hope that's not true . . .

Kurt That sounds bad. I don't mean that I'm looking for opportunities to do it, of course not. It's just that it's become a kind of ritual between us, even if she's not really in on it. It's some form of . . . closeness, actually. I mean, I wouldn't lie to just anybody! I guess that's what I'm saying.

Jess I think I understand.

Kurt . . . good. (*Beat.*) Well, I should probably get over there, then.

Jess Alright. (*Beat.*) So you're still . . . I mean, you're gonna go ahead and . . . ?

Kurt Yeah. I mean, I already did all the leg work here, might as well try to enjoy it. I can probably get a little work done . . . maybe a round of golf or something . . . (*Beat.*) Or maybe even come back early, take the kids to a movie. Who knows?

Jess That'd be nice. Weather's supposed to hold through Wednesday.

Kurt That's good.

Jess I hope the hotel's nice. It sounds nice.

Kurt Yeah, should be. I'll cancel all of your treatments at the spa there.

Jess You sure? I can call if you . . .

Kurt No, no problem. I'll take care of it.

Jess Fine, then. So, I guess I'll see you . . .

Kurt When?

Jess Ohh . . . I don't know, actually. I just said that. It's one of those things you say if you're not sure what else to say. Filler.

Kurt Right.

Jess I don't know if we will. Or should, even. Not for a while.

Kurt I figured as much.

Jess Yes. I mean, with the way I'm feeling now . . . it's . . .

Kurt Uh-huh.

Jess We should probably . . . (*Listening.*) Oh, I think they just called for . . . they're . . .

Kurt Yeah, I better get over there.

Jess Track 23.

Kurt Yep, that's it. Okay, so . . .

Jess Take care.

Kurt . . . you too, I guess. (*Beat.*) Hey listen, I just . . . lemme ask you something, quick, and be honest . . . it seems like it's time for that. Right now. Honesty.

Jess Alright. If I can.

Kurt Did you . . . in all these months together, did you ever feel that type of thing for me? What you described about the cereal and your husband . . . with his tie in the milk there? Did you?

Jess Well . . .

Kurt I'm not saying that exact same kind of 'pleasure,' but something. Anything. Did you? From what I ever did, or, or . . .

Jess . . . ummmmm . . .

Kurt . . . from us together? (*Beat.*) You can tell me. It's okay, I'm curious, that's all.

Jess It's not really a fair . . .

Kurt Even once. Just one time. (*Beat.*) *Once?*

Jess No. I didn't. No. Not ever.

Kurt Oh. Okay. Alright, I was just wondering . . .

Jess I'm sorry.

Kurt No problem. It's . . . so, I'll see you, then.

Jess Yeah, fine. Some time.

Kurt Some time soon?

Jess Maybe. Hope so.

Kurt Be nice if it was soon.

Jess I know.

Kurt I'm just saying, my opinion – that'd be nice. 'Soon.'

Jess We'll see. (*Smiles.*) Say 'hello' to the ocean for me!
Have a lobster roll, or . . .

Kurt Will do. (*Beat.*) Okay, see what happens . . .

Jess Sounds good. (*Beat.*) I just can't promise – listen, we
bump into each other all the time. Not just us but people,
all of us, back and forth across the world and sometimes
it's all life-and-death and other days we barely even notice.
That's what we do. We pass each other and maybe next
time I'll cling to you, never let you go or, or, or maybe
we'll act like we've never even met . . . so why don't we
just wait and see, okay? Life's funny that way . . . you
know?

Kurt Yep. So, I'll call ya when I get there . . . or . . .

Jess No, don't do that. Don't call.

Kurt You're right. Fine. I'll just, ummm . . .

Jess Okay then.

Kurt Okay.

Jess Good-bye.

Kurt . . . 'bye.

> *The man remains where he is. Watching the woman
> slowly disappear into the crowd. He doesn't move.
> After a moment, the man checks his watch and then
> moves off in another direction.*
>
> *Silence. Darkness.*